PRAISE FOR *RARE BIRD*

"Maria Mudd Ruth's engaging, scientific detective story bristles with humor, curiosity, frustration and passion as the accidental naturalist tracks the history of this elusive seabird, which flew from obscurity to star on the endangered species list and, in the process, rescued thousands of acres of old-growth Pacific Coast forest from the logger's ax. A fascinating avian odyssey, recounted with ferocity and grace."

—*The Los Angeles Times*

"How the mystery was solved and the implications of this discovery in the ongoing battle between environmentalists and loggers in the Pacific Northwest are conveyed in Ruth's infectious tale. . . . The story of the discovery of the nest is alone worth the price of the book."

—*Booklist*

"Heartfelt and thoughtful, inspired and well-written, *Rare Bird* is a rare book. It will transport you into a world you didn't realize existed."

—Carl Safina, author of *Song for the Blue Ocean* and *Eye of the Albatross*

" . . . [T]his is one of those tales where the science of natural history and a sense of wonder at the world around us come together; ultimately, like the author, we are seduced by a seemingly ordinary creature that manages the most extraordinary feats . . . "

—American Birding Association

"Fine nature writing, good science, and compelling historical anecdotes spanning the time of Captain Cook to contemporary naturalists, loggers, and fishermen combine in an engaging narrative."

—*Library Journal*

"*Rare Bird* is a rare book—not because it is hard to obtain, but because it tells its story so well. . . . The Marbled Murrelet is a rare bird in that, once you get to know it a little, it can change your life."

—Santa Cruz Bird Club

"Ruth's details of the hunt for bits of information about the bird—from dissecting specimens to counting birdcalls in the predawn light—provide rare insight into the trials and joys of scientific discovery."

—*Publishers Weekly*

"It is not often that you find a natural history book you can't put down. *Rare Bird* is such a book. This lyrical, sprightly tale of a remarkable bird and the woman who fell for it shows how a small piece of the natural world may climb into the soul and lodge there, changing us forever—and how, if we lose that piece through inattention, we lose some critical part of ourselves. A marvelous story beautifully told."

—Jennifer Ackerman, author of *Notes from the Shore*

"The result is a fascinating and inspiring detective story."

—*Birder's World*

"Maria Ruth tells a story as fascinating, as appealing, and as peculiar as the marbled murrelet itself. *Rare Bird* is a unique and delightful book: too passionate for ordinary journalism, too well-researched for a personal essay, and far too witty for natural history."

—Peter Cashwell, author of *The Verb 'To Bird'*

"Mixing history, personal observation and environmental science into a readable narrative, Ruth details why the bird is endangered and what can be done to change that. . . . An important addition to birding and environmental literature."

—*Santa Cruz Sentinel*

"In *Rare Bird* [Ruth] tells us not only about this intriguing seabird, but also about the dedicated people drawn into its world. The murrelet becomes a symbol of wildlife endangered by people who do not yet realize their own lethal power in a world they barely understand . . . for readers who adore birds or find fascination in nature's subtle charms, *Rare Bird* is a gem. All in all, it is a neat little book about a neat little bird and a tale well told."

—*Kenai Peninsula Clarion*

" . . . [I]t's an eminently readable book for birders . . . a good mystery . . . and a focused case study of this one single species and its endangered existence. Other species are more endangered, all are fighting their own particular battles, but understanding this one bird and its challenges drives the broader lesson home for the readers."

—Forsyth County [North Carolina] Audubon Society

" . . . Ruth does an outstanding job of telling the tale of the discoveries of the marbled murrelet's nesting ecology and highlighting some of the important players. Whether you know a lot or a little about this fascinating bird, I know you'll enjoy the book."

—*Monterey Bay Birds*

"Beautifully and deftly written. Truly captures the mystery and excitement of the murrelet's story."

—Joan Dunning, author of *From the Redwood Forest*

RARE BIRD

Pursuing the Mystery of the Marbled Murrelet

MARIA MUDD RUTH

MOUNTAINEERS
BOOKS

Mountaineers Books is the nonprofit publishing arm of The Mountaineers, an organization founded in 1906 and dedicated to the exploration, preservation, and enjoyment of outdoor and wilderness areas.

MOUNTAINEERS BOOKS 1001 SW Klickitat Way, Suite 201 · Seattle, WA 98134
800.553.4453 · www.mountaineersbooks.org

Originally published by Rodale
Copyright © 2005, 2013 by Maria Mudd Ruth

Printed in the United States of America

16 15 14 13   5 4 3 2 1

Cover Design: Karen Schober
Illustrations and cover artwork from the field notebooks of Paul Harris Jones

Library of Congress Cataloging-in-Publication Data
Mudd-Ruth, Maria.
  Rare bird : pursuing the mystery of the marbled murrelet / Maria Mudd Ruth.
    pages cm
  "Originally published in hardcover in 2005 by Rodale Inc."
  Includes index.
  ISBN 978-1-59485-835-2 (pbk) — ISBN 978-1-59485-836-9 (ebook)
  I. Title.
  QL696.C42M83 2013
  598—dc23
                                        2013013142

♻ Printed on 100% recycled paper using vegetable-based inks.

ISBN (paperback): 978-1-59485-835-2
ISBN (ebook): 978-1-59485-836-9

For Mike—unstinting, unfailing, unbelievable

CONTENTS

PROLOGUE

Aloof in the icy-cold water off Alaska's rugged southern coast, a solitary bird—dark head, chubby body, stubby tail—paddles frantically against the waves as it moves toward shore. In one swift and sudden gesture, it lifts its pointed bill into the air, stretches its neck, and dives. Stroking its wings as if flying, it moves rapidly through the water. Within seconds, it catches a fish, swallows, and returns to the surface. Shaking droplets off its feathers, it begins preening, stopping only to glance in all directions, ever alert to changes on the water.

As spring turns to summer, the bird will lose its black-and-white feathers and don its breeding plumage, which—at a distance and in a word—is brown. Close up, though, brown becomes sooty brown, brownish black, chocolate, rufous, rusty-buff, light tan, and cinnamon on the bird's back, head, and wings. Brown becomes light brown marbled with soft whites on its throat, flanks, and breast. When its new set of summer feathers is fully grown, the bird flies closer to shore, where it joins others of its kind loosely scattered across the water, some in small groups, most in pairs, some remaining ever aloof.

Summer evenings at dusk, birds with one or two small fish held crosswise in their bills rise up off the water and fly toward the forested hills. Some mornings before dawn they return to the water, uttering strange calls as they fly through the fog hanging thickly along the coast. The calls are high-pitched, piercing, and plaintive.

One morning, after a spate of rough storms along the rocky coast, dawn breaks clear and the cries of dozens of birds stir up from a sheltered cove. There, in the cove, is a large ship—a wooden sailing ship at anchor. Three men have lowered a small skiff into the water alongside the ship and are rowing toward the birds. As the skiff nears, the birds scatter—diving quickly or darting off. The men in the boat curse, laugh, and then stop rowing. They let their boat drift slowly toward a pair of foraging birds that seem oblivious to their approach. But with a sudden, loud noise from the boat, the birds plunge beneath the water. As the gunsmoke clears, the men are left gaping at rippling rings on the surface and a trail of bubbles below—an ephemeral trail that leads down to two birds they no longer see.

The year is 1778. The pursuit has begun for a bird then too abundant to be considered rare, yet too tantalizing to ignore.

PART ONE

ENIGMA

CHAPTER 1

The auk family is on the move. Millions upon millions of these surface-diving seabirds—puffins, murres, dovekies, razorbills, guillemots, auklets, and murrelets—have left their winter feeding grounds off the Pacific Coast to follow the changing currents and the upwelling of cold, nutrient-rich waters that occurs closer to land. Here the birds find a summer banquet of zooplankton, shrimp, squid, and small schooling fish. Here most find a solid piece of ground—a rocky outcrop, islet, cliff, talus, or wedge of soft earth among tree roots—and stake their claim. Every ledge, nook, cranny, crevice, and crack is soon occupied. Bare rocks wear feathers; cliff faces wear beaks. From Alaska to California, every space large enough for a pair of webbed feet becomes a nest. Some birds are scattered in small colonies of ten or twenty pairs; others are crowded shoulder to shoulder in large colonies of several thousand pairs. All of them are mating, laying and incubating eggs, defending mates, attacking predators, retrieving runaway eggs, foraging in the water, and making crash landings on the rocks and each other. And the noise! Depending on the species of auk, their vocalizations have been described by scientists as screaming, whistling, mooing, whinnying, screeching, growling, grunting, creaking, and chattering. To be sure, they are spectacularly loud.

Set apart from the raucous crowds are the quieter members of the family—the marbled murrelets. Breeding season is in full swing for them too, but their behavior is more discreet, subtle, muted. In their brown breeding plumage, the robin-sized murrelets gather in loose aggregations—nothing as tight or as bawdy as a flock.

Males and females of breeding age begin a courtship ritual, a highly synchronized affair that takes place on, in, and above the water. Potential mates join closely together, extend their necks skyward, and point their bills in the air—a movement that lifts their marbled breasts out of the water and grants the pair a touch of avian elegance before they swim rapidly across the water together, two sets of webbed feet flapping and slapping as they go. The two dive, resurface in unison, and extend their necks again, making cooing sounds. Sometimes a murrelet will extend its wings half-open over its back to form a V while swimming next to its potential mate and making a unique buzzing call. This apparently inspires the two love-birds to chase each other in the air just above the water's surface—a flight that ends with one bird crashing into the water and the other flying a bit higher up before plunging in nearby. When the birds resurface, they fly off together, a bonded pair, to mate elsewhere on the water or in the old-growth coastal forest—the unlogged forests—on an accommodating branch in an ancient, towering Douglas fir, western hemlock, redwood, Sitka spruce, or cedar. Some birds will fly nearly forty miles inland to find that branch.

Male and female birds do not, as far as scientists can tell, reveal the secret of their gender through their courtship behavior. Only during copulation might it be possible to tell male from female: The female is probably the one being mounted. I say probably because although this mating position is typical for other birds, researchers have caught marbled murrelets *in flagrante delicto* only a few dozen times—not enough to put forward any credible theories about who mounts whom. All researchers really know, and perhaps all they need to know, about the fifteen-second event is that it occurs on the water or in trees and, according to at least one witness, is accompanied by "an emphatic, nasal *eeh-eeh* call."

Once mated, a marbled murrelet pair will select a nest site and begin regular flights to and from the old-growth forest, together and apart, announcing their presence to each other and to the world with a full-throated, high-pitched *keer keer keer.* The birds fly at a speed of around 50 miles per hour but have been clocked on radar at 103.

Male and female take turns incubating their one egg per breeding season, leaving it unattended for only very short periods of time, if ever. When unattended, the pale-green, dark-speckled egg is camouflaged against the mossy branch where it rests. When it hatches, the chick is on its own for all but the few moments when its parents return to the nest to feed it. Alone, on a wide branch in the top of a two-hundred-foot-tall tree, the chick is silent, still, and camouflaged by its mottled buff-colored feathers. When the chick is ready to fledge, it waits until just after dusk, spreads its wings, and departs from the nest, flying (for the first time) through the forest, on a route not necessarily taken by either parent, for some as yet unknown distance to the sea (which it has never seen) to begin to swim, to dive, and to catch fish (which it has never done), on its own.

In a perfect year—one without predators, disease, or natural disasters—a pair of marbled murrelets have a good chance at producing one chick and increasing their population by 50 percent. But none of us, marbled murrelets included, lives in a perfect world. Despite various adaptations and instincts, predation rates are high, especially by ravens, jays, crows, hawks, falcons, and owls. Eggs and chicks are commonly taken at the nest; adults are preyed on at the nest and in flight. In an average, less-than-perfect year, most marbled murrelets do not successfully fledge a chick. Over their ten-year life span, though, a pair should be able to produce at least two chicks and thus replace themselves in the population. At this rate, marbled murrelets should today be common birds, abundant birds, a thriving species. But this is not the case. Commercial logging of the old-growth coastal forests of the Pacific Northwest that began in the 1830s has left the marbled murrelet with only 10 percent of its historic habitat. Unfortunately, the marbled murrelet doesn't just prefer old-growth and mature forests; it depends on them. In only a few cases have researchers discovered marbled murrelet nests in trees less than two hundred years old, only one nest has been found in a deciduous tree, and only a handful have been discovered on the ground or on cliff faces.

Scientists in the 1980s discovered that the northern spotted owl, another species they once believed depended exclusively on old-growth forests, could adapt and nest in second-growth forests. But compared to the marbled murrelet, the spotted owl can be considered an opportunist, or what one biologist called a "habitat whore." Marbled murrelets stay true to a specific type of tree, and in many cases to one specific tree, and even to one particular spot on one specific limb, year after year. In one sense this loyalty—called *philopatry* when exhibited by wild animals—should help the marbled murrelet's productivity rate, since finding a new nest site every year takes time and energy. But suitable nest trees vanish from one breeding season to the next, as stands, groves, and entire forests become stumps, roads, housing developments, and shopping centers. Birds seeking out a new nesting tree may find a suitably wide limb elsewhere, but one that exposes them to more predators or is too far from the Pacific, where they forage.

Marbled murrelets also face serious threats from man at sea, where they spend 95 percent of their time. Catastrophic oil spills, chronic oil pollution, and certain commercial fishing practices take their toll on these birds throughout their range. In light of these threats, the United States and Canada have placed the marbled murrelet on their lists of threatened species. In Washington and Oregon, the bird has been accorded threatened status at the state level. In California, where only remnants of the old-growth coastal forest remain, the marbled murrelet is listed as an endangered species.

At the beginning of 2005, there were 518 animals on the U.S. Fish and Wildlife Service's list of threatened and endangered species, 90 of them birds. Many are perilously close to extinction. The population of California condors, for instance, is down to 111; Attwater's prairie chicken numbers only 44; piping plovers struggle to survive at 2,800. Before it became extinct in November 2004, a Hawaiian bird called a po'ouli had a population of only a few dozen. The most recent population estimate for the marbled murrelet, one calculated by scientists in 2004, is 947,500.

A number like this is unlikely to cause casual activists to panic and chain themselves to a redwood—or to worry about the marbled murrelet at all. But the number is misleading. Most marbled murrelets—an estimated 860,000—live in Alaska, with a sizeable population of 66,500 living in British Columbia. The numbers drop to 12,300 in Washington, where the length of the coastline and the amount of remaining old-growth forests also drop. The decline continues southward, with only 7,502 birds in Oregon, and 4,598 in California.

Still, the numbers seem relatively high compared to the condor, prairie chicken, and plover. Why *should* anyone be worried about the marbled murrelet when other species are in greater peril? Because scientists have evidence that this number is a fraction of what it was historically, and because they have documented a dramatic decline in the bird's population over the past ten years. In some areas, populations have plummeted 40, 50, even 70 percent. Some scientists are convinced that it is not a matter of *if* but *when* the marbled murrelet will become extinct. This event, they predict, will occur during the next century. The marbled murrelet—now rare because its behavior and biology are unusual, unique, distinctive, fantastic, and incredible—will become even more rare because it will be decimated, scarce, unviable, and unrecoverable.

The tragedy of the marbled murrelet, and that of other threatened species, is not that its extinction will go unreported, but that it will go largely unmourned. Even today, with nearly a million birds on the earth, this strange seabird is little known outside the scientific community or beyond the coastal towns and cities of the Pacific Northwest. The majestic

bald eagle, the swift and powerful peregrine falcon, the pho-
togenic spotted owl, and even the enormous-though-unsightly
condor are more familiar to the general public.

Familiarity would certainly help conservation efforts, but
the marbled murrelet is not a birder's bird; it is a challenge to
observe in the field. Flying over forest, a marbled murrelet is
more an apparition than a real bird, a fleeting glimpse of
something resembling a baked potato with a beak, as one
biologist describes it. Swimming at sea, a marbled murrelet is
a distant form, an eyestrain, a splash, and a trail of bubbles.
Only with a great deal of planning, time, effort, and stamina
can a person encounter a marbled murrelet in the wild in a
way that is satisfying. And as the species becomes less abundant, such encounters will become rare for even the most
dedicated birders and scientists.

I've thought about this a lot—why the fate of this
chunky, baked potato of a bird concerns me. Me, a woman
who lived forty good years without ever seeing a marbled murrelet, who has lived most of her life on the East Coast, who is
not married to a logger, ornithologist, or eco-activist, and
whose life would be the same with or without any knowledge
of marbled murrelets. Or would it?

At one time in my life, a connection *with a bird* would
have seemed superfluous, ridiculous. Most of my close con-
nections have been to people, and to places such as a particular stream, rocky outcrop, garden, or childhood home, with
a few family pets and the occasional injured animal interesting
me in passing. Not until I turned forty—fortuitously? coincidentally?—did I find that I craved a connection to something
wholly other. Amazingly, this *something* turned out to be a

bird—a bird I had never seen, whose name at first I couldn't pronounce, whose very existence was previously unknown to me, and whose habitat was nearly three thousand miles from my own.

Why this bird? Why me?

This was the first mystery.

CHAPTER 2

The truth is, I am not a birder. I admire birders, but I am no more naturally inclined to wake before sunrise, dress in layers of drab clothing, and sit in a field to wait for the *possibility* of seeing a bird than I am to don a wet suit and readily plunge into the sea to look for sharks. I can identify the dozen birds that come to my feeders, but I cannot tell the difference between a crow and a raven or the many types of gulls without a field guide. I am an accidental naturalist, raised by a mother who worshipped Annie Dillard and a father who worshipped the truth. I am the wife of a scientist, the mother of two young tree-climbing boys, a sucker for a good field guide, a dilettante, an enthusiast. I am a writer with attention surplus disorder.

I did once try to become a real bird-watcher by joining other aspiring birders on guided walks and field trips. I spent one snowy winter weekend counting cardinals and nuthatches during a backyard bird count. I have bought my share of bird-seed, suet cakes, and hummingbird feeders. I acquired a pair of starter binoculars and recordings of common bird songs. All of it was fun for a while, but I couldn't shake the feeling I was missing something while I was looking at birds. The idea of focusing on birds to the exclusion of everything else in the natural world left me uninspired and uncommitted. Until I met the marbled murrelet.

Our first encounter was in 1999, on the Internet, while I was writing a book for young readers on Pacific Coast ecosystems. Soon after I began searching *old-growth forests*, I was linking to sites describing the marbled murrelet. In the several articles I found online, this bird was invariably described as "mysterious," "elusive," or "secretive," and the forests they nested in as "ancient," "enormous," and "threatened." Apparently, it had taken naturalists, professional birders, and ornithologists 185 years to finally discover the bird's nesting site. The location of the nest had been dubbed one of the last great ornithological mysteries in North America. I didn't understand how a bird's nest could generate such drama.

I turned to my bookshelf, to my copy of Peterson's 1989 *Field Guide to Western Birds*, where the marbled murrelet is described as "a small, chubby, neckless-looking seabird . . . dark above, and white below" in winter, "dark brown; heavily barred on underparts" in summer. Succinct, yes. Satisfying, no. There was no description of the 185-year nest mystery, just the punch line: "Breeds inland on mountains near coast, mainly high on limbs of mossy conifers."

I consulted two dozen other field guides and bird books. None told the full story of the bird or the nest mystery. The marbled murrelet, I did learn, inhabits the cold waters of the Pacific Coast from southern Alaska to southern California and usually forages within two miles of shore. It is one of twenty-four species of marine diving birds known as auks, or alcids. All were unfamiliar to me—all but the puffins and the great auk. I had seen puffins while hiking on the coast of Scotland in 1985, and again in 2001, as artwork on a box of organic "puffed" rice cereal at the grocery store. As for the great auk, the largest and only flightless member of the family, it had been hunted to extinction in the 1840s.

The story of the marbled murrelet's critical and dynamic relationship with old-growth forests became a short chapter in my book on Pacific Coast ecosystems. In the conclusion of that chapter, I ventured to hope that the biologists studying the birds and all those contributing to the destruction of the bird's habitat could work together to save the marbled murrelet from extinction. I sent the chapter to my editor and, several months later, received copies of the published book. That, I thought, was the end of that.

But it wasn't. I had really just scratched the surface of the story I was looking for. Why had it taken 185 years to find that nest? It was that number, 185, that perplexed me the most. It meant that the search that began in 1789 ended in 1974. Considering all that was going on in the world in 1789—the French Revolution and the election of George Washington, for instance—I wondered who would be out looking for a bird's nest in the first place.

I also was surprised at how little information I could find about this bird—how many eggs it laid, what kinds of old-growth trees it preferred, what it ate, at what age it bred, where it mated, how it fed its chicks, how and when the chicks fledge, its migration patterns, its longevity, and its role in the coastal ecosystem. Surely, I thought, these basics of a marbled murrelet's life had been learned long ago and were well-documented in some book I didn't happen to have on my shelf. But I was wrong; the libraries and bookstores I visited had nothing on their shelves to answer my questions and satisfy my mounting curiosity. So I began e-mailing and phoning biologists studying the marbled murrelet to find some answers. I learned how to pronounce the bird's last name—it's *mer*-lit, not mer-*let*, or *muir*-a-let—but no one seemed to know much about what happened in 1789. I requested their published papers and names of other murrelet-savvy biologists. I joined a seabird conservation group that had spearheaded the research on the bird back in the 1980s. The more I found out—and couldn't find out—about this mystery, the more obsessed I became. I Googled the bird day and night. I talked about it incessantly to anyone who would listen. My family and friends were intrigued but confused: *Murbled Marlettes? Marbled Merlot? Marbled Merrilat? What's it called again?* I nearly wept with joy when my four-year-old niece asked, "Can you tell me again the story about the bird no one knows about?"

Allowing a bird to take up residence in my life wasn't enough, apparently. I would have to let this bird *change* my life. I would have to live and breathe alcids, make frequent trips to the West Coast, interview more scientists, buy an expensive pair of binoculars *and* learn to call them "bins." Naturally, I resisted. I thought of all the things I'd be missing.

Over the years, I have written about a dozen books for young adults on natural history topics ranging from individual animals—snakes, owls, hawks—to entire ecosystems such as the tundra, deserts, and oceans. I plunged into my research for each book, learned as much as I could about each topic, charged toward the manuscript deadline several months later, and then celebrated when I had finished and could move on to something else. There were hundreds of thousands of organisms on the earth worthy of attention, but somehow, once I heard about the marbled murrelet, I couldn't focus on anything else. Tracking down information about this mysterious bird made me feel exhilarated, dedicated, focused, and confused, all at once. So, I started reading the bible.

Not *the* Bible. I mean the marbled murrelet bible—a technical report officially titled the *Ecology and Conservation of the Marbled Murrelet* but considered a "bible" by many seabird biologists. This report was published in 1995 by the Pacific Southwest Research Station, a branch of the U.S. Forest Service, and is available through them and university libraries. I ordered a copy, thinking that all of my questions would be answered in one concise report, and then I would be able to turn out a book on the marbled murrelet in less than a year to get it out of my system and return to the clamoring world.

Then the four-hundred-page book arrived in the mail. It was actually a compilation of thirty-seven separate technical papers written by forty-five different authors. The authors were field biologists from Alaska, British Columbia, Washington, Oregon, and California who had spent years studying the marbled murrelet at sea and in the forest. The book was intimidating, to say the least. It was days before I summoned the courage to begin reading the first report.

I am a dedicated reader of nonfiction and had managed to live a happy life without reading a single technical scientific report. Such reports don't require readers as much as decoders to translate the sentences replete with scientific terminology, symbols, and numbers (many in parentheses) that act like potholes in otherwise readable sentences. For example, "The majority (86 percent) of nests in North America ($n = 52$) had substrates that were >2 cm in depth with a large number of nests ($n = 16$) having substrate depths between 3.1 and 4.0 cm (*fig.8*)."

I read the study wide-eyed and drop-jawed. I looked up words. I converted centimeters into inches. I stared at charts and figures until they made sense. I read passages out loud to my husband. I highlighted it. I dog-eared it. The study—all three pounds of it—displaced several volumes of poetry and three novels on my bedside table. This was all I needed of non-fiction, fiction, and poetry. That anyone had ever laid eyes on a marbled murrelet nest was incredible to me. That biologists were able to glean one page—let alone four hundred pages—of information about this one bird was mind-boggling. That I would be sitting in a meadow in the Santa Cruz Mountains the following summer, in the dark, wearing four layers of drab clothing, waiting to *possibly* catch a glimpse of a bird I had never seen before, was plain shocking.

But there I was.

This chunky little seabird had stolen my heart. It had arrived in my life silently, in dim light, wearing cryptic plumage. When I finally woke up and realized what was happening, I could feel the spread of this bird's wings in my soul.

CHAPTER 3

The odyssey of my infatuation with the marbled murrelet began in the rural village in Virginia that my husband, two young sons, and I called home for ten years. Our elementary school was at one end of the village, the post office and tiny general store a quarter mile away at the other. A sidewalk connected the two ends, and our house sat in the middle. Neighbors were friends, and my large extended family was nearby. Life was good. I filled my time with family, freelance writing assignments, volunteer work at the school, projects to revitalize our village, and efforts to protect the open spaces of the rapidly growing county in which we lived. I didn't know how to get uninvolved, to pass the torch, to say no. Perhaps I could have tried to bow out gracefully, project by project, so that I could have written about the marbled murrelet without leaving Virginia, but this wasn't just about the bird.

For a writer, a never-before-told story is a gift on a silver platter. For me, the story of the marbled murrelet was a golden key, a key that might open the door to a new world, new discoveries, a new life. I wanted to experience the marbled murrelet in the field and create the necessary space in my life to write about it full time. I knew that in order to commit myself to this bird, I would need to uncommit elsewhere. I would, as Annie Dillard said, need to go at my life with a broadax if I wanted to write. I never thought I would leave my native Virginia and all that had become familiar. Neither did my husband.

When I first intimated that I was ready to go West, my husband ignored me. He didn't say so, but I knew he thought my passion for the marbled murrelet would soon fade. It didn't. The silver platter and the golden key gleamed constantly in my mind. A year later, my husband started looking for jobs on the West Coast. My only requirement, I told him, was that we had to live within the marbled murrelet's breeding range. The job market was tight, he said. Would I consider living a few hours from the southern edge of its winter range? There was a job opportunity waiting for him in southern California.

We sold our house, packed up our bags, and after a marathon of long and teary goodbyes, drove our two boys and dog across the country to a place where nothing was familiar and where we knew not a soul. This was our first big move and represented a quantum leap of faith for all of us—my husband's faith in my somewhat daring career move, my boys' faith that three thousand miles would not separate them from family and friends forever, and my faith in myself that I would have the energy and stamina to follow the marbled murrelet wherever it would lead me.

Once you take a broadax to your life, clean up the debris, and find yourself in a clear space, you cannot start shoveling everything back in with the first pangs of loneliness. I worked hard to ignore the fact that the phone never rang, that I didn't know my neighbors or my children's classmates, that I couldn't jump into other projects and jobs, and that we were going to see family and friends only when transcontinental flights were involved.

After a few weeks of unpacking boxes, I set up my computer and bookshelves, found the local libraries and natural history museum, and began planning my first trip north to murrelet country.

Our home was a long day's drive or a short flight from the Santa Cruz Mountains, the southernmost marbled murrelet breeding area. After more than a year of learning about the marbled murrelet, I was anxious to see one in the wild. I put in a call to Steve Singer, a biologist, environmental consultant, and birder who lives in the city of Santa Cruz. Steve has been involved with marbled murrelet studies since the 1970s and had written some of the early and intriguing articles I had read about the bird. Steve kindly invited me to join him in the meadow where he regularly conducts scientific surveys of marbled murrelets in the summer.

To do things right, I needed to adjust my schedule to be on Pacific Murrelet Time. I checked into a tent-cabin north of Santa Cruz, ate dinner at 5 P.M., and then went to bed at 8 P.M. after setting the alarm for 4 A.M. I woke and dressed in my birding costume—long underwear, leggings, sweatpants, waterproof hiking pants, two cotton T-shirts, a fleece jacket, wool socks and hat, hiking boots, and gloves. It was, after all, July on the foggy central California coast. The temperature was not too different from Iceland's in October, where I first assembled this cold-weather costume for a five-day getaway with my husband to explore the country's volcanic terrain. I have an aversion to being cold—and to listening to myself whine about it—so I wear this costume whenever I think the mercury might dip below fifty degrees.

I drove up the two-lane coastal highway toward the town of Pescadero and then turned onto a narrow, winding road that led through a deep forest to the rendezvous spot, a locked gate, where Steve said he would be waiting in his pickup truck. I pulled my car over to the side of the road, parked, and walked toward the truck. We shined our flashlights at our own faces and introduced ourselves. Steve wore a plaid flannel shirt, jeans, and a knit cap and had a salt-and-pepper beard. Had he been leaning on an ax, he would have been a dead ringer for a diminutive Paul Bunyan. I hopped into Steve's pickup, and we drove down a nearby dirt road and parked.

Steve handed me a plastic lawn chair from the back of his truck and led me to the middle of a half-acre meadow encircled by towering Douglas firs and coastal redwoods whose spiky, silhouetted tops jutted into the sky. We set up our chairs, sat down, then slouched further and further down until our heads rested on the backs of the chairs and we faced the sky. The circle of trees was too large to take in all at once, so I rotated my head, gazing from treetop to treetop and then straight up. I waited, staring up at the stars fading in the pre-dawn sky—a window of pixilated light, a swirling wash of pin-pricked black, blue, brown, beige, and white surrounded by the dark wall of soaring trees. It was magnificent even without marbled murrelets.

Still, I waited, a mere point in the 30 million years of human evolution, waiting for a bird that represented 205 million years of evolution. Soon my life would intersect with the marbled murrelet's in the present, in a single moment, in this meadow. I smiled. I was on course, in the right place at the right time, focused. I was so full of hope and anticipation that I felt I could will a wild bird out of an ancient forest.

"There's one," Steve whispered. It was 5:15 A.M. A small, dark shape came hurtling across the sky just above the tops of the 150-foot-high trees. The bird was flapping its wings rapidly and audibly. It streaked across the meadow to the west and disappeared. I had seen it—my first marbled murrelet. I felt as if I had discovered the first bird on the planet. I imagine birders seek that euphoric feeling as much as they seek the birds themselves.

A few minutes later, we heard a high-pitched *keer keer keer*, and then a pair of marbled murrelets flew by. A few minutes later, another. Soon I could recognize the birds' calls and turn my head toward the sounds as they emerged from dark forest into brightening sky. The birds were like fragments of the forest, dark pieces of the dark trees breaking off into pale space.

For about an hour, Steve Singer and I watched marbled murrelets cross and circle over the meadow before they headed to the ocean or into the forest behind us. Sometimes the birds flew low and silently. Other times we never saw them, but we heard their calls in the distance. When the sun lit up the meadow and forest, the show was done. This morning was a gift from the forest, one of nature's fleeting but breathtaking spectacles. I didn't want to leave. I wanted to will the sun back down so the show would start over.

My consolation prize was a visit later that afternoon to

the nearby Big Basin Redwoods State Park, an eighteen-thousand-acre gem of a park founded in 1902 to preserve an old-growth forest threatened by logging. The park is nestled in the Santa Cruz Mountains and spills down to the Pacific Ocean at Año Nuevo Bay. As remote and secluded as the park feels, it is a backyard forested playground for millions of people living in the San Francisco Bay Area. Roads in the park are paved, trails are wide, and RVs are welcomed. This was where the first marbled murrelet's nest was discovered in 1974—at a campground right off the park entrance road, adjacent to a parking lot, restrooms, and staff housing. How could an elusive bird hide its whereabouts here? How could anything remain a mystery with ten thousand visitors camping, hiking, and milling about each year? I would have understood the 185-year-long search effort had this discovery site been on some remote and uninhabited island—a little sand spit in the Aleutians, for instance. But Big Basin Redwoods State Park? This was yet another mystery.

In the 1970s, Steve Singer had worked as a park ranger here at Big Basin so he knew the exact location of the tree where the first marbled murrelet nest was spotted. Steve sent me directions to the site and a black-and-white photograph of the Douglas-fir. When I arrived at the park, I marched into the campground, expecting to find the tree within minutes, take a photograph, and then explore one of the park's hiking trails. I spent a good hour looking for that tree—one with a metal plate covering the place where the 148-foot-high nesting branch had been removed. When I found some Douglas firs that seemed to qualify, I scanned their upper branches with my binoculars. No luck.

The sun was getting low, but I was determined to find the tree before dark. I ran up to the park headquarters to call Steve for more specific directions. He assured me I was in the right place and gave me a few more landmarks and details. I went back down to the campground, took the first trail to the left after the parking lot, walked west toward a fallen tree and a picnic table, turned around, faced east, and looked up. There, catching the last light of the setting sun, was the metal plate. In those few moments before sunset, it shone like a beacon on a lighthouse.

As I gazed at the metal plate, it slowly dawned on me how high up 148 feet was. Imagine twenty-five six-foot-tall men standing on each other's heads. The person on top could rest his chin in the nest branch. A branch so lofty was accessible to only a few types of people—tree surgeons, loggers, people who work as professional cone harvesters, and very determined tree sitters. However, these were not the types of people involved in the search for the marbled murrelet's nest. Most of the people who *were* searching—naturalists, ornithologists, biologists, birders—did not have the skill or the guts required to climb two-hundred- and three-hundred-foot-high trees.

Had I been camping in the meadow or here at Big Basin the night before, alone and ignorant of the existence of marbled murrelets, I might have heard the early morning *keer* calls from inside my tent and assumed they had come from a gull, hawk, or dream. Had I been clearheaded and bright-eyed and staring at the open sky at 5:15 A.M., I might have seen the silhouette of something speeding past. A bat? A bird? A mote in my eye? I might have tried tracking the dark shapes streaking across the sky but I would have remained clueless. This bird gives so little of itself; the uninitiated observer just doesn't know what to think. That the mystery took 185 years to solve was suddenly understandable. That the number 185 would lead me aboard the HMS *Resolution* and to Captain James Cook confirmed my suspicions that the marbled murrelet had me under its spell.

CHAPTER 4

To arrive promptly in 1789, when the search for the marbled murrelet nest apparently began, you have to get a running start, in 1776, when the HMS *Resolution* and the HMS *Discovery* set sail from England for the Bering Sea under the command of Captain James Cook in search of the fabled Northwest Passage, a navigable waterway believed to connect the Pacific to the Atlantic. This four-year voyage—Cook's third and final voyage of discovery around the world—took the ships from Cape Town to Tasmania, New Zealand, Tahiti, Hawaii, and then northward along the uncharted coast of North America.

The ships reached the coast of Alaska in May 1778, where they encountered a spate of foul weather: fog, rain, and strong, impetuous gales. Under the strain, the *Resolution* began to leak. When the weather calmed, Cook ordered the ship into a sheltered cove in Prince William Sound where it was moored for repairs. The crew keeled the ship to port and, upon inspecting its bottom boards, discovered that rats had chewed holes through the wood right down to the copper sheathing.

For three days, the crew worked to plug the holes and repair the torn sheathing, no doubt cursing the rats mightily all the while. During this time, other crewmates boarded skiffs to explore the sound and to hunt waterfowl and game for food.

Dr. William Anderson went along to hunt in the name of science. Anderson, the ship's chief surgeon and naturalist, shot birds and small mammals to bring back to England for scientific study. Because the voyage had been undertaken at the command of King George III and in His Majesty's ships, everything Anderson collected was property of the British Admiralty. Upon return to England, officers of the admiralty would distribute the specimens to scientists, esteemed scholars, collectors, and museums in London and elsewhere in Europe as they chose.

Anderson may have been the first to spot the chunky little birds bobbing on the water, their heads and short tails cocked at a jaunty angle, but it likely took more than a few men to collect them. What the crew figured out soon enough was that the birds were adept at avoiding boats and diving out of sight at the first (missed) shot. In his expedition journal, Cook wrote of the ducks, geese, and other birds in the sound as "so fearfull that it was hardly possible to get a shot at them." But shoot they did, and eventually with some success.

When the *Resolution* returned to England in 1780, three—possibly four—small, web-footed seabirds were on board. The preserved birds arrived among hundreds of wooden crates and casks, jars, and bottles that held four years' worth of collected zoological and botanical specimens. They arrived without labels, identification numbers, or any kind of codes linking them to the published description, but it was these birds, scholars now believe, that are referred to in the description of Prince William Sound published in 1784 in the official account of Cook's third voyage:

There is likewise a species of diver here, which seems
peculiar to the place. It is about the size of a partridge;
has a short, black, compressed bill; with the head and
upper parts of the neck of a brown black; the rest of a
deep brown, obscurely waved with black, except the
under-part, which is entirely of a blackish cast, very
minutely varied with white; the other (perhaps a
female) is blacker above, and whiter below.

Neither Anderson nor Cook survived to match bird to
word. Dr. Anderson died of illness shortly after the boats left
Prince William Sound, and the good captain was murdered
in Hawaii the winter after the sightings. Anderson's
notebooks are now in the Zoological Library of the Natural
History Museum in London, but the third volume—the one
that could have contained the description of the "divers"—
was lost sometime after the ships returned to England.
William Ellis, the surgeon's mate and artist on the voyage,
kept a detailed journal of his observations and produced
many illustrations of the animals he encountered, but none
included a bird resembling a marbled murrelet.

Though the expedition account reads as if it all flowed
from the pen of Captain Cook, the description of the birds
does not appear in Cook's original journals. Scholars believe
that Captain James King, who commanded the expedition
upon its return to England in 1780—and who compiled and
wrote the official account—excerpted a description from Dr.
Anderson's now-lost journal. Anderson was not credited; it
was customary in the writing of expedition accounts for the

commander to make free use of every crewmate's journal without any obligation to attribute information to its original source.

Authorship aside, there now existed a published description of the marbled diver—the first to circulate among the learned of Europe. King George III was presented a much-coveted copy of the expedition account, as were the high-ranking officers of the British Admiralty and members of the British Royal Society and the Royal Academy of Sciences.

One of the birds was given to Sir Joseph Banks, the renowned English naturalist who had circumnavigated the globe as the official naturalist on Cook's first voyage, in 1768. A man of science and letters, Banks maintained an enormous library, herbarium, and collection of natural history specimens in his London home. His newly acquired seabird doubtless earned a place in one of his collection cabinets, perhaps on a shelf alongside other birds of similar provenance. News of the seabird spread by word of mouth. Naturalists and gentlemen collectors paid frequent visits to Banks's home to exchange the latest natural history news and to consult his books, drawings, and preserved specimens.

Captain James King presented two of the divers, along with many other items from the third voyage, to Sir Ashton Lever, an obsessive collector, unschooled naturalist, and friend of the late Captain Cook. According to one British historian, Lever was the "man to whom you gave or sold any eight-legged cats, stuffed crocodiles or Polynesian nose flutes that came your way." Lever's collection of artificial and natural curiosities, including many items from Cook's second Pacific voyage, filled his very popular and very eclectic Leverian Museum in London.

ENIGMA 31

Exactly how Lever displayed his two new nameless birds is not known, though he provided some sense of his curatorial style in a catalogue he published listing other articles he had acquired from the voyage. The divers may have appeared in one of several rooms featuring "admirable and curious articles collected by Captain Cook on his third and unhappily last voyage." Or they may have been displayed in a glass case "furnished with miscellaneous articles" including nests and eggs of birds—"some of them very curious . . . some of them labeled." How they were displayed was of little importance to the public. The birds were admired for other reasons: They were unfamiliar; they had come from halfway around the world, from the strange and frozen land of the Esquimaux; and they were a real connection to the lost and heroic Captain Cook.

Today, the only known extant specimen from the voyage can be found in the ornithology collection of the Natural History Museum in Vienna, Austria. In 1786, Sir Ashton Lever sold his museum and its collections to a Mr. James Parkinson, who moved the museum to a new building. When the museum failed to pay its way, Parkinson sold its contents at auction in 1806. The curator of the Imperial Collections in Vienna purchased several birds at the auction, including a diver in breeding plumage. This bird is now considered the type specimen of the marbled murrelet, meaning that it is *the* bird scientists first claimed to manifest the features of the marbled murrelet. When naturalists were unsure of the identity of a bird they had collected, they could visit this specimen for a careful examination of the real McCoy.

I have not traveled to Vienna to see the world's oldest

marbled murrelet, but I have spent some time with the marbled murrelet specimens at the natural history museum located just four miles from my home. Two of the specimens—adults in summer plumage—are posed to appear in flight as they hang from a nylon line in the Hall of Birds at the San Bernardino County Museum. Six marbled murrelet specimens are stored in a drawer in the museum's bird collection.

The collection is on the ground floor in a large room behind heavy-duty gray metal doors. The doors are tightly sealed to prevent insects from flying or crawling in and chewing and damaging the preserved animal specimens. Should any insects find their way in, mothballs placed in the collection drawers usually do them in. Some visitors, especially schoolchildren on field trips, never make it through the doors. The waft of mothball-scented air, and the sudden realization that they are entering what is essentially a bird morgue, sends them to the nearest chair for a breather or to a door leading to fresh air. The smell of isopropyl alcohol triggers the same reaction in me when I step inside a hospital, but my association with the scent of mothballs is an entirely pleasant one from my childhood. It is the fragrance of my stored wool sweaters, unchewed by moth larvae, on the first chilly day of autumn.

The first time I visited the museum's bird collection, I stared at the murrelet specimens for a few minutes, wondering, waiting. I imagine this is how Captain Cook, Dr. Anderson, and many of the visitors to the Leverian Museum felt staring for the first time at something they sensed was interesting or important without knowing exactly why.

The birds laid out before me weren't exactly birds, they were bird skins. Skins in this and every other bird collection assume the shape of real birds, but they are missing their soft tissue, organs, fat, and most of their bones. What's left after these are removed is a thin, feathered skin that looks like an empty coat—flaccid and shapeless. The birds regain their chunky figures when the skin is stuffed with cotton batting and sewn shut. No special treatment is given to the beak, wings, or webbed feet, as these parts do not contain fat or other rottable parts. Except for its eyes—small protrusions of white cotton—it would be easy to mistake a well-prepared skin for a recently lifeless bird, stretched out like a mummy, wings at its sides.

From the small handwritten tags tied to each bird's leg, I learned that five of the birds were collected in the Aleutian Islands in 1970 and 1971; one was collected in 1959 near San Luis Obispo, California. Three of the birds are male, three female. Two are in their brown breeding plumage; four are in subtly varied black-and-white winter plumage. A cryptic note on one female in breeding plumage reads "o. not e." After trying out some "o" and "e" words for a few minutes— *olfactories not even, organs not eviscerated, obviously not exemplary*—I figured this could only mean *ovulation not evident*. It must have been a young bird, or one who had yet to lay her first egg that year.

I picked up the specimen and turned it over to look at its torso. The feathers were mostly a soft white color, but there were what appeared to be someone's false eyelashes tucked here and there between the feathers. Each set of dark brown eyelashes had perhaps six or eight individual lashes—each lash was straight, delicate, and separate. When I looked closely, I saw that the lashes were actually the very fine tips of the white feathers.

I picked up another bird to see how many colors of brown and white I could distinguish in its plumage. Like real marble, there were too many colors to name. Many birders, naturalists, and ornithologists can read a bird's plumage and tell you the age of the bird, its breeding status, its molt cycle, and its health, and describe for you the behaviors you could expect to observe of a bird in a certain plumage. I sat there frustrated that I could do little more than admire the feathers. I knew there was a story in these feathers, in the colors and patterns they made, but I couldn't read it. The feathers were like tea leaves, and I was no mystic.

What "skin readers" can also tell about a marbled murrelet is whether or not it is a breeding bird. Careful examination of the feathers on the bird's abdomen may reveal a patch of exposed skin, called a brood patch, where the body heat of the adult is efficiently transferred to its egg during incubation and, later, to its newly hatched chick. While Dr. William Anderson, Joseph Banks, and Ashton Lever may have been aware of brood patches on the marbled murrelets they acquired, their interest in these birds surely would have had less to do with anatomy and behavior and more to do with taxonomy—where the birds fit in the grand scheme of things, how they were related to other birds. But just by collecting, preserving, storing, and displaying these "objects of curiosity," they told the world that the birds were somehow important and that they held secrets worth learning.

CHAPTER 5

O f the thousands of people who examined the marbled murrelet skins at the Leverian Museum and in Sir Joseph Banks's home in the 1780s, two men took an unusually keen interest in the divers from Prince William Sound. One was Dr. John Latham, an ornithologist, illustrator, naturalist, and successful physician from Kent. In 1780, Latham was nearing the completion of the first volume of his comprehensive *A General Synopsis of Birds*. In it he would provide the first published names and descriptions of many birds, including dozens collected on Cook's voyages.

Of all the birds that John Latham had studied in the field and in Swedish botanist Carl Linnaeus's *Systema Naturae*, Latham believed the unusual marbled birds were guillemots— medium-sized auks that, in winter plumage, bear a striking resemblance to the divers from Prince William Sound. Latham included them in his book as "marbled guillemots."

Welsh naturalist, antiquary, and author Thomas Pennant also lingered over the specimens in London. Pennant was a close friend of Latham, Banks, and Lever and, like Latham, he was anxious to learn of the latest zoological news for a book he was writing. The four men were undoubtedly in agreement about the marbled birds because, in 1784, when Pennant published his *Arctic Zoology*, he

listed them as "marbled guillemots" and described them
much as Latham had:

> *With a black bill: crown dusky; throat, breast, and*
> *belly, mottled with black and white: back and sides*
> *very glossy, and marbled with black and rust-color:*
> *wings dusky; greater coverts edged with white; tail*
> *black: legs yellow; webs black. LENGTH nine inches.*
> *Inhabits* Prince William's Sound *on the western coast*
> *of* North America, *and probably Kamtschatka.*

The description is about as straightforward as they
come. What makes Pennant's treatment of the "marbled
guillemot" unique is that it features a beautifully detailed
engraving of two birds. One is a pied-billed grebe sitting on
the rippling surface of a vague body of water; the other is our
"marbled guillemot" displaying in exquisite detail the distinctive marbled pattern of its throat and breast. The grebe
looks off into the clouds. But something is dreadfully wrong
with the "guillemot," and the whites of its eyes show it. It is
standing on the platformlike bank of the shore, its webbed
feet firmly planted on the ground, in the strange company
of the grebe. Stranger yet is the thrust of its head, the splay
of its legs, and the angle of its body. Our "marbled
guillemot" looks like a prairie chicken.

No one in the eighteenth century would have found the
image of the bird odd or criticized it as implausible, unscientific, or at all comical. Few Europeans had ever seen the bird
alive and in its natural habitat. Based on what was known of
web-footed diving birds at the time, the image seemed correct.

Despite the name Pennant gave the bird or what he wrote about the "marbled guillemot," I have a theory that his readers were more likely to remember this engraving. This earth-bound, shore-hugging image of our bird—Pennant's and others'—would persist for the next two hundred years. Until quite recently, every engraving, watercolor, pen-and-ink drawing, and even a photograph (amateurishly doctored in an early scientific journal) of this seabird appeared at home by the sea—on the ground at the edge of the continent. Every published image reinforced the same wrong ideas about this bird's behavior on land—ideas that would hamper the search for its mysterious nest.

The fact that the bird now had a name did not take the world by storm. It did not require anyone to initiate a study, send a collecting expedition back to Prince William Sound, or plan to exploit the bird and its eggs as a food source. Like many of the zoological specimens collected on Captain Cook's three round-the-world voyages, the marbled murrelets were merely clues for the scientists, curiosities for the public, pieces of a puzzle, souvenirs from the far side of the newly rounded earth. It did mean, however, that word of the bird's existence could spread. There is no evidence to prove or disprove this, but I like to think that Sir Ashton Lever placed a new label next to his marbled murrelets—a small hand-written tag for visitors to squint at as they streamed past. And I hope that Sir Joseph Banks showed his bird to his fellow scientists with a flourish not unlike that of a sommelier presenting a fine French wine. "Gentlemen . . . the marbled guillemot." It is not out of the question that Banks talked of the bird to his friend and confidant, King George III, if only to make sure he knew the bird had been collected in Alaska in a place Captain Cook had named to honor the king's son, Prince William, whose name in French is *Guillaume*.

Word spread far beyond London as copies of Latham's *General Synopsis of Birds* and Pennant's *Arctic Zoology* were shipped to university libraries and imperial collections throughout Europe. Sometime before 1788, these two treasured texts found their way to Gmelin.

When I first encountered this odd name, I wasn't sure if *Gmelin* was a person, place, or typo. In most of the scientific papers I had been reading on marbled murrelets, the name Gmelin and the date 1789 usually appeared together in parentheses just after an author's first reference to the marbled murrelet, as in "Studies of the marbled murrelet (Gmelin, 1789) are being conducted in Alaska." The few biologists I asked (and seemed to catch off guard) knew that Gmelin was a man, probably a German. No one knew Gmelin's first name or exactly why his name became cemented to the marbled murrelet's.

To solve this new mystery, I first had to learn to pronounce Gmelin: *gmay-leen*. Discovering Gmelin's first name was not so easy. The *Larousse Dictionary of Scientists* listed three Gmelins: Johann Georg Gmelin, who in 1789 had been dead for thirty-three years; Samuel Theophilus Gmelin, who had been dead for fourteen years; and Leopold Gmelin, who was just one year old that year. All belonged to a family of distinguished scientists from the ancient city of Tubingen, Germany (where a university had been founded in 1477), and all were accomplished scientists in their day—but not in 1789. The Gmelins I found in the online version of the 1911 edition of the *Encyclopedia Britannica* brought to nine the total number of scientifically inclined Gmelins. Only one of the nine had a birthday that qualified him as a candidate for accomplishing *anything* in 1789. This was Johann Friedrich Gmelin, who would have been forty-one that year. This was my man.

Following closely in the footsteps of his grandfather, father, and uncle, Johann Friedrich was a student and then professor of medicine at the university in Tubingen. Like all doctors of his time, he was knowledgeable in all fields concerning natural science and published widely on chemistry, medicine, botany, zoology, and mineralogy. Gmelin distinguished himself as the chair of medicine and chemistry at the university in Gottingen. In 1788, he was offered the job of updating the twelfth edition of Linnaeus' *Systema Naturae.* Linnaeus had died ten years earlier and the twelfth edition, now more than twenty years old, was badly outdated. Gmelin accepted the position and spent an entire year on the project, relying heavily on the works of Pennant and Latham to revise, name, and reclassify many species, especially the birds.

In 1788, the thirteenth edition of *Systema Naturae* was published in Latin. Gmelin retained the English name marbled guillemot and assigned the bird its official two-part Latin scientific name: *Colymbus marmoratus.* Though Pennant and Latham had already placed the bird in the *Colymbus* genus, had first used the descriptive term "marbled," *and* had published a description of the bird, Gmelin gets the credit. Why? According to the 1958 International Code of Zoological Nomenclature, species became species only when they were given two-part Latin names and described in the tenth or subsequent editions of Linnaeus's *Systema Naturae*.

And as for 1789? Gmelin's thirteenth edition of *Systema Naturae* was actually published in 1788 in Leipzig, Germany. It was the English translation that was published in London in 1789.

So much for blissful mornings spent spotting murrelets in picturesque meadows. I was spending more time than I planned Googling Gmelins, hunting down rare books, and reading articles in publications such as the *Journal of the Society for the Bibliography of Natural History*. And yet when the librarian at the UCLA Bio-Medical Library's Rare Book Division brought me Pennant's 1784 *Arctic Zoology*—a copy signed by the author, no less—I wanted to kiss her hands, so grateful was I for the opportunity to hold this book, to turn its thick, irregular pages, and to find yet one more clue to the mystery of the marbled murrelet.

I didn't feel quite so grateful when confronted by the bird's taxonomy. Taxonomy is the naming and orderly classification of living organisms based on such things as habitat, food habits, locomotion, and physical appearance. Thanks to Linnaeus and other scientists, every living thing has been classified with other living things into a series of groups, called taxa—kingdom, phylum, class, order, family, genus, species. You may recall the mnemonic King Phillip Came Over For Good Spaghetti. Human beings, for example, belong to the kingdom of Animals, phylum Chordata (living things with spinal cords), class Mammalia, order Primate, family Hominidae, genus *Homo*, species *sapien*.

Taxidermy, of course, is the art of preserving, stuffing, and mounting the skins of formerly living things. While you may go peacefully to your grave without ever dealing with taxonomy, it's harder to escape the art of taxidermy: It is what brings us the glass-eyed elk heads in pool halls and bars, the glistening marlins on seafood restaurant walls, and most every animal on display in natural history museums around the world. Both taxidermy and taxonomy are messy, but in the case of the marbled murrelet, the early efforts of taxonomists ironically seem to have worked against the understanding of this bird's breeding behavior and, ultimately, against its survival as well.

From the moment the crew of the HMS *Resolution* collected the marbled "diver," this seabird was a conundrum. No one knew what kind of bird it was. Not until 1837, after much taxonomic shuffling, was the marbled murrelet placed in a new genus and given its current scientific name, *Brachyramphus marmoratus*, which derives from the Greek *brachy*, or "short," and *ramphus*, for "beak," and from the Latin *marmoratus*, meaning "marbled." On paper, the marbled guillemot officially became the marbled murrelet—so named because it appeared to someone as a diminutive version of the much larger murre.

The marbled murrelet is not the only murrelet. There's also the Japanese murrelet, the ancient murrelet, Craveri's murrelet, Xantus's murrelet, the long-billed murrelet, and Kittlitz's murrelet. Where their ranges overlap in Alaska, the marbled murrelet and the Kittlitz's murrelet are nearly impossible to tell apart. In size these murrelets are but an inch apart in wingspan and a fraction of an ounce apart in weight.

Their black-and-white winter plumage differs by but a few splashes of white, their summer plumage by a few dashes of brown.

And, because they looked alike, nineteenth-century naturalists assumed these two murrelets would behave alike. They expected them to appear during breeding season in the well-known landscape of European alcid intimacy—the bare ground along the seaward side of the coast.

In 1838, a pair of marbled murrelets appeared before hundreds of naturalists and bird enthusiasts. The birds were seen—close up and as clear as day—sitting upright, penguin-style, on the edge of a flat cliff, their yellow webbed feet planted flatly on the ground. One bird was an adult feathered in brown, the other a juvenile in black and white. Both stared fixedly at something just beyond the tips of their dagger-like beaks. The hundreds of lucky naturalists stared for a long while, savoring the rare glimpse of such creatures . . . then turned the page. They had been looking at engraved prints of the paintings of American naturalist John James Audubon in his just-published *Birds of America*.

Hundreds of people purchased copies of Audubon's engravings in 1838. In the following years, thousands more came upon copies as they were reengraved, reprinted, recol- ored, and retouched. Audubon, apparently unaware of the bird's "official" name of 1837, referred to the birds as "slender-billed guillemots," a name that further tangled the bird's taxonomic lineage. Audubon was not the first—nor would he be the last—to give *Brachyramphus marmoratus* a different common name. It's been called a marbled guillemot, Townsend's murrelet, marbled auk, and Wrangell's murrelet.

Today, even though marbled murrelet is the accepted common name, there are several common names—nicknames, really—by which the bird is still known: fog lark, dip chick, buzz bomb, Australian hummingbird, kiss-me-ass bird, and little hell diver.

Audubon drew from life when he could, but in this case he did not. His decision to paint the birds at the sea's edge with their webbed feet flat on the ground was based on information from other naturalists who suspected that the birds must have behaved this way . . . when they weren't looking. Though Audubon's portrait of the marbled murrelet never enjoyed the popularity of his Carolina parakeets or flamingos, the image of the bird impressed fellow naturalists. It was a beautifully detailed vision, one that corroborated their thoughts about this species' behavior. It was a vision they hoped would appear before them on some afternoon ramble along the Pacific, in a scramble out to that remote cliff, that narrow ledge, that precipitous rock. There, when their footing was sure and their ocean-misted glasses wiped dry, they would look up and behold two marbled murrelets just like Audubon's.

Nothing in Audubon's portrait or in the minds of any naturalists in the mid-nineteenth century tied the birds to inland hills or the forests that spilled down to the ocean. These were seabirds. They were alcids. Their world was the sea, the air, and the merest wedge of land between the two. As long as these murrelets faced the sea in the minds of the artists, naturalists, and taxonomists, they would be untouched by the changes happening at their backs. For as these seabirds were swimming in the cold waters of the Pacific, untold numbers of explorers, gold miners, trappers, loggers, farmers, builders, and railroad workers were heading west.

Not until 1896 did anyone turn inland to ponder the behavior of the marbled murrelet or its strange, clandestine flights over the deep forest of the changing landscape.

CHAPTER 6

In 1896, a nineteen-year-old college student from Pasadena, California, caught a ride on a sailing sloop headed two thousand miles up the coast to Sitka, Alaska, where he would spend the summer exploring its island-studded waters, rocky shores, and ancient spruce forests. The young man was Joseph Grinnell, already a skilled bird collector and naturalist and on his way to becoming one of California's greatest ornithologists.

In Alaska, Grinnell found work in Sitka's newly opened Sheldon Jackson Museum, where he was paid $1.50 a week to assist in the museum on "boat day," when the weekly boatload of tourists arrived to see the exhibits of local artifacts. But mostly, he collected birds for display and study at the museum. In some of his early letters home, the young Grinnell's energy and enthusiasm for birds—and life—are wonderfully evident.

I have fine company now—A Prof. and Mrs. Hindshaw from the University of Washington who are collecting plants, birds, bugs, & everything else. . . . We get up great meals I tell you. My! But the spread we had last night! Flapjacks! 16 Plover roasted in a Dutch Oven, the finest meat I have ever tasted; Venison, Salmon, etc. And after supper we went a few yards back

of the house and picked all the Huckle-berries and
Salmon-berries we could eat, and plenty for pies. . . . It
is very pretty weather here now. I never was so well and
happy in my life. Think of it! In a new country, collecting
new birds every day. It's my idea of a good time.

After reading this letter, excerpted in a 1940 issue of the journal *Condor*, I wondered if such enthusiasm, such appetite, was a requirement for anyone pursuing marbled murrelets in the field. Certainly, the murrelet researchers I have met seem to have taken a page from Grinnell's notebook. I, too, can feel every one of Grinnell's exclamation points when I reflect back on my own move to California— my "new country"—to pursue this bird.

Once Joseph Grinnell had collected enough of the conspicuous puffins and murres in the waters around Sitka, he set his sights on birds he would later describe as the "tiny, timid Murrelets, which would not allow themselves to be taken so easily." Grinnell had attempted to collect his first marbled murrelets from his friend's sailing sloop, but the birds flew out of range as the boat approached. After Grinnell befriended the native Tlingit and mastered the use of their "rolling treacherous Indian canoes," he had better luck. But still he found that the wind had to be just right and the water rippling just so in order for him to secure even one bird out of every three shots.

Grinnell worked at it all summer. He observed and collected marbled murrelets at dawn, midday, and dusk; in the open bay, in sounds, and inlets; upwind and downwind; when the breezes shifted; when the water was erratic. He knew the birds on the water, in flight, and starting upwards "uttering their weird, wild cries." Grinnell collected enough marbled murrelets to notice that all the adults he collected in July and August had brood patches. He knew this meant that the birds were incubating an egg or warming a newly hatched chick somewhere. But where? Grinnell asked his native Tlingit companions on the island. No one knew.

In May 1897, Grinnell published a lengthy and detailed article about the marbled murrelet in a short-lived ornithological journal called the *Osprey*. In the article, he included an intriguing story from the Tlingit who, though they did not name the birds specifically, told Grinnell that they heard the birds "at night passing high over the mountains and islands" and that they were "wonderful, strangely-colored birds which raise their young in hollow trees high on the mountain side, just below snow line; but nobody has ever reached them." Grinnell made no comment on the information, but the fact that he included it at all is significant. It was the first inkling published in scientific literature that the marbled murrelets might not behave like other alcids.

Close upon the heels of Grinnell, George G. Cantwell arrived in southeast Alaska in 1897 to survey birds and mammals for the U.S. Biological Survey, the precursor of today's U.S. Fish and Wildlife Service. Cantwell was one of hundreds of sportsmen, ornithologists, field collectors, and nature enthusiasts recruited for a national inventory of fauna. Cantwell stepped onto the shores of Prince of Wales Island and set up camp at a native Haida village near present-day Ketchikan, not far from Grinnell's stomping grounds in Sitka.

One May morning, a young Haida who had befriended Cantwell asked to borrow his gun to shoot ducks. Cantwell loaned him his gun with the instructions to bring back some "divers" if he could. The boy returned from the water that afternoon with four marbled murrelets, one of which appeared to have an egg in it. Before Cantwell could stop him, the boy squeezed the bird's abdomen and broke the egg within. Cantwell opened up the bird and discovered a large, fully formed green egg spotted with black and brown. Recognizing this rarity, Cantwell patched it up the best he could and sent his "almost perfect specimen" to the Smithsonian Institution in Washington, D.C.

When Cantwell asked the Haida elders what they knew about the bird, they told him that they thought the bird bred "high up on the mountains in hollow trees." One man declared that "he had found the young in such places." Cantwell searched the woods for many hours, but he had no success finding a nest site. His report, published in the January 1898 issue of the journal the *Auk*, raised the eyebrows of William Leon Dawson, a well-respected naturalist and egg collector.

"The 'hollow tree' touch is doubtful," Dawson wrote of Cantwell's story, "for no bird in this group could 'dock' in a hole in a tree with sufficient accuracy to guarantee a continuance of the race." Despite his lighthearted skepticism, Dawson's own exploration of Washington State's Olympic Peninsula in the early 1900s yielded strikingly similar stories. The Quileute Indians told Dawson that the birds "do not nest like the other seafowl upon the rocky islets, but that they colonize upon some of the higher slopes of the Olympic Mountains where they lay their eggs in burrows." In his authoritative *The Birds of Washington*, published in 1909, Dawson included this story, Cantwell's story, and word from the Aleutian Islands that marbled murrelets nested in holes and crevices along with ancient murrelets. And, in his charming and disarming style, Dawson introduced an intriguing anecdote:

"It sounds fishy, I know," he begins, "but I have one slight confirmation for such a hypothesis. At Glacier, on the North Fork of the Nooksack River, and near the foot of Mount Baker, having risen before daybreak for an early bird walk, on the morning of May 11, 1905, I heard voices from an invisible party of marbled murrelets high in the air as they proceeded down the valley, as tho to repair to the sea for the day's fishing."

The town of Glacier, where Dawson heard the birds, is twenty-four miles inland from the nearest salt water. Why were the birds so far inland? Dawson did not pretend to know. He knew enough, however, to declare the nesting of the marbled murrelet "an engaging mystery." No longer was the bird's nesting behavior and nest site merely considered "unknown" or "not known as yet" in the scientific literature. In 1909, it had become a mystery.

In May 1914, Dawson was camping with a party in the foothills of the Santa Cruz Mountains in California, where he encountered marbled murrelets again.

I roused at early dawn to see a dark meteor crossing the sky and going down the valley in a fashion which suggested an Auklet or a Murrelet; but because the bird was silent, I let the incident pass unchallenged. When,

however, some fifteen minutes later I heard cries, meer,
meer, *as familiar as the voices of childhood, I sprang to
my feet. Two pairs of marbled murrelets passed overhead in full cry, each going straight down the valley at
a height about twice that of the surrounding redwoods.*

The cries woke Dawson the next morning, and he arose
in time to observe six birds descending from the forested
hills. "Somewhere on the slopes of Ben Lomond," he wrote,
"there is a nesting colony of marbled murrelets, and these
birds were returning to sea-duty after spending the night
with their mates or young."

In the summer of 1916, Dawson was camped in
northern California, half a mile from the ocean near
Trinidad in Humboldt County. Over several days, he heard
and observed marbled murrelets flying directly overhead in
the evening and in the early morning. Remarkable to
Dawson was that at night the birds were *"bound for the
interior."* Dawson's italics indicate how important this observation was—that inbound nighttime flights suggested the
birds were not just flying over the forests but were perhaps
roosting away from the sea. A few weeks later, while visiting
friends in Carlotta, an outpost of a town in the heart of
northern California's redwood country, Dawson heard the
birds again, this time flying down a nearby valley toward the
ocean. Dawson and the birds were twenty miles inland.
There was no turning back. Once Dawson had published
these observations of marbled murrelets in his *The Birds of
California* in 1923, any well-read naturalist searching for a
marbled murrelet nest went inland.

But even after eliminating the coastal cliffs and rocky out-
crops from the search, the potential territory was incompre-
hensibly vast, the terrain often rugged and inaccessible, and
the forest the perfect hiding place. The mystery of the marbled
murrelet was no less mysterious. The same year Dawson's book
was published, forty-six-year-old Joseph Grinnell, now
California's top ornithologist, began a series of observations of
the marbled murrelet's inland behavior. His notes begin in
Carlotta, at the same home of H. E. Wilder visited by
Dawson.

"Each morning since I've been here," Grinnell wrote in
his 1923 field journal, "I've heard cries of some sort of birds
high overhead in the fog. . . . At first I thought they might be
hawks. Then I began to remember some of the same notes
years ago, on Pescadero Creek in the Santa Cruz Mountains,
and, I think, Sitka, Alaska—*marbled murrelets!* This morning,
the fog was higher than usual and also the producers of the
cries were out later than usual, up to 5:35 A.M. And I saw
them! Birds with small chunky bodies, and rapidly, continu-
ously beating small wings, like a small duck, very high, sometimes entering the fog. . . . They swung in great circles
overhead, or seemed going straight-away. It would be easy to
imagine them passing between the ocean to the west of us and
the forested slopes of the mountain within half a mile of us.
Truly a mystery!"

Middlepoint Bight
The juvenile with
adults in attendance
close by. Aug 26 97

To imply, as I have, that Dawson and Grinnell knew the most about marbled murrelets at the turn of the century is but a half-truth. To state as a fact that the official naming of the bird by Gmelin marks the beginning of knowledge of the bird is misleading. To declare that the history of man and murrelet begins aboard the HMS *Resolution* with Captain Cook or Dr. William Anderson in 1778 is specious.

Most of what I have learned about the early history of the marbled murrelet is from books, published copies of ships' logs, field notes, texts, and scientific journals. What *really* began aboard the HMS *Resolution* is the paper trail that chronicles events of man and murrelet. Only by writing down what they knew—and publishing it—did these early naturalists receive credit for their knowledge. But Anderson didn't collect the first marbled murrelet, nor did Gmelin or any other European give the bird its first name, nor were Grinnell and Dawson the first to share their observations of these birds year after year on the Pacific Coast.

I cannot name the man or woman who deserves credit for these firsts. No one will ever know who heard the first *keer* call or who caught the first glimpse of the birds at dawn; marbled murrelets evolved into their present form millions of years before the first humanlike beings appeared. But there are stories of the marbled murrelet, human stories, that can be traced back thousands of years before anyone took pen to paper. These stories are held in the earth, in the archaeological record, in piles of bones left behind by prehistoric cultures.

Archaeologists have unearthed skeletal remains of the marbled murrelet dating from 1,600 to 4,000 years ago at numerous sites along the West Coast of North America. In British Columbia, digs at Hesquiat Harbour and Yuquot on Vancouver Island contained leg and wing bones, as did the St. Mungo Cannery Site in the Fraser River Delta on the British Columbia mainland. Archaeologists unearthed bones at the Hoko River Rockshelter and at an Ozette site on the tip of Washington State's Olympic Peninsula. Excavated sites at Yaquina Head and Seaside along the Oregon coast also yielded marbled murrelet bones.

The Yuquot site on Vancouver Island is particularly interesting, as the number of murrelet bones is dispropor-tionately large compared to those of other alcids and seabirds. All of the marbled murrelet bones unearthed were intact; none had butchering marks indicating the birds had been prepared for cooking or used for making weapons, tools, or decorative items. Why, with so many other larger-boned, meatier, and easier-to-catch seabirds available, would the natives have gone out of their way to pursue a marbled murrelet for a meal? According to some archaeologists, no one did. The birds were most likely caught unintentionally with other seabirds and then perhaps tossed whole into the stew pot.

Not all coastal-dwelling people ate marbled murrelets. For some, the marbled murrelet carried spiritual significance. The marbled murrelet figures prominently in Tlingit mythology. One story involves a man named Murrelet, who possessed the power to move swiftly up cliffs no other men could scale. As a child, Murrelet had been trained to run up steep cliffs by having a heavy mountain sheep's hoof tied to his leg or around his neck while he tried to climb up the walls of his house. As a young man, Murrelet was captured during the First War in the World—a war between two Tlingit groups. His captors took him by canoe to a steep cliff along the shore and demanded proof of his climbing skills. Murrelet failed three times and fell back into the canoe, complaining that he didn't have the necessary ax, staff, flint, and grease he always climbed with. After his captors equipped him properly, Murrelet stepped out of the canoe, called like the murrelet, and went flying up to the very top of the mountain.

Through other stories in other Native cultures, it is evident that the marbled murrelet was a revered and familiar bird. Some Tlingit groups considered the marbled murrelet the "mother of Raven"—a great position of power and mystique. One translation for one of the Tlingit names for marbled murrelet is "they just ruffle up the water." William Leon Dawson reported that *Tichaahlukchtih* was the ancient name used for the birds by the Quileute people he visited on the coast of Washington.

Paul Jones, a writer and marbled murrelet researcher from British Columbia, says that the bird also figures prominently in the culture and mythology of the native people of British Columbia. For the Tsimshians, Jones learned, the marbled murrelet had "special significance because it knew the mysteries of the deep and communed with the spirits of the unseen world beneath the sea." *Spipiyus* is the name the native people of the

Sunshine Coast gave to this bird; Spipiyus Provincial Park in the Caren Range was so named because it preserves the ancient forests where the bird nests. An elder of the Sechelt Indian Band told Jones that his people "revere the murrelet" and "know its mischievous nature and its close association with fishing."

One story of man's spiritual associations with marbled murrelets can be drawn out of a hat. This particular hat is carved out of cedar and is painted red, green, and black. On the top of the hat is a carved bird—a marbled murrelet— whose carved wings are partially open as if it is preparing for flight. Tufts of human hair, six to eight inches long, have been fitted into the wood in the front part of the wing where the quill of the feathers would be attached on a live bird. When the person wearing the hat moved, as in walking, dancing, or advancing in battle, the tufts of hair would move and could create the impression of the fluttering movement of the mur- relet's wings. This stunning hat belongs to a Tlingit tribe of southeast Alaska, the Brown Bear House of the Kaagwaantaan Clan, whose crest symbol is the marbled murrelet.

In 1998, the Tlingit clan hat made the national news. After being on display for more than ten years at the Eiteljorg Museum of American Indians and Western Art in Indianapolis, Indiana, the hat was brought back to Alaska by representatives of the clan. Under the Native American Graves Protection and Repatriation Act, the hat—an item of cultural, historical, and traditional importance to the Kaagwaantaan Clan—rightfully belonged to the clan. The hat is now back home in Haines, Alaska, where future genera- tions of Tlingit can marvel at the carved bird and its ethereal wings.

CHAPTER 8

William Leon Dawson went further out on a limb than most of those involved with the great mystery of the marbled murrelet. According to fellow naturalist Harry Swarth, Dawson did not "feel called upon to serve some such abstraction as Truth or Science." Dawson laid out evidence and told stories that made sense to him in the here and now—even when they were secondhand, anecdotal, or just plain fishy. Most weren't. Dawson's books were scientific, entertaining, and extremely popular. Copies of his books sold out quickly and were must-haves for ornithologists and amateur naturalists alike.

In his *The Birds of Washington* and *The Birds of California*, Dawson combines a scientific description of the marbled murrelet and exclamation point–rich stories of his efforts to solve the nest mystery. Dawson's well-organized accounts summarized some seventy years of evidence in several pages of cohesive paragraphs with tidy, justified margins. Anyone reading Dawson's accounts—and they can be read and absorbed in less than ten minutes—might conclude that the study of the marbled murrelet was well-organized, cohesive, and tidy and that Dawson was just one of the many ornithologists purposefully studying this bird.

Marbled murrelet research has always been an untidy

science. I spent about a month trying to create a chronological summary of early marbled murrelet breeding records—sightings of adults flying inland, chicks on the forest floor, nests on the ground, clutches of eggs, and evidence of tree nesting. I tracked down back issues of naturalist club newsletters, bulletins, and scientific journals such as the *Murrelet* (now *Northwest Naturalist*), *Auk, Condor, Victorian Naturalist, Canadian Field-Naturalist,* and *Wilson Bulletin*—journals still in publication today. Some of these are published monthly, others quarterly, still others less frequently. Most of the articles appeared between 1918 and 1956—years that cover two world wars and the Great Depression, a time when news about a mysterious bird would have been a pleasant diversion. Reports came from well-known ornithologists, serious birders, professional egg collectors, and regular folks with a soft spot for orphaned fledglings.

I laid out all the reports on my office floor in what I thought would be chronological order based on the date of the publication. I found that the date the evidence was collected—the bird sighted, the chick found, or the egg discovered—bore little relation to the date news of it was published. There routinely were three months of lag time and sometimes as many as thirty years between the two events. This is not unusual given the situation the world was in during the first half of the twentieth century and given the incremental nature of scientific discoveries—the years of small events that lead up to the grand "eureka!" Should anyone have been trying to track the mystery of the marbled murrelet in print in real time beginning in the early 1900s, they would not have known what to think about this strange bird and its nesting habits. The evidence just didn't add up. Though the records were reported in well-respected journals—and often by well-known ornithologists—there was often no way for a reader to know if the authors were credible or if the news they shared was valid, dubious, significant, apocryphal, or scandalous. Ironically, though you can now find on the Internet all the information you could possibly want with a few clicks of a computer mouse, the problem of credibility still exists.

One of the most widespread and misleading reports came from the remote Queen Charlotte Islands in British Columbia where, in the 1920s, professional egg collector Solomon John Darcus had been working and observing marbled murrelets. After searching for marbled murrelet nests on the rugged islands for four years, Darcus announced in a 1927 issue of the *Canadian Field-Naturalist* that he had discovered the marbled murrelet's nest site. The find supposedly came after hours of climbing on the steep cliff faces of tiny Cox Island, where he said he came upon a colony of twenty pairs of marbled murrelets and several deep underground burrows about two hundred feet above sea level. Darcus reports reaching into the three burrows, causing the adult bird within to back farther into the burrow and allowing him to secure three eggs from within side chambers lined with dry grass and leaves. Darcus also reportedly collected a fourth egg from a deep crevice in the rock the following day. "The eggs are all in my collection," Darcus writes at the end of his four-page article. The editors of the *Canadian Field-Naturalist* swallowed the story, but Reverend C. J. Young did not.

I learned this from Gary Kaiser, an ornithologist who was working in British Columbia for the Canadian Wildlife Service in the 1990s when a set of original handwritten letters to and from Darcus and two other ornithologists was being purged from the service's files and sent to the trash. Gary saved the letters and kindly loaned them to me to piece together this scandal of the "scrambled eggs."

Reverend Young was an ornithologist who had traveled with Darcus to the Queen Charlotte Islands the year before the "discovery." But Young did not recall that Darcus showed any interest in marbled murrelet nests during their trip. When the reverend read the news in a British oological bulletin that Darcus had sold two marbled murrelet eggs to a collector in England for $1,000, he was flabbergasted. Such a huge price tag on the eggs—the equivalent of a new Studebaker Roadster at the time—raised questions in Young's mind about Darcus' credibility and motivation. In the 1929 annual *Report of the Provincial Museum*, Reverend Young described Darcus's marbled murrelet eggs as "quite doubtful." That was not enough to deter Darcus from collecting more eggs, nor did the doubt the reverend cast on the authenticity of the "marbled murrelet" eggs affect Darcus's sales.

In 1932, however, R. A. Cumming of the British Columbia Ornithologists Union wrote a letter to F. A. Munro, the chief federal migratory bird officer of Canada's western provinces. Cumming's letter purports that Darcus had in fact been collecting the eggs of the ancient murrelet and intentionally selling them as marbled murrelet eggs. Cumming had become suspicious of Darcus's motives when he serendipitously encountered him in the Queen Charlotte Islands and noticed that Darcus "seemed evasive." When Cumming later brought up Darcus's name to the native Haida people of the Queen Charlottes, he learned that many knew Darcus, but none spoke well of him, especially a man named Pavic. Darcus had hired Pavic to guide him to various bird nests and to scale the local cliffs and collect eggs for him in recent years. In fact, Pavic was about to burn an entire box of eggs he had recently collected for Darcus since Darcus had failed to pay him his month's wages for guiding him around the island. In the box Cumming found the eggs of seven song sparrows, five guillemots, nine puffins, one oystercatcher, fourteen cormorants, and twenty-six ancient murrelets—but not a single marbled murrelet egg.

News of Darcus's wheeling and dealing should not have surprised Munro. In a letter he had received from Darcus before the *Canadian Field-Naturalist* article was published, Darcus provided specific details of the location of the burrow, the birds within them, and the number of eggs he discovered—details inconsistent with those published in the *Canadian Field-Naturalist.*

Darcus never defended his claim publicly, never admitted to any deceit, acknowledged an honest mistake, or discovered more eggs as evidence. Darcus likely wanted to sweep the entire issue under the carpet, as his reputation and his livelihood were at stake. In a 1930 issue of the *Canadian Field-Naturalist,* Darcus presented four pages of notes on the birds he observed in the Queen Charlotte Islands in 1927. Darcus devoted only four lines to the marbled murrelets on Cox Island: "Abundant; one breeding colony found."

Since no other nests or eggs of the marbled murrelet were found and documented for nearly fifty years, no one could disprove Darcus's claim. In fact, mention of Darcus's marbled murrelets nest discovery continued to appear in scientific journals well into the 1970s, if only to be claimed as "unlikely" or "dubious."

Not all of the early clues to the breeding habits of marbled murrelets were discovered by oologists or ornithologists. In many cases, grounded chicks were discovered accidentally by motorists, hikers, and picnickers. In 1918, for instance, a Mr. A. B. Johnson picked up a dead marbled murrelet chick from a road six miles inland from the Heceta Head Lighthouse near Florence, Oregon. Though Johnson may or may not have known what kind of bird he found, he wisely gave the bird to Overton Dowell, a well-known bird collector living nearby. Dowell prepared the bird and added it to his private collection of some seven hundred local bird skins. Like Dr. William Anderson, Joseph Banks, Ashton Lever, and other collectors, Dowell may not have known the identity of the bird or its significance. For some reason, he did not publicize the find. But he preserved it. Eleven years later, in 1929, Oregon ornithologist Stanley G. Jewett visited Dowell and examined his collection. Jewett found several birds "of unusual interest," including the marbled murrelet chick. In the March 1930 issue of the *Condor,* Jewett declared the chick to be the youngest of the species yet collected and stated that it was "too young to have flown far from where it had hatched." The way science works often seems very unscientific. One day a motorist picks up roadkill, and eleven years later it becomes evidence that marbled murrelets might nest well inland.

My favorite accidental naturalist story comes from Olive Barber, who during the summer of 1940 was hiking along the Coos River in Oregon when she discovered a strange bird on the forest floor about twenty-five miles inland. She rescued the bird—a flightless chick—took it home, and after consulting some two dozen books, identified it as "that rarity, a young marbled murrelet." Barber kept the bird in a box for two weeks and fed it a "heaping tablespoonful" of minced clam every two hours during the day and twice during the night.

"He was a dirty little bird," she wrote in the summer 1941 issue of the *Murrelet*, "and by morning his box was very foul. We never did solve the problem of cleaning him. If we washed him, his feathers absorbed water like a sponge."

Though Barber gave the bird the best care she could, she sensed the bird was miserable. And so to her it was "almost a relief to find him dead on the afternoon of August 2," she wrote. Careful not to point a finger—at a hapless husband? a well-meaning child?—Barber explained the cause of death: "Another than myself had fed him, and he had evidently choked on a large piece of clam." I can picture Olive Barber now at her typewriter, writing to the editor of the *Murrelet*, x-ing out personal names, x-ing out terms that would relate her to the culprit, x-ing out every vague pronoun, until she finally came up with the perfectly passive "another than myself" to make it perfectly clear that she herself was not to blame.

Many early clues in the nesting mystery were gleaned from Native Americans living on the Pacific Coast and from local woodsmen and loggers working in the old-growth forests there. Ornithologist George Willett reported in 1926 that he had talked to dozens of hunters and trappers—"both whites and Indians"—in Alaska who told him of "murrelets' nests in hollow trees and logs, on mossy limbs of trees, and on the ground in swamps." Pretty good clues, I would say, but unfortunately, these same men also claimed that the nests held up to five eggs that varied in color from pure white to almost black. One man, Willett wrote, attempted to sell him a marbled murrelet egg—an egg Willett immediately recognized as that of the sooty grouse. Willett tossed the baby out with the bathwater—the clue about the mossy limbs with the fanciful stories about the eggs. While scientists today might seek out hunters and trappers for such valuable nuggets of information, such stories were, at the time, generally regarded as unscientific or hearsay, as were many stories from working lumbermen.

In 1925, Mr. E. J. Booth discovered a strange bird's egg in the office of a logging camp in Whatcom County, Washington. Two well-known ornithologists who examined the egg declared it was, beyond a reasonable doubt, that of the marbled murrelet. The logger who found the egg on a bed of moss was working fifteen miles inland on the Nooksack River. Apparently neither the logger nor anyone else could determine if the egg and moss were originally on the ground or had fallen from a tree, though the anonymous author added that it was "a very beautiful egg."

In Joseph Grinnell's last field notes on the marbled
murrelet, written from Carlotta, California, in 1936, he
wrote that one of his colleagues was brought a young marbled
murrelet from a tract of redwoods near Eureka, a coastal town
nearby. Other colleagues reported to Grinnell that the
"lumbermen in the area seemed to know the murrelets well
and call them 'fog larks'!" If the marbled murrelet mystery
were unsolved today, that anecdote would have sent swarms
of reporters to Eureka. But Grinnell didn't budge. Though he
seemed open to the idea that marbled murrelets nested in the
forests, he wrote that "[t]here is no evidence, though, that the
birds ever occur *in* redwood trees, as once guessed by
someone."

The most persistent problem for anyone trying to
follow developments in the marbled murrelet mystery was
tracking the latest theory on the nest location. Some scientists believed that the birds nested "on islands and on the
mainland—at moderate altitudes or even close to the sea."
Some assumed they nested somewhere "in the timber or on
the bald hills facing the Coast Ranges from Oregon northward." Others claimed that all available evidence indicated
that they nested on the forested slopes on the mainland
"within the humid coast belt, where natural recesses under
logs or mammal burrows in spongy ground may be used for
nesting places."

So convinced was ornithologist and artist Allan Brooks
that the birds nested in between rocks or under the roots of
trees that he provided step-by-step nest-finding instructions
in the January 1926 issue of the *Murrelet*. Armed with a

shovel, ax, wire hoops, net bags, and slender switches, Brooks advised, nest-searching parties should dig into tree roots and large sunken logs with suspicious-looking holes. Holes should be covered with a series of netted hoops that will catch the bird either entering or leaving the hole. "Patience and determination," Brooks wrote, "would in all probability bring success the first season."

Ornithologist Stanley Warburton of Tacoma, Washington, certainly was patient and determined, though in 1931 he was searching the rocky slopes above timberline on Alaska's Chichagof Island for marbled murrelet nests. Warburton had been seeing and hearing the birds there; so had Earl R. Osburn, an engineer at a mining site on Chichagof Island. Osburn agreed to lead Warburton and his wife on an expedition to find the nests. As the trio clambered up the rocky slopes above timberline, Osburn flushed a bird from under the scrub and a windblown spruce tree. The bird whizzed past Osburn—who called "Murrelet, murrelet!"— and then it flew down toward the timberline about two hundred feet below where he was standing. The group approached the scrub and spruce tree and found a single egg on a bit of moss among the rocks—the first nest, they believed, of the marbled murrelet.

Though Warburton was a respected ornithologist, his evidence of a discovery was deemed weak on several counts: Neither Mr. nor Mrs. Warburton had actually seen the adult bird, it was dusk when Osburn flushed the bird, Osburn had not actually seen the bird sitting on the nest, and the egg they found closely matched the color of one indisputable egg of a

Kittlitz's murrelet, which had been found on the ground in the Aleutian Islands in 1913.

To prove that the egg did not belong to a Kittlitz's murrelet, Warburton took the egg, the moss, and a few feathers from the nest to the Museum of Vertebrate Zoology in Berkeley, California, where the museum director just happened to be Joseph Grinnell. Grinnell examined the feathers and confirmed that they belonged to the marbled murrelet. The egg, however, was another story. Because no indisputable marbled murrelet egg had yet been collected, Grinnell was unable to tell Warburton what he wanted to hear. Warburton kept the egg in his collection but never published any information on its identity nor made claims to have solved the nesting mystery.

Years later, in 1959, biologist-authors Ira Gabrielson and Frederick Lincoln announced in their *Birds of Alaska* that the first marbled murrelet nest had been discovered in Alaska. It was Warburton's egg from 1931. Before publishing this news, Gabrielson and Lincoln had made a careful study of all the breeding records, including the records of eggs taken from the oviducts of marbled murrelets collected by Cantwell, Willett, Jewett, and others. The evidence somehow convinced them that the Warburton egg belonged to the marbled murrelet. The "news" of the Alaska ground nest was picked up in the second edition of Roger Tory Peterson's *Field Guide to Western Birds*, published in 1961. But the news didn't stick. That same year, two Canadian ornithologists suggested that the egg perhaps belonged to the Kittlitz's murrelet. The only way to settle the issue was to compare the eggs of both species. But there weren't any indisputable marbled murrelet eggs to use for comparison.

So, the egg made its way to the Puget Sound Museum of Natural History (now the Slater Museum of Natural History) in Tacoma, Washington. In 1978, an ornithologist published a photograph of the egg and described its color to a colleague as "bluish-green." That was enough for the colleague to declare that the egg was *not* that of a marbled murrelet because it did not have the yellowish background color typical of many marbled murrelet eggs. That declaration stuck; the Warburton egg did not make a published list of known and probable nests of the marbled murrelet—or of the Kittlitz's murrelet—published in 1983. But it came unstuck several years later when the ornithologist who had initially examined the photograph retracted his statement, admitting that the quality of the photograph was really too poor to decide which species of murrelet laid the egg. So the egg sits in the Slater Museum's collection among eggs of other auks, some collected by Cantwell, Willett, Booth, Jewett, Dowell, and Gabrielson, and two belonging to the ancient murrelet, collected from a burrow on Cox Island in 1927 by Solomon John Darcus.

By the 1950s, scientists had a mountain of clues to the marbled murrelet's nesting site, but the clues just weren't definitive. Evidence of possible ground nesting seemed to contradict evidence of possible tree nesting, and evidence for either was weak, often circumstantial, and frequently anecdotal. For one Canadian seabird biologist, the fact that the evidence wasn't adding up was not confounding, merely intriguing. In his words, it was "nice"—"nice to have a bird of mystery such as this upon which to conjecture." That man was Charles Guiguet, a rare bird himself, a biologist from British Columbia who had begun his pursuit of the marbled murrelet back in the summer of 1935. Beyond what Guiguet knew about this seabird, he knew that what the marbled murrelet mystery needed was attention—media attention. It was time for the marbled murrelet to move into the limelight.

PART TWO

DISCOVERY

CBC 662 600 New
August 10th '93

first bird carrying
fish arrives w/o any
seeing it at appx
am. The chick takes
the Sandlance after the
second bird arrives with
fish at appx 7:05
and 7:02 resp. The
chick takes the second
Sandlance at 7:15 and
the adult leaves after

and there's an 8-10 Knot
wind blowing from the
NW.
By 11:20 am things
have completely socked
in. It is not our

Sitting
on the
(W) u
for the
its fi
'tween 9:45
7/F 1
Kn 17
aweth
(ca
at
from
mis

One man, Charles Guiguet, knew more about marbled murrelets than anyone. Guiguet (pronounced *gee-gay*) was the curator of the Birds and Mammals Division at the Royal British Columbia Museum in Victoria. Apart from the war years, he had spent every summer since 1935 on zoological expeditions in coastal British Columbia. Guiguet knew the inlets, bays, and sounds like the back of his hand. He had explored islands and islets—Cox, Langara, Frederick, Hippa, Moresby, Bardswell—some too small for most maps. Guiguet, who had lived and worked most of his life in the remote coastal settings, was relentless. He spent "nights on shores and skylines, listening for the cry of the marbled murrelet," and had searched "in the talus slopes and rock slides of the alplands" and on "hand and knee crawling with digging irons through the Pacific West Coast salal jungle."

Guiguet knew the marbled murrelets in their summer and winter plumage and all stages in between. He studied the birds' habits in the day, night, dawn, and dusk. He knew their postures on the water, how they dove, and how they flew low over the timber. Guiguet could recall every probable breeding record of the marbled murrelet—every egg taken from an oviduct, every partially incubated egg, every flightless downy chick picked up on land. His ever-widening circle of friends included biologists, naturalists, fishermen, hunters, island natives, and loggers—people with intimate knowledge of the water and land where the marbled murrelets held their secrets. If anyone was qualified to discover a marbled murrelet nest, it was Guiguet.

But qualifications didn't seem to matter to the marbled murrelet. Guiguet was no closer to solving the nesting mystery than was the weekend birder, the accidental naturalist, and the day-tripper touring the redwood parks in high-heeled sandals. No one had seen a marbled murrelet egg *in situ*, a newly hatched chick on the nest, or an adult bird incubating its egg or feeding its chick.

It may take a scientist to reclassify a species, to publish a peer-reviewed article in an ornithological journal, or to prepare a museum-quality bird specimen, but it doesn't take a scientist to report a bird, an egg, or a nest. Ornithology was, and still is, one of the few sciences in which the nonscientist can make a significant contribution; but he or she has to be familiar with developments in the field. News of the marbled murrelet rarely reached anyone who did not subscribe to one of the obscure specialist journals.

That changed in 1956, when Guiguet published an article entitled "Enigma of the Pacific" in *Audubon* magazine. That magazine reached thousands of birders, citizen-scientists, and accidental naturalists who were also members of the National Audubon Society. *Audubon* readers enjoyed the outdoors, wildlife, birding, and articles full of information—but not too much. Guiguet's five-page article appeared in the same issue as "How it Got its Name—The Praying Mantis," "Insecticides—Boon or Bane?," "How to Attract Birds," and

"Johnny F. and The Birds." It included three images. One was an aerial view of a suspected nesting area in the Queen Charlotte Islands, the second was a photograph of three marbled murrelet skins laid out to highlight their plumage variations (winter, summer, and juvenal), and the third was a painting of three birds on the water. The text of the article was written for the layman without scientific terminology, symbols, citations, or figures. After chronicling the nest-finding exploits to date, Guiguet presented an intriguing story he heard in 1953. A logger and amateur bird-watcher named Walter Feyer was working in an old-growth forest in the Queen Charlotte Islands when he discovered a stunned marbled murrelet in the debris of an enormous hemlock he had just cut down. Feyer saw that the bird had a brood patch and so he searched in the debris, where he found the fragments of the bird's egg.

One would think, as I did, that those three pieces of evidence—felled tree, adult, egg—would add up to a nesting marbled murrelet. But no. Guiguet concluded his article wondering, "Whether the tree had fallen upon a nesting site or whether the egg and the bird were in the tree before it was felled, we don't know. But there seems little doubt that Walter Feyer was very close to a nesting marbled murrelet that day."

How exasperating—not for Guiguet but for me. He was so close. Why didn't he just put two and two together and declare the mystery solved? Because Guiguet was a scientist, and though Walter Feyer had examined the nest site carefully, he couldn't provide Guiguet or anyone else with strong and conclusive evidence. Or, perhaps Guiguet knew exactly what he was doing, recognizing just how tantalizing Feyer's story would be to Audubon's readers.

One of those readers was Eleanor Pugh.

Pugh was an early riser and an avid amateur birder whose husband, Robert, was a California State Park ranger. In the 1950s and 1960s, Eleanor, Bob, and their young children moved from state park to state park where Robert spent a year or two reorganizing staffs and trimming budgets. Everywhere they went, Eleanor participated in Christmas bird counts and annual migration counts. At each new park, she assigned herself a project of keeping track of the distribution and activities of a number of bird species. She kept a field journal and shared her observations about the birds with the parks' rangers and naturalists. Eleanor also sent her observation notes in regularly to "The Season," a region-by-region report of bird sightings published at the time in the magazine *Audubon Field Notes* (now *North American Birds*).

In 1956, the Pughs were assigned to Portola State Park, one of the "big-tree" state parks in the Santa Cruz Mountains. On one of her early morning rambles, Eleanor heard unfamiliar gull-like calls—an odd sound, she thought, in a forest ten miles from the ocean. Soon she began seeing small birds circling over the old-growth forest making the same gull-like calls. She watched the birds zipping into the forest—where exactly, she couldn't tell. Perplexed, Eleanor called Howard Cogswell for help.

Cogswell taught biology and ornithology at Mills College in Oakland. He also compiled and edited "The Season" report for the Middle Pacific Coast Region. He knew Eleanor Pugh from the notes and sightings she had dutifully sent him from parks all over the state. When Cogswell heard Eleanor's description of the calls and the behavior of the mysterious birds in Portola, he knew they belonged to the marbled murrelet. He had first heard and seen the birds back in August 1949 when on a bird-collecting expedition in Big Lagoon, a coastal site in Humboldt County at the edge of the old-growth redwood forests. The leader of the five-day expedition was Alden Miller, then director of the Museum of Vertebrate Zoology at Berkeley. At dawn and dusk, Cogswell recalled, Miller pointed out the birds and their distinct calls and told stories of the futile efforts to find the birds' nests.

Intrigued by what she heard, Eleanor decided to keep careful records of the birds she observed in Portola. Perhaps, she thought, she would be the one to solve the great mystery. Eleanor wrote her notes on the five-by-seven index cards kept on file at each park to track first-time or unusual sightings of plants and animals.

In 1959, the Pughs landed in Big Basin Redwoods State Park near Santa Cruz. There, Eleanor watched marbled murrelets fly over the redwoods and firs at daybreak, often in the fog, but she was unable to follow them to their nesting sites. One day, Eleanor got a call from one of the park attendants whose child had found an immature bird on the forest floor and had taken it home. Eleanor paid the bird a visit. She knew it must be a marbled murrelet chick. They "had it swimming around the bathtub for a short time, feeding it tuna fish," Pugh recalls, "and then let it go swimming down the creek." While stationed briefly at Prairie Creek Redwoods State Park in northern California one winter, Eleanor often saw these "small dumpy birds flying through early morning fog, calling as they flew, and winging it rapidly over the treetops."

Eleanor Pugh had the discipline, skill, and curiosity to solve the mystery of the marbled murrelet. And her round-the-clock presence in the park gave her an advantage over more casual birders. I am convinced that had the Pughs remained in the park for the summer, Eleanor would have been the one to solve the great mystery. Prairie Creek Redwood State Park is a marbled murrelet breeding hot spot and, not coincidentally, one of most important old-growth redwood sanctuaries in California. Alas, after just seven months at Prairie Creek, Eleanor's husband was promoted to superintendent of San Simeon State Park, near the famous castle of recluse William Randolph Hearst but well south of the forests that held the secrets of the reclusive marbled murrelet.

Not long after the Pughs' departure, budget cuts in the early 1970s eliminated funding for on-staff naturalists in California state parks. Park rangers were being cross-trained as law enforcement officers. They carried guns and focused more on keeping the peace than on keeping track of unusual birds.

Eleanor Pugh is now eighty-three, recently widowed, and living part time in her yurt in southern Oregon where, since 1971, she has been part of an intentional community called the Lichen Co-Op. Ever since my first phone conversation with Eleanor in 2001, I had wanted to meet her—not only because of her involvement with the marbled murrelet, but because she was breathless when she answered the phone. Octagenerians have many reasons to be breathless, but Eleanor's reason was that she had just walked in the door after a morning of pulling invasive Scotch broom from a degraded wetlands she was helping to restore near her home.

In the summer of 2004, I finally made arrangements to meet Eleanor at her 140-acre, mostly wooded property in Oregon. I followed her directions off Interstate 5 and found myself on a narrow dirt road—or was it a wide hiking trail? I drove on a distance before seeing a parked car but no driveway, mailbox, or sign that someone lived nearby. I parked and began following a narrow pathway up a rise, then down past a large fenced-in vegetable garden, and then up again. Suddenly, a woman appeared on the trail just ahead of me. She looked about sixty and was walking briskly toward me.

"Maria?" the woman asked.

"Eleanor?"

Eleanor was not the granny I had conjured up from her thin, slightly reedy voice on the phone. She was a lean, sturdy woman with short, wavy hair wearing sturdy-looking clothes and shoes. Eleanor's short-sleeved shirt revealed tan, muscular arms.

"I thought you'd be older," she said.

"I thought you'd *look* older," I replied.

We laughed and then walked up the trail a bit farther to Eleanor's spacious and furnished circular yurt, where she lives without electricity but with running water from a sink. From a cooler on the front porch, Eleanor fixed me a delicious sandwich; from a saucepan, she served me a glass of orange juice. We sat at a cozy table and talked for a long while.

Eleanor Pugh was born and raised in Ohio and majored in chemistry at Ohio State University. When she moved to Rochester, New York, after college to work at Eastman Kodak,

Eleanor's landlady noticed that she was always out walking and hiking. One spring morning, as Eleanor was heading out for a hike in the Genesee River Gorge south of Rochester, her landlady offered Eleanor her binoculars. "They were German-made," Eleanor said, "from World War II. The eyepieces had individual focusing." Eleanor borrowed the binoculars—her first pair ever—and she recalls hearing a rustling noise behind her one day when she was hiking.

"I slowly turned around and raised up my binoculars to see a black, white, and blue bird," Eleanor told me, her eyes lighting up. "Man! It was beautiful!"

Those binoculars opened up a new world for Eleanor and sent her directly to the library, where she checked out all the birding field guides she could. The bird Eleanor had seen was a black-throated blue warbler—a male in full plumage. I had no idea what one of those birds looked like, but seeing how it excited Eleanor—sixty years after the fact—I was tempted to give bird-watching another try.

In 1982, Eleanor purchased her first recording equipment and began recording, editing, and producing commercial audiocassettes of birdcalls. Today she still keeps busy supplying nature gift stores, bird clubs, and ornithological societies with her twenty-five different cassettes and compact discs. Eleanor is not going to hang up the binoculars or recording equipment anytime soon. Shortly after my visit, Eleanor and a friend went to Alaska for a few weeks, taking along her friend's teenage grandson and his cousin to hike, rent an RV, and explore Denali National Park, taping some birdcalls along the way.

When I left Eleanor, I told her I'd be in touch.

"You can catch me at home between seven and nine most mornings," she said. "But I warn you, I'm not always there in the springtime." There are few people I call and hope *not* to catch at home. But whenever I reach Eleanor's answering machine, it makes me happy to think that she is out in the world with her binoculars, seeing something that will put a twinkle in her eye.

Even if Eleanor Pugh had spotted a marbled murrelet nesting in a tree back in the 1960s, there is a good chance that no one would have known what to think. In 1959, news of the first ground-nesting marbled murrelet appeared in print. But no one was entirely convinced that all marbled murrelets nested on the ground. In 1967, a Canadian Wildlife Service biologist named R. D. Harris received a call from a woman reporting that two young, flightless birds with webbed feet had dropped out of a cedar being felled by loggers on Vancouver Island. Harris asked the woman to send him the surviving bird by air the next day. As soon as Harris received it, he verified that it was a marbled murrelet in its juvenal plumage, ready to fledge. Harris kept the bird, feeding it a wet mixture of fish, dried prepared dog food, and milk, but it died three days later. It was impossible for anyone on the scene to determine whether the nest was in a tree cavity, on one of the tree's branches, on the ground, or in a burrow disturbed somehow during logging. Tree nest? Ground nest? Still nobody knew which was more probable.

Skeptics of the ground-nesting theories wondered how it was possible that not a single ground nest had been discovered along the well-examined coasts and well-trod forests of British Columbia, Washington, Oregon, and California. Skeptics of the tree-nesting theory wondered how marbled murrelet chicks found their way from the forest to the ocean when they fledged. In 1968, Russian biologist A. A. Kishchinskii theorized that the birds simply dropped out of their nesting trees and found their way to the nearest stream or river and then floated to the sea.

As the nesting mystery deepened, the theories grew crazier. Since marbled murrelets had been seen inland on lakes, some biologists wondered if the birds might nest *in* the lake in burrows with underwater entrances, like those of muskrats and beavers. Such an underwater nest—one that slopes upward to a nesting chamber above water level—was at least biologically possible for a diving bird. And indeed, at this point in the long and futile search for a nest, it seemed *anything* was possible. As crazy as some theories were, the scientists who developed them deserve credit for thinking creatively and for thinking about the mystery at all.

But a theory is just a theory until enough evidence is gathered to prove it true or false. With the marbled murrelet, there just wasn't enough evidence to decide either way. So, in October 1970, the editors of *Audubon Field Notes* offered a $100 prize for the first verified and documented discovery of the nest of the marbled murrelet—a bird they dubbed a "stubborn holdout." Of the seven hundred–some birds known to nest in the United States and Canada, the marbled murrelet was the only one whose nesting habits were still unknown. The editors also believed that the monetary award—unprecedented in the history of American field ornithology—"would add a very modest extra incentive to the glory that will undoubtedly accrue to the discoverers." The illustration accompanying the announcement was Audubon's marbled murrelets from 1838—the penguinlike birds standing at the edge of a sea.

News of the reward traveled fast. Birders began flocking to sites along the Pacific Coast where the birds had previously been observed. Special nest-search expeditions were organized, with participants camping out in coastal forests and along ocean-bound streams with hopes they might hear the birds at dawn and be able to track them to their nests.

In May 1971, *Woman's Day* magazine ran news of the hundred-dollar prize and encouraged its readers who found themselves "in the top of a redwood tree or on an inaccessible cliff" along the Pacific Coast to "hang on and take a good look around" in case they should see a marbled murrelet's nest. To help the magazine's readers identify the little-known bird, the editors thoughtfully printed a photograph with the article. Unfortunately, it was a photograph of a parakeet auklet—a bird that, even to me, looks nothing like a marbled murrelet.

The mystery was now becoming an embarrassment. That no one had yet found a nest was considered by some as "incredible," "absurd," and even "preposterous." But Charles Guiguet didn't seem to mind. In 1972, in one of the many handbooks he published on the birds of British Columbia, he wrote, "I have little doubt that a serious effort will reveal the location of the marbled murrelets' nesting-site, and that the story of life history, downy young, and the rest will follow."

The serious effort Charles Guiguet had in mind no doubt included a large group of energetic biologists, lots of funding, much strategizing, and no sleep. As with other mysteries humankind has endeavored to solve, this kind of effort—exerted over a period of months, years, even decades—eventually leads to a discovery. Guiguet made an enormous effort and, though he did not find a marbled murrelet nest, he did demystify much about the bird's behavior and biology. This contribution—and those made by Grinnell, Cantwell, Dawson, and all the others—should have eventually led directly to a nest. But they did not. As it happened, the ultimate discovery had little to do with effort and more to do with chance and a strange series of events.

On January 3, 1974, a serious snowstorm blasted through California's Santa Cruz Mountains, dumping up to three feet of heavy snow over two counties and wreaking havoc in an area that receives only the occasional winter dusting. Thousands upon thousands of snow-laden trees fell onto power lines, across highways, and crashed down to earth, causing the deaths of at least two people and stranding eight thousand away from their homes. Six thousand homes were left without power, some for as long as a week. Highways connecting small mountain towns were closed;

scores of waylaid motorists abandoned their cars and trucks and trudged toward emergency refuges. The communities of Bonny Doon, Lompico, and Boulder Creek were hardest hit. An estimated quarter million acres of land were left in fire-hazardous condition because of downed timber.

The effect of the freak snowstorm on the forests of Big Basin Redwoods State Park was cataclysmic. Weak trees simply collapsed under the weight of the snow. Large branches cracked under the white weight and became tangled in standing trees. Giant coast redwoods remained upright, but the heavy, wet snow snapped off their tops. Trees were falling at such a rate that one lumberman said, "I felt like a fly, with a thousand fly-swatters slapping down around me." Along a one-mile stretch of the park's entrance road, more than 250 trees fell, trapping park staff for seven days until they could chainsaw their way out.

While the storm can be explained in meteorological terms, I like to imagine that after 185 years, Mother Nature had completely lost her patience with all those bird people searching in the wrong places for nests. Now, with a dramatic bit of weather, she seemed to be shouting "Yoo-hoo! Up here!"

Her handiwork certainly got attention, but not as she may have intended. For three months, the park was closed to the public for cleanup. Work crews cleared fallen trees and broken branches from roads, hiking trails, campgrounds, and park buildings. From all the trees they inspected and all the branches they cut and hauled away, workers offered no reports about marbled murrelet nests. The birds themselves were out at sea. Though the attentive listener might have heard an occasional *keer* call over the forest, the birds would not return to the forest in great numbers until later in the spring to breed.

In April, Big Basin reopened to the public, well before the warm weather and summer crowds.

In May, the park superintendent called in forestry experts to inspect the trees in the park's campgrounds and high-use areas. They tagged more than one hundred trees they judged to be potential hazards to park visitors. Some still held storm-damaged branches, others were decayed, and still others loomed threateningly over campsites and picnic tables.

In June, the park superintendent opened the bidding for the job of trimming those one hundred trees.

In early July, the Davey Tree Company of Livermore, California, won the trimming contract with the lowest bid. In mid-July they sent one of their young tree surgeons and a groundman to the park to begin what they estimated was a month of work. The team worked apace for the first few weeks, tackling dozens of tan oaks, live oaks, and madrones—the "small" fifty- and eighty-foot-high trees. When they reached the big trees—twenty two-hundred-foot-tall Douglas firs and coastal redwoods—the crew began to lag. The big trees were harder than they thought to manage; each took a full day to climb and trim. At this rate, work would drag on another week at least. The Davey Tree supervisor saw his profit turning to sawdust, but he knew better than to try to rush a tree surgeon, so he called the one man he wouldn't have to rush.

On the morning of August 5, Hoyt Foster, age forty-seven, arrived at the park ready to work. Six feet tall, 160 pounds, wiry, and strong, Foster had been trimming trees since he was twenty-one years old. He excelled in the big ones that daunted other climbers—the ones beyond the reach of cherry pickers, hydraulic lifts, or ladders of any kind. In a good ten-hour day, Foster could climb and trim two big trees to every one of his colleagues, even the young climbers half his age. It wasn't that he was that fast, it was that he was extraordinarily steady and patient.

Foster had operated his own trimming business in Seattle in the 1950s, but after several nearly fatal falls from big trees, he sold the business and moved back to his home state of Idaho, where he served as a minister for the Assembly of God church. But Foster missed the big trees. In 1972, he moved to San Jose, California, with his wife to take a job with Davey clearing trees from power lines in the Santa Clara Valley.

"I considered the job at Big Basin an honor, really," Foster told me by phone. "Most men who would have been called for the job would have been twenty or thirty years old. By age forty-five, most tree surgeons are considered washouts. They're worn out, or they've come to their senses and taken jobs as supervisors. I kept at it because tree climbing has always been fascinating to me—and a challenge."

Foster paused.

"I'm kind of a nut, in other words."

On his first two days at Big Basin, Hoyt Foster and Ray Johnson, a nineteen-year-old novice groundman, climbed and trimmed five trees. On the morning of August 7, the pair carried their gear and equipment to an idyllic tent-only campground not far from park headquarters. Walking beneath redwoods and firs, they followed a wide dirt path that led to several campsites set among dense huckleberry bushes. During a normal week in August, the campground would have been alive with the sounds of campers, tent fly zippers, and Steller's jays squabbling over every bit of dropped picnic food. But during the tree trimming, the campground was closed for safety reasons, so Foster, Johnson, and the jays had the place to themselves.

Foster strolled around to size up the flagged trees, finally deciding to start on a Douglas fir whose high and massive branches extended over four separate campsites. Foster gazed up the trunk. The lowest limb was ninety feet above his head. Above that, the branches were widely separated and mostly dead or dying. In tree-surgeon parlance, this tree was overripe.

Around 9 A.M., Foster began his routine. He pulled on his blue coveralls, laced up his knee-high arborist's boots, and buckled his wide leather climbing belt. He clipped a few D-rings onto the belt and tied on his ropes: a 110-foot climbing line to his left side, an 18-foot flipline to his right. He clipped on his pruning saw, strapped on his hard hat, and approached the Douglas fir. At the base of the tree, Foster put on his climbing spurs and wrapped his flipline around the trunk, holding an end in each hand. Taking a deep breath, he set his spurs into the bark, worked his flipline around the back side of the tree, and started climbing. From the ground, Ray Johnson watched as a man more than twice his age walked up the trunk of that fir almost as if it were horizontal. Foster climbed with no belay—only with rope, spurs, strength, and stamina.

As Foster climbed, he wasn't thinking about how far he had to climb or how far he might fall if his skills or equipment failed. He wasn't thinking about his last near-fatal fall, from a big tree twenty years earlier. He wasn't reliving the pain of every broken rib, punctured organ, compressed vertebra, or fractured skull he had suffered in falls over the years. Instead, he was listening to the tree. He was listening to the sound of the bark under his spurs. He was listening to the sound of his flipline as it coiled around the back side of the tree. He was feeling the subtle changes in tension and position of his rope in his hands as it reacted to the tree. He was paying attention to the muscles in his feet, calves, thighs, arms, neck, and back.

Foster reached the first branch in fifteen minutes. Assisted below by Johnson, Foster hoisted up a pole pruner, chain saw, and a second 110-foot line and then continued climbing. By noon, he had removed a dozen or so branches as he worked his way up the tree. By 2:30 P.M., he was 148 feet above the ground, perched in a cluster of limbs the size of telephone poles. Here Foster paused. He tied himself into the tree and signaled down to Johnson to send up his sandwich and canteen of water on his climbing line. As Foster ate, he did not gaze out over the forest canopy to enjoy the vista from his lofty perch. He kept his focus on the trunk of the tree, on his climbing line, and on the position of the branches and his feet. His body was in the tree. His mind was in the tree. Foster finished his lunch and prepared himself for another few hours of climbing higher into the tree. As he turned to adjust his rope, he discovered a problem.

It would have been a small problem, really, but in a Douglas fir tree 148 feet above the forest floor, such a problem became significant. The problem was alive and sitting on a branch right where Foster planned to place his foot. He paused.

Because it had a beak, Foster figured it was a bird. He'd encountered thousands of birds in trees during his career, but never one like this. "It looked like a squashed up porcupine with a beak sticking out," he recalled later. "I'd never seen anything like it."

The creature was covered in brownish downy feathers and possessed a few darker, quill-like feathers on its wings. A pair of black eyes and a slender beak jutted out from the squat, fluffy mass. Its neck was nowhere to be seen, but sleek, dark feathers suggested a head. And there it was, hunkered down in a shallow bowl of moss on a branch just wide enough to hold it. Foster stared, bewildered. The creature sat, motionless.

Foster didn't know what to do. He had a soft spot for young animals. Over the years, he had rescued dozens of animals from trees—including three baby squirrels he once took home, raised, and released. It was not just that Hoyt Foster was a nature lover; by showing some sensitivity to the wildlife on this job, Foster figured he might be helping Davey Tree Company win additional trimming contracts. California had dozens of state parks where chain saws and wildlife conservation needed to go hand in hand. But Foster was a practical man. He knew from experience that dealing with wildlife on the job could be, as he put it, a "hassle and a time killer." He had been hired to trim trees, not to save animals. Foster's employer wasn't going to look favorably on the time he wasted trying to rescue this odd-looking bird. Though he hated doing it, he had kicked his share of pigeon squabs out of their nests in situations where trying to save them would have compromised his safety. But Foster's policy for dealing with wildlife on the job was simple: Always try to find a way around hurting or killing them.

Perhaps, Foster thought, he should just ignore the bird and try to avoid stepping on it or clobbering it with his flipline as he continued working. Or maybe if he moved around a bit or made some noise the bird would fly away. While contemplating his options, Foster noticed appendages along the creature's sides. Wings, perhaps? A gentle nudge might send the creature flying, or—if they weren't wings—hopping down to another branch. Either way, no one would ever know. What happens twenty stories up in ancient trees are secrets kept in the furrows of the bark and in the conscience of the climber. So Foster did what any good tree surgeon would have done: He took out his saw.

Foster's favorite hand saw was a twenty-four-inch-long, four-teeth-to-the-inch, curved pruning saw. It was fast and versatile and known in the industry as a speed saw. In capable hands, the vicious-looking tool could cut through a branch as thick as a man's arm in fifteen seconds. "I have never seen anything that walks, howls, climbs, or scratches that wasn't terrified of a speed saw," he told me. "Especially if you swing it, it makes the neatest whistling sound you ever heard. Dogs just leave. I mean big dogs."

Foster removed the saw from its thick leather scabbard and moved it slowly toward the bird, aiming the tip in the direction of the appendages he hoped were wings. "Before I even got close to him, he reached out and pecked the saw," he remembered. "I thought to myself, 'Why, you little rascal! If you're that feisty, maybe you're durable. Maybe it'll be worthwhile to fuss with you a little bit.'"

Foster retracted his saw and then moved it slowly toward the bird again. This time, the bird pecked aggressively at the saw and then clenched the edge of it in its beak. He raised the saw up a few inches and the tenacious bird actually rose up with it. That's when he saw its feet. Webbed feet.

Foster was no birder, but he knew this was strange. He knew that wood ducks had webbed feet and nested in cavities in trees. But this bird wasn't *in* the tree, and it didn't look like a duck. Besides, he told himself, wood ducks didn't nest so high up or so far from water—there was no stream or pond in sight. He was intrigued—and certain that the park would be interested in such an odd creature. Foster radioed down to Ray Johnson to find a ranger. Within a few minutes, Johnson had found a park maintenance worker who called up to park headquarters for a ranger.

Ranger Dan Friend picked up the call. One of Friend's jobs was handling any orphaned or injured wildlife found in the park, most often squirrels, jays, and robins brought to headquarters by visitors. Uninjured animals were returned to the forest to fend for themselves. Injured animals were given temporary homes in cages or cardboard boxes in Friend's office until a wildlife rehabilitator picked them up. But a raptor or rare animal—injured or not—required a call to the local Department of Fish and Game. Ranger Friend had handled mostly fledging jays, crows, and the occasional squirrel. He didn't know *what* to expect at Jay Camp.

Standing beneath the Douglas fir moments later, Friend gathered what little information there was—that Hoyt Foster had found a strange and extremely pugnacious little bird. Friend instructed Johnson to send a T-shirt up to Foster on his

220-foot line. Foster could wrap the bird in the T-shirt and then lower the bundle back down to the ground. It seemed like a reasonable plan, but the bird wouldn't cooperate. When Foster moved the T-shirt toward the bird, the bird scuttled backward off the wide branch and fell silently toward the ground, flapping its rudimentary wings, bouncing, skidding, and sliding between several pendulous limbs before Foster lost sight of it. The men on the ground, with their heads cricked back, witnessed the hundred-foot free fall.

The bird, they said, fell like a felt hat—softly, silently, almost in slow motion. It landed on the ground about twenty-five feet south of the tree, where Ranger Friend was amazed to find it alive and apparently unharmed. He also didn't have a clue about what this bird was. He wrapped the T-shirt around the bird, drove it back to park headquarters, and found a cardboard box in his office to set the bird in. Friend tried to call the Audubon Society, but he couldn't find any phone numbers for a local office. He then called the Santa Cruz Animal Shelter and got the phone number of a local wildlife rehabilitator who agreed to pick up the bird later that afternoon. Were it not for a strange coincidence, the unidentified chick would have been given away and the whole incident at the park forgotten.

Though August 7 was his day off, Ranger Denzil Verardo showed up at park headquarters late that afternoon to pick up his mail. As Verardo was sorting through his letters, he overheard talk of a bird in the next room. He listened, only half interested, until he heard someone mention webbed feet.

Denzil Verardo was not only a ranger, he was the park's historian and had just published a history of Big Basin

Redwoods State Park. He had spent the past few years reviewing early park records, archived articles, and hundreds of the five-by-seven-inch natural history cards. He remembered the ones written by a certain "E. A. Pugh" in 1959. He remembered her descriptions of the marbled murrelets' dawn flights over the forest. He remembered a note she made about their webbed feet. Denzil moved quickly to the next room and to the box, where he saw the chick. When he picked it up and saw its feet, he knew exactly what he was looking at.

Verardo immediately called Steve Singer in Santa Cruz. When Singer was a ranger at the park the previous winter, a camper had turned in an injured bird at park headquarters. For several hours Singer and Verardo had worked to identify the bird, the first of its kind they had ever seen. Once they had figured out it was an adult marbled murrelet in its winter plumage, Steve began a search of the scientific literature for information on the species' ecology. What he learned about it he passed on to Denzil Verardo who was now very grateful for that knowledge.

Steve Singer dropped what he was doing and drove to the park. When Singer laid eyes on the bird, he knew Verardo was right. He in turn called Bruce Elliott, a biologist with the local office of the California Department of Fish and Game, the agency that regulates the state's rare and unusual wildlife. As news of the chick traveled fast—one bird club threatened to "kidnap" the bird so it could share the "glory" of its discovery!—Elliott suggested the rangers safeguard the chick in one of their residences until he could get to the park first thing the next morning.

Meanwhile, Foster continued working in the trees,

unaware of the commotion his find was causing at park headquarters, unaware that the bird he had found was a seabird
called a marbled murrelet, and unaware that the patch of moss
the chick had been sitting on was actually the bird's nest—the
first such nest ever to be discovered in North America. With
a bit of curiosity and his twenty-four-inch speed saw, Hoyt
Foster had accidentally and unwittingly solved one of the last
great ornithological mysteries in North America.

CHAPTER 11

The downy chick now lay lifeless in Laurence Binford's hand. Its body fit snugly into his outstretched palm, its slender beak at his fingertips, its delicate webbed feet extended back and lightly touching his wrist. Binford had never held such a bird, nor seen one, even through binoculars. He was thrilled when Bruce Elliott, a longtime birding pal, had phoned him about the bird, though he was saddened that he couldn't have seen it before it died—just one night after its discovery. Bruce Elliott, Denzil Verardo, and Steve Singer had no doubts that the bird was a marbled murrelet, but Laurence Binford was the man who would prove it scientifically.

Binford, then thirty-nine, was an ornithologist and a recognized authority on the birds of California and Mexico. He was also the assistant curator of birds and mammals at the California Academy of Sciences in San Francisco. Binford had seen marbled murrelets—adults and juveniles—at sea many times. He had even written about the great nest mystery in his *Birds of Western North America*. Binford didn't have the time or the inclination to spend searching for a nest, even though his office was less than an hour's drive from the old-growth forest where the chick had been found. He spent his time with other birds, more than one hundred thousand of them, all preserved as study skins in the academy's collection. Binford knew that a birder or ornithologist would come upon a marbled murrelet nest someday, but he never imagined it would be so high in a tree, so out of sight and reach.

Binford was aware that evidence was mounting to support the theory of tree nesting, but only a handful of ornithologists believed it possible, or probable. Alcids were notoriously fast but awkward fliers with poor records for smooth, precision landings. How could a marbled murrelet navigate its way in and out of the deep forest without hitting trees like a pinball? How could the bird survive dozens of flat-footed crash landings on the short runway of a tree branch? Binford's colleagues were skeptical. Yes, he acknowledged, a tree was a bizarre place for a web-footed seabird, but he also knew that nature embraces the anomalous, unlikely, and strange with arms wider than the human imagination.

By placing the bird in Binford's hands, Bruce Elliott—and, by extension, the California Department of Fish and Game—had given him the responsibility of describing the chick and its nesting habits to the world. Binford had to create the document, an article in a peer-reviewed scientific journal, that proved the chick was in fact a marbled murrelet, and that the mossy patch on the limb was in fact its nest. Every feather, bone, organ, bit of moss, and chunk of branch was evidence requiring examination, comparison, and analysis.

The nesting site would no longer be unknown or mysterious. Rangers and biologists would return to the discovery site to measure the height and diameter of the nest tree; the diameter, length, and orientation of branches near the nest limb; and the distance from the tree to the nearest point on the Pacific. They would provide the names of the trees and bushes surrounding the nest tree, the percent of canopy closure, the names and location of nearby streams, climate and fog data, and the pattern of sunlight at the campsite. Once everything relating to the discovery of this chick became factual and familiar, Binford's report would be reviewed by several of his peers and published according to the same time-honored approach used by Charles Darwin and generations of scientists for documenting discoveries.

The job of documenting the evidence found by Hoyt Foster—the work that turns a find into a discovery—fell to Binford. It was a job that would require several months of work, but a job that Binford happily accepted.

Binford's first step in the process of discovery fell on the roof of the California Academy of Sciences building overlooking Golden Gate Park. Set in the center of the roof is a small structure resembling a garden shed. Inside this humble structure is the skinning lab, where freezers full of dead birds and mammals awaited "preparation." Inside hung the stench of animal carcasses and a chaos of plastic buckets, cardboard boxes, metal trays, and tables covered in piles of papers and books familiar to today's natural historians. At a central table, preparators hunched like surgeons over sea otters, red-tailed hawks, and rufous hummingbirds. With a variety of tools not usually found in a garden shed, they disassembled, dissected, examined, cleaned, stuffed, and reassembled these animals for study or display.

Had the marbled murrelet chick been of less potential significance, Binford might have handed it over to one of the staff preparators to skin in the rooftop lab. But Binford wanted to skin the fragile bird himself, to learn its secrets firsthand. He had skinned thousands of birds and was confident in his skills—meticulous and thorough—and what mysteries they would reveal not only about this unusual bird, but about the entire species.

Binford entered the lab and picked up a metal tray on which he placed a dissecting kit, gram scale, calipers, borax, cotton, needles, and spool of thread. He returned to his basement office where he laid out the lab equipment, opened a notebook, removed the dead chick from its ice-packed cooler, and placed it on the scale. The bird weighed a mere 95.6 grams, or 3.3 ounces. This could be considered normal, but Binford was careful to note that the numbers did not take into consideration loss of weight from unusual exertions, starvation, and freezer desiccation. There would have been no way to calculate the cost of the chick's battle with Hoyt Foster's speed saw, the flapping fall from the Douglas fir, and the two days of being handled and ogled. No equation exists to account for such loss. No numbers, however small, can quantify such trauma.

Before Binford reached for the scalpel, he found a pencil and made a rough sketch of the pattern of spots on the chick's head and neck. The pattern might hold the code for determining the chick's age when it could be compared with other downy chicks—if and when others were found. In 1974, no natural history museum in the world had a downy marbled murrelet chick. Most had dozens, even hundreds, of adult and juvenile marbled murrelets in their collections. A few had downy chicks of other murrelets. What Binford had was unique.

As Binford sketched the dappled chick, he noticed that the down was attached to the tips of nearly full-grown feathers. It was apparently undergoing its first molt into juvenal plumage. That the chick retained its down while molting was not so unusual; many birds retain wisps of downy plumage even after fledging. What was strange was that the chick retained so much of it so late. When Binford gently stretched open one of the chick's folded wings, he discovered developed primary flight feathers, primary and secondary wing coverts, underwing coverts, and alular quills. This was a bird ready to fledge, but a bird still mostly covered in its natal down.

The chick's small, pointed wings angled out perpendicularly from its body and then swept sharply back at their midpoint. This was the high-speed wing design typical of falcons, swifts, terns, many shorebirds, and most alcids. Binford measured the small wing of the chick and the length of its tail and bill. He measured the tarsus and the middle toe. He measured the bird's egg tooth—the tiny protuberance on its bill that helped it peck its way out of its shell some weeks earlier. The chick now had a set of numbers that gave its body weight and size. Without another marbled murrelet chick to use for comparison, the numbers meant little; they were just numbers. Binford took the same measurements from six male marbled murrelet skins in the academy's collection. His comparisons revealed a chick that was more than three-quarters its adult size. Despite his careful measurements, Binford had no way to estimate the bird's age. No growth pattern for this bird had yet been established.

Binford set the young bird on its back. He separated the feathers along its midline and cut through the bird's thin skin from sternum to vent with his scalpel. Binford snipped the bones in its breast, wings, and legs, and then opened up the bird. Binford carefully examined the organs. The chick was, by evidence of paired testes, a male. Finding these organs (or ovary in the female) was the only way at the time to determine the gender of a marbled murrelet. There is no known difference in size, shape, or plumage between males and females—a trait that scientists refer to as sexual monomorphism.

When Binford examined the chick's digestive tract, he found some partially digested egg yolk—not the usual fare for a fish-eating seabird. During the chick's twenty-four hours in captivity, the wildlife rehabilitator caring for the chick had used the standard meal for orphaned birds. In retrospect, it was a poor choice for a seabird, but grounded marbled murrelet chicks found after 1974 also refused to eat the ground-up seafood they were fed. Not until 1991 did researchers first observe a marbled murrelet chick eating: It swallows whole, small fish in one gulp.

Binford's chick had also eaten a few whole down feathers. Downy chicks of many species will pluck their own feathers and peck at and snap up loose feathers around the nest.

Binford weighed and measured the chick's organs and then placed them in a jar of preserving alcohol. He measured the fat on the inside of the skin near the feather bases. There was a moderate amount of fat, which Binford scraped away, careful so as not to tear the skin or loosen the feathers from their bases. He wondered if the unusually late retention of the down—rather than a thick layer of fat—allowed the chick to stay warm and still be light enough to fly to the sea on young wings. Certainly a heavy, fatty chick would drop like a stone from a lofty nest without a chance to get airborne.

Next Binford detached the muscle tissue from the bones and wings, gently rubbing the skin with borax to remove traces of fat so that the preserved skin would not rot. He stuffed small rolls of cotton into the skull and body cavity until the chick assumed its original volume and shape. With a zigzagging stitch, Binford sewed the bird closed. He spread open the webbed toes of one foot and gently closed the toes of the other. He crossed the bird's legs, left over right, and tied them together with a string attached to a small paper tag. On the tag in indelible ink, Binford wrote the bird's serial number (CAS 68895); the collection location (California, Santa Cruz Co., Big Basin State Park, Campground J-1); and the collector (Hoyt Foster). On the back of the tag, in pencil, he wrote the name of the bird: marbled murrelet, *Brachyramphus marmoratus.*

Binford looked at the bird. The downy feathers were still soft and fluffy, the juvenal feathers glossy and intact, and the head tucked and cocked naturally. Were it not for the chick's white cotton eyes, the bird looked poised to fly right out of Binford's hand. It was lifelike to be sure, but Laurence Binford's work was just beginning. He had to work quickly to describe the colors of the chick's feathers before they began to fade. He could have taken the easy way out and described the chick as "buff colored with some black spots on the head," but as birders, artists, and housepainters know, one man's buff is another man's beige, and black isn't necessarily black.

To describe the color of the chick, Binford needed a color standard—a set of colors created through a scientific system.

Color standards usually take the form of a chart, wheel, or book of color plates. Not all color standards are created equal. Some are created for artists, others for housepainters, mineralogists, botanists, printers, mapmakers, textile dyers, crayon manufacturers, and anyone needing to match or reproduce a certain color exactly. Binford found most color standards were too bright, too electric, and too acrylic for the subtle variations of hues and tints of feathers. For Binford and most every ornithologist, there is only one color standard for birds. It is Robert Ridgway's *Color Standards and Color Nomenclature.*

Since its publication in 1912, Ridgway's book has found its way onto a shelf in every natural history museum library in North America. Robert Ridgway was an ornithologist, author, and painter in the era after Audubon and before Kodacolor. From 1874 to his death in 1929, he was the curator of birds at the Smithsonian Institution in Washington, D.C. Ridgway knew birds, and he knew firsthand the problems of reproducing and naming the colors of the natural world. Ridgway worked on this problem for twenty years, including three years on the reproduction of the color plates alone. He based his system on thirty-six pure, solid colors, to which he added carefully prescribed amounts of black and white pigments. The resulting 1,115 colors are presented on one-inch-square plates cut and glued to thick pages separated by sheets of vellum. Each color, including twenty-two shades of black, has a name. Using Ridgway's book, an ornithologist in Baton Rouge can describe a bird as having an Olivaceous Black nape and a Buckthorn Brown supercilium, and every other ornithologist east and west of the Mississippi will know exactly what he means. The book is a masterpiece, indispensable.

It is also unstable. "CAUTION!!!" Ridgway warned readers on the page preceding the color plates, "DO NOT EXPOSE THESE PLATES TO LIGHT FOR LONGER THAN NECESSARY." Ridgway had gotten his colors onto paper in 1912, but he couldn't guarantee they would remain fixed there. He took great pains to use the most durable pigments available at the time, but certain colors could only be reproduced with pigments that were light sensitive. "Green and violet aniline dyes are all very evanescent," he wrote, "rapidly fading and eventually disappearing." To avoid such a fate and the corruption of the color standard, most libraries wrap the book in black cloth and store it in a locked cabinet. The book is never used in direct sunlight and is only viewed for very short periods of time. How well this book suited the secretive and crepuscular marbled murrelet.

Binford brought Ridgway's book from the academy's library into the natural, indirect light of his office. Glancing between bird and book, plumage and plate, Binford found exactly what he was looking for. The feathers on the chick's head and neck were Light Ochraceous-Buff marked with twenty-seven spots of Sooty Black. Its throat and upper parts were Pale Ochraceous-Buff. Its abdomen was feathered in Pale Smoke Gray and Light Buff. Its sides and flanks were shaded in feathers colored Pale Smoke Gray at the base, Deep Mouse Gray at the middle, and Light Ochraceous-Buff at the tip.

Plate by plate, this chick acquired the weight and beauty of poetry, the rich language of color. The open vowel sounds were luscious and soothing: *Ochre* evoking iron ore, *Buff* the color of bare skin, *Smoke* the ephemeral world. *Pale* and *Light* are suitably subduing modifiers for a bird of the dawn and dusk.

As fanciful as the names sound, they are not Ridgway's color names. With the eye of a scientist and artist, he selected them carefully from two existing sources. One was a color standard commissioned by the American Mycological Society for identifying mushrooms. The second was a collection of colored Japanese silks, taffetas, velvets, and other dress goods sent to Ridgway from the now defunct Woodward & Lothrop department store in Washington, D.C. The color names had associations and stories, and now every feather and bit of weightless down held them, too.

Satisfied that he had named every visible color and had left nothing unmeasured or undescribed, Binford placed the bird in the lid of a cardboard box and carried it toward the metal collection cabinets. He placed the chick in a corner of a drawer holding two dozen marbled murrelets—all adults, all laid out in rows on their backs in the mothball-scented air. Nothing could have been further from the mossy branch of a Douglas fir.

Now, Binford had to make sense of the nest. The day after the chick was found, Hoyt Foster climbed back up the Douglas fir to remove the limb and lower it in sections to the ground, taking special care to keep the nest intact. What Binford ended up with—what was now sitting on his desk— was a foot-wide chunk of the limb covered with moss and bird droppings that were redolent of fish and, to Binford, not unpleasantly reminiscent of a marine bird colony.

The nest was little more than an oblong depression or "bowl" in the bark of the limb. Binford judged this bowl to be natural since he detected no bill or claw marks that would indicate a bird had shaped the nest by removing flakes of bark.

The bowl was large enough to accommodate one of the marbled murrelet's chicken-sized eggs, or one chick—no more.
The size of the nest supported evidence that this species laid
single-egg clutches.

Hoyt Foster had reported that moss grew thickly along
the entire length of the branch—green on most of its length
and then brownish as it surrounded the nest bowl. But no
moss grew inside the nest bowl. A botanist at the academy
identified the moss as *Isothecium cristatum*, a species commonly found in California's moist coastal forests. The botanist
could think of nothing that would prevent the natural growth
of moss in the bowl or that would turn the moss around the
bowl brown. Nothing, that is, but marbled murrelets. Binford
suspected that the moss had been worn off inadvertently by
chicks and adults over a period of time, not in just one nesting
season. The missing moss was the first evidence of philopatry
among marbled murrelets.

Binford examined the moss, which apparently served as
an underlying meshwork for the thick layer of droppings that
ringed the bowl. In terms perhaps more poetic than the subject deserves, Binford described the droppings as "smooth,
rounded, slightly glossy hillocks that varied in color from
buffy-white to Cream-Buff." The latter color (a Ridgway
color) was strikingly close to the Pale Ochraceous-Buff of the
chick. Through his painstaking color matching, Binford had
broken a code, tapped into a secret language in which colors
reveal secrets and relationships tell stories. Binford was a code-
breaker, a listener, a scribe, a translator.

The buff colors told Binford of a chick adapted for
survival on the nest. As long as the chick retained its buff-

colored downy plumage, it remained camouflaged against buff-colored droppings. The buffy down hid the chick's striking black-and-white juvenal feathers as they emerged from beneath it. In a world of Cream-Buff and Light Ochraceous-Buff, the chick would be rendered nearly invisible to predators—whoever they were. Had the chick lost this down as it molted into its dark, juvenal plumage, the chick would have lost the protection of camouflage. This would explain the late retention of the down that Binford noted.

Binford reached for the tweezers. From the ring of droppings and surrounding moss, Binford fastidiously picked out approximately 165 eggshell fragments ranging from smaller than the head of a pin in diameter to the size of a raisin. With the naked eye, hand lens, and microscope, Binford noted the colors of the fragments and the spots that marked some of them. The background color of the egg, according to the Ridgway standard, was Pale Glass Green. The spots were Lavender-Gray, Deep Madder Blue, Sepia, Bone Brown, and Saccardo's Umber. The names alluded to and commingled the worlds of wine bottles, fragrant herbs, pigment-rich plant roots, cuttlefish ink, fossilized skeletons, and made a nod to Pier Andrea Saccardo (1845–1921), a man who spent thirty-five years of his life compiling a 160,000-page list of all the common and scientific names that had ever been used for fungi.

These richly evocative color names described an eggshell, but, Binford wondered, were they the colors of a marbled murrelet eggshell? Binford turned to a brief scientific article, written in 1941 by ornithologists G. M. Sutton and J. B. Semple, that described an egg taken from the oviduct of a female marbled murrelet they had collected in British Columbia. These authors also cited Ridgway's colors, ones that closely matched those that Binford had chosen and were unlike the colors of the eggs of any other alcid species.

On the nest, a marbled murrelet is almost chameleonlike in its coloration development from egg to chick to juvenile to adult. The egg blends in with the dappled moss freshly green after winter rains. The downy chick matches the colors of the tree bark, the fallen brown needles of the tree, and the ring of droppings surrounding its nest. Adults in their cinnamon-brown breeding plumage blend in with the bark of the nesting trees and the browned moss and needles around the nest. All the clues, all the pieces of the puzzle, were fitting together. Finally. Buoyed by the strength of the evidence at hand, Binford turned to the scientific literature. Here, in the journals of natural history clubs and ornithological societies, he found plenty of evidence for tree nesting. All of it, however, was indirect or circumstantial.

Beginning with George Cantwell's stories from the Haida in 1897, Binford followed the evidence presented in articles by Darcus, Dawson, Gabrielson, Guiguet, Harris, and others. What he found were stories of nest searches (many, failed), egg discoveries (one indubitable, several questionable), chicks found on the forest floor (a handful, possibly fallen from trees), sightings of marbled murrelets flying inland (hundreds, destination unknown), nesting theories (many, all unproven), and a wealth of information about the bird's biology and breeding behavior (now, in hindsight, pointing to one inevitable conclusion). The most recent article he read had been published in January 1974 in the journal *Auk*. "Evidence for tree nesting in the marbled murrelet is mounting," wrote a young Canadian ornithologist named Spencer Sealy.

In January 1975, after months of laboratory and library work, Laurence Binford drove down the coast highway to visit the nesting site at Big Basin Redwoods State Park. He met with Steve Singer, Denzil Verardo, Bruce Elliott, and others who had been involved with the nest-finding events the previous summer. He walked up the path to the campground and to the Douglas fir. Binford gazed up the trunk at the metal plate covering the cut where Hoyt Foster had removed the nesting limb. The height was astonishing. There would have been no way for Binford or anyone else on the ground to see a nest of any sort on a limb that high. Even if Binford could have seen it, he still wasn't sure he would have believed it. It was a strange place for a seabird's nest.

Binford completed his report in March 1975 and submitted it to the *Wilson Bulletin*, the quarterly journal of the Wilson Ornithological Society. Binford had considered other prestigious journals, *Auk* and *Condor*, but the *Wilson Bulletin* was the only one that could publish the color photographs he had—ones of the live chick in all its buffy glory taken by Bruce Elliott and one of the humble nest on the cut limb. The article was reviewed by two ornithologists and accepted in May. In September 1975, "Discovery of a Nest and the Downy Young of the Marbled Murrelet" appeared in print. Laurence C. Binford's name appeared as the first author, but to acknowledge their work collecting data in Big Basin, Binford listed Bruce G. Elliott and Steven W. Singer as well.

The report ran eighteen pages with two color photographs, one black-and-white photograph of the entire 225-

foot Douglas fir; and a sketched profile of the spotty-headed chick. It was the official announcement of the discovery of the first marbled murrelet nest. The chick and its nest had been written into the record, introduced to the world. The chick was no longer a porcupine with a beak sticking out. It was a bird, an alcid, an auk, a marbled murrelet, *Brachyramphus marmoratus*, a bird found and then discovered. Its nesting site was no longer a mystery, a vexation, a Holy Grail, a "stigma on oologists" as one naturalist called it. It was a bowl in a mossy branch, a natural depression, a Cream-Buff ring of droppings, and a very small niche on a large planet.

Twenty-five years after Binford's report was published, I stood in the basement of the California Academy of Sciences in San Francisco holding the marbled murrelet chick in my own hand. It was about the size of a starling—larger than I imagined it would be. It looked less like a downy chick than it did a dark-feathered juvenile hiding (badly) in a too-small fur coat—like a wolf in sheep's clothing.

I had brought Binford's article with me. I opened up to the photograph taken of this tiny bird, alive, on the day of its capture. There on the table before me were two chicks. One was a twenty-five-year-old preserved specimen under fluorescent lights; the other was a live chick sitting in dappled sunlight captured in color print made from a Kodachrome slide. Which chick did Binford describe? Which one did Hoyt Foster reach for in the Douglas fir? Which chick was closer to the truth? The true colors of the chick now existed only on the small color plates of Ridgway's masterpiece. I picked the chick up in my hands.

I held the bird for a long time. I stood there, treelike, with my arm extended, branchlike, my hand cupped like a nest. I imagined the chick warm and alive in the Douglas fir. Had this chick eluded all predators and tree trimmers during its first summer, the mystery of the marbled murrelet would have ended with another bird in another forest somewhere on the Pacific Coast. This chick would have remained on the tree limb in the Santa Cruz Mountains, waiting for food, waiting for flight. At dawn and dusk, its parents would have appeared with fish for their rapidly growing chick. Very gradually, the down would have disappeared from the chick's forehead and mandibles. A week later, from its belly. And in another week from the sides of its body. The chick would have felt a sudden burst of energy and the need to preen, scratch, and flap its wings. In its last eight to forty-eight hours on the nest, the chick would have lost its last bit of camouflage. Some of the down covering its back would have been scattered over the moss or trapped in the droppings. Most of it would have floated to the forest floor.

I imagined the chick exposed and vulnerable on its nest in black-and-white plumage, its instincts shouting, "Fly!" Where did the bird hold these instincts? In its brain or muscles, or in the feathers or spaces between? Were they lost in the wind, or was I holding them in my hand? Somewhere still was the urge to step to the edge of its nest. Somewhere lingering was the longing for the fish, the salt water, its parents. What no scientists knew in 1975—but what scientists would learn many years hence—was what happened next: Just after dusk, the chick would have spread its wings, flown off the nest, and headed west to the sea in one direct, original, and beautiful flight path.

In the faintly glowing western sky, someone—a camper, a birder, a logger—might have seen the small bird whirring over the old-growth forest and down toward the bluffs. Someone might have pointed, marveled, wondered about the fleeting shape. Someone—a boater, a fisherman—might have turned toward the splash on the water. No one would have guessed it was the sound that marked a successful fledging, a mission accomplished, and the end of a perilous journey.

I set the chick back in the box lid. With this small creature, the great mystery of the marbled murrelet's nesting site had been solved. But the mystery of this bird was far larger than the discovery of a patch of moss. Scientists knew little to nothing about this bird's life history, breeding range, breeding behavior, parental care, incubation period, characteristics of its nest sites, diet, feeding ecology, seasonal movements, migration, vocalizations, territoriality, causes of mortality, predators, or life span. And they didn't know how difficult it would be to unravel these still remaining mysteries.

9 05 - 9 22 feeding

After a flurry of stories in local newspapers, birding magazines, and bird club bulletins, the marbled murrelet resumed its life as a secretive, elusive, and enigmatic bird. The preserved chick and the mossy tree limb from Big Basin were stored in the basement of the California Academy of Sciences. They were never put on display in the academy's popular museum, where a curious public could marvel at them as "natural curiosities" the way the crowds did back in the days of the Leverian Museum. To see the long-sought-after chick, birders and academic researchers alike were required to make an appointment with the curator. Few went to the trouble.

No one ever claimed the $100 Audubon discovery reward. Laurence Binford resumed his work on other birds and mammals at the Academy. Bruce Elliott took on another California Department of Fish and Game project at a marshland north of Oakland. Denzil Verardo returned to his historical research and writing. Hoyt Foster gave a few interviews and picked up his old job trimming trees over power lines. Steve Singer continued his teaching job but returned to the park frequently to look for more nests, sometimes bringing fellow birders along for weekend camping trips in the old-growth groves. It was 1975, and Spencer Sealy, a young professor of zoology at the University of Manitoba, had just published two full-length scientific articles—the first any scientist had ever dedicated exclusively to the marbled murrelet. In 1970 and 1971, Spencer Sealy had traveled to British Columbia to study the breeding and feeding ecology of ancient murrelets at sea for his PhD. This species of murrelet nested in burrows, crevices, and under tree roots and logs along the coast. Like the marbled murrelet, it was a little-studied bird; unlike the marbled murrelet, it was a colonial and wore black-and-white plumage during the breeding season. As soon as Sealy had motored his pneumatic boat out to the colonies on Graham and Langara Islands to begin his study of these birds, he was struck by an unexpected sight.

"What were all these little brown birds doing here on the water?" he wondered.

They were "the marbleds," as Sealy calls them—a bird he knew little about. Because marbled murrelets didn't nest in colonies along the coast or exhibit any recognizable breeding behavior at sea, Sealy had never given them much thought. But the marbled murrelet has a way of working itself under your skin. Sealy decided to take the opportunity to learn something about them. In June, he began his first excursion— the first of one hundred trips he would make to the inlets, bays, and passages between the islands over the next two years. He spent long days observing marbled murrelets foraging, loafing, and bobbing on the water. On many occasions, Sealy observed birds sitting on the water holding whole fish cross-wise in their bills. He watched and waited, but the birds didn't swallow the fish or feed them to other birds on the water. He saw the birds flying off the water, still holding the fish, to some destination beyond the range of his binoculars.

On the water, Sealy also noticed that marbled murrelets appeared singly and in aloof pairs early in the season and in small, gregarious groups later in the season, with the young and adults separate. At certain times during the season, there were birds on the water in brown breeding plumage, in black-and-white plumage, and in various stages of molt in between. Sealy found it impossible to tell male from female and difficult to distinguish breeding adults from non-breeding subadults. He observed birds in pairs; but he was unsure if they were mated pairs. Despite his two hundred hours of observation of the birds at sea, Sealy never witnessed marbled murrelets copulating. He never saw what looked like a marbled murrelet family group—two adults and a chick together on the water. How was he going to uncover any secrets about the bird's breeding behavior?

Sealy had neither the interest nor the time to search the forest where at least he would have had a chance of observing the mysterious breeding behavior directly. He wasn't even tempted to look for a nest. What Sealy wanted to learn about marbled murrelets he was going to learn from their feathers and flesh—from his boat and with his collecting gun.

Without ever searching for a nest in the hemlock and cedar forests, Spencer Sealy determined that the marbled murrelet breeding season in the Queen Charlotte Islands ran from late April to September. Without ever seeing a single marbled murrelet egg, he deduced that marbled murrelets laid their eggs over six to seven weeks from mid-May to early July. Without ever observing an adult bird sitting on a nest, he calculated that the incubation period for marbled murrelets was about one month long.

My idea of a nightmare is to be put in an inflatable Zodiac raft with a shotgun, a pair of binoculars, a few measuring devices, and instructions to learn something about a bird's breeding behavior. The very idea that Spencer Sealy or any other field biologist could produce such data from such basic equipment was astounding. To me, this was like giving someone a box of crayons and saying, "Here, see what you can find out about the Milky Way."

Over two years, Sealy collected dozens of marbled murrelets during the spring and summer. Once he had the birds in hand, he examined each for the presence of a brood patch—a single, centered, and relatively small (1-by-1½-inch) oval patch large enough for incubating one or two eggs, no more. Not all brood patches Sealy examined were alike. He made detailed notes on the amount of down and contour feathers missing from each patch. He measured the area of exposed skin. He compared the amount of vascularization of the exposed skin from one bird to the next. Then he devised a simple scoring system—one scientists still use today—to rate the brood patches according to their development. A Class One patch, for instance, is small with little loss of down or contour feathers and belongs to a bird in the early part of its breeding cycle and probably preparing for egg-laying and incubation. A Class Three patch is fully defeathered and heavily vascularized and suggests that the adult is fully engaged in incubation duties. A Class Six patch is mostly refeathered with new down and contour feathers and belongs to a bird well past the end of its breeding cycle.

When Sealy dissected the adults with brood patches, he found that roughly half possessed testes, and the other half had ovaries—an observation that supported the theory that males and females both incubated their egg. Sealy then examined the reproductive tracts of twenty females to see whether he could determine when each might be laying its egg. Each ovary contained a cluster of spherical follicles (the part of the ovary that produces the egg) of varying sizes. The larger the follicle, Sealy knew, the closer the female was to producing an egg. One female had an unshelled egg in its oviduct—evidence that she was within a day or two of her laying date.

Sealy then plotted the size of the follicles against the collection date of each bird. He looked at the brood patch scores. He studied the dates he had seen birds flying toward the forest with fish in their bills and the dates he had first seen newly fledged chicks on the water. From his data—measurements, dates, charts, and scores—emerged his answers. And some advice. Anyone planning to look for a marbled murrelet nest in the Queen Charlottes should get out his or her calendars and pens. Chances of finding a nest would be greatest during the incubation stage, when Sealy observed the adults flying to and from the nests regularly, and afterwards, during the chick-feeding stage, when both adults made flights at least once a day into the forests with fish.

Spencer Sealy offered the advice freely, but he was never tempted to get caught up in solving the nest mystery himself. He had set out to study ancient murrelets and marbled murrelets at sea, and he was determined to keep it that way. Of course, this didn't mean he couldn't look at the forests. He did. He spent much time staring up at the majestic hemlocks and spruces of the Queen Charlotte Islands, at their dark trunks, at their moss-covered limbs, and asking himself, "Is that where they nest?"

In January of 1974—the same month and year that the cataclysmic snowstorm hit the Santa Cruz Mountains— Spencer Sealy published his first major paper on the marbled murrelet in the *Auk*. In the article, under the subhead "The Nest Site," Sealy describes his idea of the bird's likely nesting trees. They were "large evergreens, both hemlock and cedar, which, in addition to having many large crotches suitable for a nest, frequently have large accumulations of moss on horizontal branches. Such moss 'beds' often measure up to a meter across and would surely support a nest, but the murrelet's rufous-colored back would certainly not afford the incubating bird concealing coloration. Also prevalent in these forests are freshly broken hemlock and cedar trunks, the inner wood of which, to my eyes, matches perfectly the rufous of the adult marbled murrelet's backs. If indeed the marbled murrelet does nest in trees, as the number of potentially suitable nest sites in the coastal forests is almost infinite, some method of location of their nest other than chance sightings is desirable."

No scientists would call this prescience—just good science.

Sealy was not too surprised when, eight months after his article appeared, the nest and chick were discovered in Big Basin—on a mossy limb of a large evergreen tree, one with many large and suitable crotches. Spencer's surprise came two months later, in October, at the annual meeting for the American Ornithologists' Union in Norman, Oklahoma. There, in a crowded conference room, a colleague approached him and invited him up to a hotel room to "see a couple of chicks."

When Sealy got to the room, he was greeted by a group of distinguished ornithologists and two chicks—the downy marbled murrelet from Big Basin and a downy Kittlitz's murrelet from the ornithology collection of the University of Kansas. Sealy and his colleagues spent the rest of the evening studying the two *Brachyramphus* chicks—the similar buff color on their backs, rumps, and heads; the same light buffy-gray of their breasts and abdomens; and the strong pattern of blackish variegations on their heads. It was a night Sealy has never forgotten.

Sealy shies away from the title of "father of marbled murrelet studies," a title his younger colleagues have conferred upon him. He will admit, after acknowledging the contributions of several colleagues, that he was "probably the first one to show that marbled murrelets were something worth studying." Sealy is as humble as he is accomplished. The fact is that in the 1970s, when the field of marbled murrelet research was wide open, Spencer Sealy was the only ornithologist in it. Since then, he has authored or coauthored more than a dozen articles on the marbled murrelet—articles that are now and will forever be cited in the scientific literature on this species.

When I first met Sealy, it was in a large crowd at a seabird conference. He was in his late fifties, tall, lean, and bespectacled, with a full head of wavy, gray hair. His face was neatly chiseled and wrinkle-free. In a crowd, Sealy holds himself a bit aloof—sometimes standing singly, sometimes in a pair with one of his many admirers. He talks and listens with care. Despite all the prestigious awards Sealy has received recently for his contributions to ornithology in Canada and on the Pacific Coast, he remains modest. He is a soft-spoken intellectual, a man whose body language says he'd rather be birding.

Since 1972, Sealy has been teaching courses in chordate zoology, ecology, ornithology, and mammology at the University of Manitoba in Winnipeg, where he also supervises PhD and master's students. Two of his graduate students are currently prominent marbled murrelet researchers. Though Sealy still makes trips to the Pacific Coast to study alcids, his home and family are in Winnipeg. There, he has developed an avian research program on the shores of Lake Manitoba and conducted long-term studies of yellow warblers, least fly-catchers, and brown-headed cowbirds. He recently became editor of the *Auk*. How, I wondered, did a young man raised on the landlocked prairies of central Canada start pursuing seabirds on remote islands off the Pacific Coast?

During Sealy's elementary school days in Saskatchewan, he took an interest in raptors—a first favorite of many young boys who find aerial predators and the ancient art of falconry irresistible. Unlike most boys, Sealy didn't outgrow his interest in birds. During his first year in high school, he learned that Stuart Houston, a medical doctor and well-known bird bander from Saskatoon, was recruiting volunteers to help with a study of hawks and owls across Saskatchewan. Sealy sent in his request for a set of numbered metal bands and was soon exploring the woods and fields near his home on foot and on his bike. After just a few days of banding suc-cesses, Spencer Sealy was hooked. When he had covered the territory near his home, Sealy's parents planned family out-ings to get him farther afield and to enjoy—but not to join—

their son in the field. Sealy's father and mother—a minister and a schoolteacher—were always thrilled when their son took an interest in something educational.

In 1959, Sealy attended his first American Ornithologists' Union meeting. The following year, he published his first article, on bats. In 1961, he applied for his own banding permit and banded more than two hundred birds with a friend that year. Some were raptors; most were gulls and other waterbirds that nested in colonies on Saskatchewan's myriad marshes and ponds.

"I took an interest in these birds," Sealy told me during one of our phone conservations, "because I think I was interested in wading through marshes and experiencing the wetland habitat."

Sealy paused. I imagined he had closed his eyes and had transported himself back to his high school days, to the edge of the marsh where he stands in his hip-waders, the shimmering water, the flocks of gulls, the summer sky, and his youth spread out before him like a feast.

"I think it was the actual act of banding, too." He paused again. "There was something less than subtle going on in my mind in that I was actually thinking that I was playing the role of a scientist. I was doing what scientists do. I enjoyed any opportunity I ever had to do what I thought was more than just a kid thing. Even though I wasn't doing a study or looking to recover banded birds over the next year, I was contributing to scientific research."

It didn't take long for Sealy to take up the role of a real scientist. With his undergraduate degree in zoology and encouragement from his advisors, he headed to Alaska to study auklets in the Bering Sea. A few years later, Sealy settled into the Queen Charlotte Islands to begin his work on the ancients and the marbleds.

That Spencer Sealy was the only ornithologist studying marbled murrelets in the 1970s did not sit well with Steve Singer, who had spent most of his weekends during the summers of 1975 and 1976 in Big Basin Redwoods State Park waiting for marbled murrelets. With his wife and several birding pals, Singer camped in the park's old-growth groves, rose before dawn, and stood staring up at the sky and into the trees hoping to learn something about the bird's breeding behavior. He also hoped to find a second nest. During those summer mornings, he and his group saw hundreds of birds flying overhead. They learned to recognize their different calls and flight patterns; they even found several grounded juveniles on the forest floor. They failed, however, to find a second nest—a nest seemingly as elusive as the first.

Singer was frustrated. He was working full time and didn't have the time or the money to launch a full-blown scientific study of the marbled murrelet himself. Where were the ornithologists? The wildlife biologists? The forestry ecologists? Singer couldn't understand why no one had taken an interest in this rare bird with the strange, almost amphibious life. Why hadn't a single seabird biologist come to the Santa Cruz Mountains after the hoopla surrounding the nest discovery had died down?

Singer knew part of the answer. The discovery of the first nest was purely by accident. There was no concerted effort by the scientific community at the time to find a marbled murrelet nest. Few people thought that the birds were—

or would be—endangered. Marbled murrelets just didn't interest many ornithologists at the time. Spencer Sealy's published articles seemed to fill the need for any immediate studies.

And there were other reasons, too. Scientific research had been growing increasingly specialized over the years. The men and women who were once naturalists became biologists, and ornithologists, then wildlife ecologists, forestry ecologists, evolutionary biologists, and seabird biologists. Members of this latter group naturally set their sights on birds that lived and nested at sea and along the coast: the gulls, terns, albatrosses, pelicans, murres, and other alcids. But not the marbled murrelet. Forest ecologists and wildlife biologists focused on the birds that lived and bred in the forest—the woodpeckers, owls, hawks, crows, jays, and a multitude of perching birds and songbirds. The marbled murrelet simply fell into a wide crack, one that kept seabird biologists on one side in their boats and forestry biologists on the other in their boots. And what the world didn't know, Singer believed, could hurt the marbled murrelet.

His greatest worry was that if the marbled murrelets were in trouble, they could vanish completely without notice. Who witnesses the deaths of birds at sea or in the forest? Who counts the downy chicks left starving in the treetops? Who stops to wonder when the dawn skies suddenly become empty and silent? Would anyone actually miss this nearly invisible bird? At times, Singer felt like the lone Lorax speaking for the trees in a forest where no one was listening.

Singer wasn't one to rant and rave and shake his fist at the logging trucks and bulldozers. Instead, he went to his typewriter on August 16, 1976, and composed a letter to Spencer Sealy—the one man he thought could help. Singer's one-page letter was a request—an impassioned plea, really—for Sealy to encourage his graduate students to come to Big Basin Redwoods State Park to study the marbled murrelet's breeding behavior before it was too late. With university backing and adequate funding, Singer reasoned, a graduate student would have little trouble locating additional nests and producing an original master's or PhD thesis. Singer was careful to explain that he did not have ulterior motives—a share of the funding, control of the project, or joint authorship. He wrote:

> I am motivated not only by the desire to increase man's knowledge about the real world but also by a desire to insure that the marbled murrelet will always be with us. If the discovered nest is typical . . . (which, admittedly, is pure conjecture at this time), then the continuing harvest of virgin timber along the western coast of this continent could, conceivably, adversely affect this species. There seems to be no immediate problem in this regard, but who knows what the future holds?

Sealy read Singer's letter with interest and sent him his recent articles, but not a graduate student. He didn't necessarily share Singer's concern about the uncertain future of the species. Sealy had found the birds to be relatively abundant in the Queen Charlotte Islands, and tree-nesting had not been proven to be "typical," as Steve noted. Sealy saw no reason to worry about marbled murrelets. But Spencer Sealy had yet to meet Harry Carter.

CHAPTER 13

Ｉf you had to pick Harry Carter out of a crowd today, you would look for a clean-shaven man in his late forties, a man with blue eyes that had seen plenty of open sky and ocean, a man who seems capable of inhaling salty air and exhaling data sets. You would look for a serious and sturdy man who carries himself as though he's had his sea legs from the moment he took his first steps. Blindfolded in a boat, Carter likely could tell you exactly where he was on the Pacific Coast simply by smelling the breeze, feeling the ocean swells, and listening to the cries of the seabirds.

Harry Carter grew up in Victoria, British Columbia, with the Strait of Juan de Fuca as his backyard. He spent much of his youth aboard his family's thirty-foot fishing boat, the M/V *Tedmac*. From an early age, Carter knew fish and the fishermen catching them, seabirds and the biologists studying them. Carter's high-school girlfriend was Suzanne Guiguet— the youngest daughter of biologist Charles Guiguet of the Royal British Columbia Museum. Carter saw his first marbled murrelets while visiting the Guiguets on Vancouver Island during the summer of 1973. It was Suzanne who pointed out the birds to him one evening as they cruised along the shores of Barkley Sound in a Zodiac. Later, Suzanne's mother told Carter of her discovery a few years back of a marbled murrelet chick on an inland logging road nearby. The next day, Charles Guiguet himself introduced Carter to the great mystery of the marbled murrelet and recounted some of his nest-searching exploits over the past three decades. Carter was intrigued, but the ocean was full of intriguing seabirds, and his life among them was just beginning.

Carter attended the University of Victoria for one year, then the University of British Columbia for three years and spent every summer as a student intern at the Royal British Columbia Museum working with a team of museum biologists. Carter's main job was to conduct the first complete survey of the seabird colonies along the entire coast of British Columbia.

Though the noncolonial marbled murrelets weren't included in the survey, Carter couldn't help noticing the birds on the water everywhere along the coast. Nor could he help hearing Guiguet and Campbell tell (and retell) the story of their quest for the nest of the marbled murrelet. When Carter began compiling a bibliography of British Columbia birds, he kept a special list of papers on marbled murrelets.

Carter didn't develop his interest and passion for the marbled murrelet during those summers, but he did develop his approach to studying seabirds—one that places equal value on fieldwork *and* knowledge of the scientific literature and unpublished data. Carter believed that a strong grasp of historical data helped biologists put their own work in a broader context, design better and more insightful field studies, and reduce the risk of reinventing some very expensive wheels.

During those summers in the museum library, Harry Carter wasn't just reading the scientific literature on British Columbia birds or merely alphabetizing thousands of articles by the author's last name. He was absorbing the literature. He was evaluating the data, analyzing methods, weighing the evidence, and filing the articles in chronological order—in his mind. The young Harry Carter was becoming a walking database, a gold mine of historical data. If a person called out "Grinnell 1897," "Guiguet 1956," or "Sealy 1970," Carter could, I believe, describe the contents of the article and offer an opinion on its merits.

Needless to say, a person with this kind of mind stands out in a classroom, especially if he also has a way of engaging his peers and generously sharing his knowledge. Such was the case when Harry Carter walked into a seabird biology class at the Bamfield Marine Station in 1976. The teacher, Spencer Sealy, knew almost instantly that Carter was a peer. A spark ignited between the two—that rare spark that turns a student and teacher into lifelong colleagues and collaborators.

In the fall of 1978, Harry Carter had a degree in zoology, four summers' worth of seabird colony surveys, a rudimentary understanding of marbled murrelets, and no job. In the fall, while Carter was finishing up a volunteer project at the museum, in walked Spencer Sealy on sabbatical from the University of Manitoba to begin a study of ancient murrelets. In no time, Carter had a volunteer job, and Sealy had an eager assistant.

As the two studied ancient murrelets over the next year, they frequently discussed marbled murrelets because both birds had associations with the old-growth forest. As they

examined ancient murrelet study skins in various ornithological collections on the West Coast, they took the time to
examine marbled murrelet skins as well.

When Carter was ready to begin his graduate work in
1979 (with Sealy as his advisor), he proposed studying the effect of old-growth logging on murrelets—ancient murrelets in
the Queen Charlotte Islands. It was a worthy and original
topic, but Carter couldn't find funding for the study. So Carter
joined Sealy and another graduate student for an already
funded project on common murres in Barkley Sound on the
west coast of Vancouver Island.

As soon as the team began their fieldwork, one of the
first things they noticed was the large numbers of marbled
murrelets in one particular channel. Rather than ignore the
birds, Sealy suggested that they survey the channel more
closely to see what they could learn about these alcids. Now,
Harry Carter is not an either/or kind of scientist. It's either
all or nothing—usually it's all. He spent the 1979 field season
on the water studying both the common murre and the
marbled murrelet. But while he was collecting data, something very strange happened.

Someone began dropping off bodies of dead marbled
murrelets on the wharf at the Bamfield Marine Station where
Carter lived aboard the *Tedmac*. The birds, he learned from
local salmon fishermen, had been caught in gill nets—nearly
invisible nylon mesh nets that trap fish by their gills as they
swim past. Such nets are still used. They are effective but not
selective; when fishermen haul in their catch of salmon, a hefty
bycatch of diving seabirds and other marine animals can be
hauled in with them.

Carter took the marbled murrelet carcasses to Sealy at the University of Manitoba to be prepared as study specimens. Carter was not sure what to make of this windfall of dead murrelets. Certainly they would enhance the university's collection, but when the birds kept piling up at the wharf, Carter sensed that the windfall could lead to a downfall. Over the next two years, he collected 360 gill-netted marbled murrelets. That number, he later estimated, represented about 4 percent of the total population of marbled murrelets in Barkley Sound.

Carter made another important discovery. By 1981, he had unintentionally collected more information on marbled murrelets than on common murres. After discussing the issue with Sealy, Carter decided to switch his thesis topic to marbled murrelets. His timing could not have been more fortuitous.

The Pacific Seabird Group, a professional association of seabird biologists, had just announced a symposium on the interactions between seabirds and commercial fisheries. Carter's and Sealy's records of the gill-netted marbled murrelets from Bamfield would illustrate one such interaction. In January 1982, Carter and Sealy reported their findings to hundreds of fellow seabird biologists at the Pacific Seabird Group meeting in Seattle, Washington.

There was, as Carter recalls, "a general lack of reaction to the presentation." Hundreds of marbled murrelets were nothing when compared to the thousands of gill-netted seabirds reported on at the conference or the hundreds of thousands of seabirds killed in other types of fishing nets and gear in the North Atlantic and North Pacific each year.

Carter and Sealy listened to their disbelieving colleagues, not convinced that their data from Barkley Sound were so insignificant. They simply needed more data to show scientifically what they believed: that the gill netting of marbled murrelets was not a localized threat but was likely occurring elsewhere along the Pacific Coast. After much thought and many discussions, these two seabird biologists realized that the problem was even larger than gill netting. Marbled murrelets faced numerous threats from both the marine and terrestrial environments. At sea, marbled murrelets were threatened by oil spills, oil pollution, and gill netting. Inland, they faced a drastic loss of their habitat from the logging of the old-growth forests. But neither Sealy nor Carter had the data to prove these threats were real.

Eight years had passed since the 1974 nest discovery at Big Basin, but that tree nest was still the only well-documented, indisputable piece of evidence that linked the marbled murrelet to the old-growth forest. Sealy and Carter did not have time to begin searching the forests for nests. They had only one field season to collect and write up their data. In August 1982, the International Council for Bird Preservation was holding its annual meeting in Cambridge, England, and the Pacific Seabird Group was holding its annual meeting in Hawaii. Neither man wanted to miss those opportunities to present his data-strengthened concerns to his colleagues.

In April 1982, Harry Carter returned to Victoria and refurbished the *Tedmac* to serve as a base of operations for counting marbled murrelets at sea, estimating their population, and mapping their distribution along the coast of Barley and Clayoquot Sounds. He enlisted his father, Harry Sr., to captain the *Tedmac*, while he conducted counts on the open water from the *Tedmac* and in narrow channels and inlets from a fourteen-foot inflatable Zodiac raft. The protocol was straightforward and involved little more than a map, a boat, and a pair of binoculars. Using nautical maps of the coast, Carter plotted a grid that covered the water from two to six kilometers (1.2 to 3.7 miles) from shore. Each square, or quadrat, in the grid measured one square kilometer (.62 square miles), so that marbled murrelets could be counted per square kilometer.

For four straight weeks in June, from 5 A.M. to 2 P.M., the two Harrys plied a labyrinth of channels, sounds, islets, and fjords along the coast and counted marbled murrelets. While one person steered the boat, another one or two would scan the water and count the marbled murrelets on the water or flying over water in each quadrat.

What Carter discovered was that there were many thousands of marbled murrelets distributed in large clumps—one as large as three thousand strong—in the nearshore waters. There was nothing unusual about this clumped distribution of marbled murrelets; seabirds often form clumps or flocks when the schooling fish they are preying on are concentrated in the water. For many seabirds, the clumping was a strategy that promoted more efficient foraging, but this behavior had a downside for the marbled murrelets. Large groups of foraging marbled murrelets served as beacons to local fishermen. Where there were marbled murrelets, there were small fish, and where there were small fish, there were big ones. The fishermen frequently maneuvered their boats near the murrelets and lowered their gill nets to haul in their share of the bounty.

The marbled murrelet's nearshore foraging behavior also increased the potential impact of oil spills on their populations. Even though most spills occur well beyond the birds' foraging areas, the oil eventually moves toward shore, where it usually concentrates as a thick ooze on the water's surface. A small bird like the marbled murrelet has little chance of surviving once its feathers become oiled. In two studies published in 1979 and 1981, scientists had recently listed the marbled murrelet as the seabird most vulnerable to oil spills in certain parts of Alaska, Washington State, and British Columbia. Judging from developments in the petroleum industry along the Pacific Coast, there was reason to believe that the threat to the marbled murrelet would only worsen.

But what about the logging of the old-growth forests? How could Carter or Sealy expect anyone to believe that logging was a problem for a local population of birds numbering in the many thousands in just one small area? Were there once millions of birds evenly distributed along the shore? Were the clumps of birds adjacent to old-growth forests? Did the clumped distribution imply that the murrelet-free stretches of water were adjacent to logged forests? Carter went to the British Columbia Forest Service to find out.

Using maps of logged and unlogged forests, Carter plotted the areas where he had conducted his marbled murrelet census. He reviewed logging statistics and forestry reports and found no strong correlation between the locations of the birds on the water and the dense forests of old-growth hemlocks, cedars, spruces, and firs. What he did find was that at the current rate of logging in British Columbia, the old-growth forests along Barkley and Clayoquot Sounds would be gone within fifty years. If marbled murrelets did in fact depend on these forests, the birds would simply vanish with the trees.

In July, Carter and Sealy began working furiously to put their case together—a strong case that the marbled murrelet was imperiled and needed immediate attention from the scientific community. In August, Sealy traveled to King's College in Cambridge, England to address his colleagues at a symposium on the status and conservation of the world's seabirds. Sealy describes the response as "lukewarm at best." Some of the prestigious ornithologists gathered at the International Council for Bird Preservation meeting believed that other seabirds were at greater risk than the marbled murrelet. Others felt that Sealy didn't have enough data to support his concerns. Some just didn't understand the problem. Sealy recalls that the turning point came during a potentially awkward moment at an elegant banquet dinner during the conference. In the Great Hall of the historic college—beneath the soaring arched ceiling and across the long, candlelit table draped in white linen—a highly respected colleague leaned toward Sealy and asked in a tone more incredulous than curious, "Why should we be worried about the marbled murrelet?"

Sealy laid out his concerns thoughtfully and in great detail over the din of the banquet, and again the next day at a meeting of alcid specialists. By the end of the meeting, Sealy had prevailed. The International Council for Bird Preservation officially recognized the marbled murrelet as "a species of concern because of habitat destruction in its breeding range." The awareness of the problem had suddenly grown from a few scientists to several hundred. It was a critical first step—a leap, really—in the conservation of the marbled murrelet.

Kees Vermeer was one of the alcid specialists at the International Council for Bird Preservation meeting. Vermeer was also a member of the Pacific Seabird Group, so in August, he traveled to Hawaii where he presented the council's decision on the marbled murrelet at a special marbled murrelet workshop. During that meeting, Vermeer drafted a resolution of concern for the marbled murrelet. The Pacific Seabird Group passed it and published it in its winter 1982 bulletin.

The resolution, a succinct twenty-six-line document, tackled the most critical of the three threats to the marbled murrelet: the logging of the old-growth forest. The resolution circulated among the seabird biologists and was sent to the offices of the Canadian and U.S. forest and wildlife management agencies. These agencies controlled most of the old-growth forests where the marbled murrelets were believed to breed. The resolution recommended that these agencies consider the marbled murrelet in their plans that might adversely affect the integrity of these forests.

Here it was, finally—the response Steve Singer had hoped for six years earlier when he wrote his letter to Spencer Sealy. The scientific community was rallying around the cause of the marbled murrelet. In the membership of the

Pacific Seabird Group, there were dozens of men and women willing and ready to undertake the challenging and exhausting work that would enable them to state outright what Steve Singer had only hinted at in his letter written six years earlier: that the marbled murrelet was in peril and the old-growth forests needed to be protected if this species was to survive.

PART THREE

PURSUIT

(W) when
for the first bird to deliver
its fish.
ween 9:45 & 10:35 Im at MmLk but
drew a complete blank.

At 11:15 am Im' setting beside
Km 17 looking straight up
over the roost & a murrelet
(carrying a fish?) flys
at T×1.5 right overhead
travelling N80°E. There is
mist in some of the trees

The Pacific Seabird Group is a dynamic society of professional seabird researchers and managers dedicated to the study and conservation of seabirds. Formed in 1972, its four hundred members include people from the United States, Canada, Mexico, Japan, and a dozen other countries. Initially the group's efforts were directed toward birds that lived at sea and were studied primarily by boat. When the issue of the marbled murrelet came along, however, they embraced the study of this forest-nesting bird and encouraged researchers and managers working in the coastal forests to attend their meetings.

I have attended three Pacific Seabird Group conferences since I met the marbled murrelet. I love these conferences. Most of the three hundred attendees are researchers, but many are forestry managers, conservation professionals, and representatives of the lumber, oil, gas, and fishing industries who are there to exchange ideas and concerns and to learn the latest science from their colleagues.

In a typical three-day Pacific Seabird Group conference, there are well over a hundred presentations on nearly as many species of seabirds. Each presentation is short—fifteen minutes—and requires the scientist at the podium to summarize the highlights of the previous year's research. Needless to say, these scientists talk very fast. Many of them seem to take one very deep breath and talk very rapidly while slowly exhaling. When they inhale again, they are done. Relieved, they take a gulp of water and a question or two from the audience. One popular question is, "What's the take-home message?" This requires the speaker to further reduce his or her research into one or two sentences—an accomplishment alone worth a round of applause.

At my first conference, in Santa Barbara, California, in 2002, there were fourteen presentations on marbled murrelets, making it the second-most talked about species after the threatened white pelican. Presentations on marbled murrelets ranged from the at-sea movements of radio-tagged birds to the use of ultrasound scanning to determine the sex of the birds captured at sea. Because of my attention surplus disorder, I also sat in on talks on "A Tangerine-Scented Pheromone in a Monogamous Seabird," "Aggressive Competition among Broodmates," and the "Endothermy, Ectothermy, and the Structure of Marine Communities."

During these presentations and the coffee breaks in between, I was learning some of the subtle differences between real scientists and amateurs like myself. Never once, in the dozens of high-speed, fifteen-minute presentations I attended did I hear anyone use the word "data" as a singular noun. Data *are*, not *is*. Your data are significant. His data are confusing. Rarely did I hear a scientist say that they had "good data." I talked with one biologist who was very excited about the data he had been collecting from a radio-tagging project. He started out one sentence, "We have some g—"

He stopped short. He laughed and looked over at a colleague and said, "I almost said, 'We have some good data.'" The colleague chuckled.

The biologist turned back to me, looked me in the eyes over his reading glasses, and said, "We have some data. It's as good as it gets."

Data are data. Facts are facts. Good and other qualitative adjectives may be betrayers of a scientist's subjectivity.

One of the roles of the scientists of the Pacific Seabird Group is to provide government agencies and others with expert advice on managing the threats to seabird populations. If these scientists are to be taken seriously and their data valued, they must remain objective. There is no room for opinions or biases or conclusions their data don't support. By training, scientists are not supposed to be advocates for their data, nor are they supposed to tell managers how to use their data. Ideally, researchers collect data, interpret it carefully, and present it to managers and advocates to use responsibly to make their decisions and strategies. But maintaining their professional objectivity isn't easy; human beings are all about subjectivity. In the case of the marbled murrelet, when the research is so challenging and the stakes so high to save the bird, the dreaded emotions slip in around the edges, especially when the data they have gathered so scrupulously are misinterpreted, warped, spun, or worse, ignored. It is easy to get emotional about an endearing little seabird like the marbled murrelet. Some scientists believe their objectivity is what will help this bird the most; others feel that personal compassion is a necessary part of conservation.

In less than ten years—from 1975 to 1982—the

awareness of the plight of the marbled murrelet had stirred one biologist in California, then two in British Columbia, dozens in England, hundreds in Hawaii, and now hundreds of scientists in every Pacific Coast state and province in North America. But awareness is only the beginning. Action had to follow. But none did.

The Pacific Seabird Group's 1982 "resolution of concern" fell mostly on deaf ears. There was, as Harry Carter describes it, a "general lack of reaction" among those who read it. It wasn't that the forest and wildlife management agencies didn't care about the marbled murrelet, it was that they were overwhelmed by the plight of another bird they had been requested to consider. That bird was the northern spotted owl.

Considering isn't exactly the right word to describe what they were doing. They were struggling. Scientists had reported that the population of this owl was plummeting due to the logging of the old-growth forests they inhabited. The forest and wildlife managers were struggling to remain cool, calm, and objective in the midst of a contentious owls-versus-jobs battle between the environmentalists and loggers of the Pacific Northwest. To many, this was no time to consider the marbled murrelet—a little-known bird with only one verified nest in the old-growth forest.

Four years passed before the Pacific Seabird Group rallied again and organized a meeting to discuss the marbled murrelet. In December 1986, twenty-two biologists from the Pacific Coast states and provinces—some seabird specialists, some forestry specialists—showed up for the all-day meeting on marbled murrelets. In no time, group members found themselves in agreement: They had observed marbled murrelets *only* in association with old-growth forests. In the summer and throughout the year, they had seen the birds flying well inland, in one case as far as thirty miles. They had seen them carrying fish over the forests in late summer and had records of the birds feeding in freshwater lakes nearly fifty miles from the sea. The scientists had plenty of anecdotal evidence of marbled murrelet chicks being found on the forest floor during the harvests of old-growth trees.

It didn't take long for the researchers and managers to agree on the most significant threats to the marbled murrelet populations. These scientists had recorded several hundred marbled murrelet deaths from gill netting, not only in British Columbia but also in Alaska and California. They had identified oiled marbled murrelets killed in January 1986 when a disastrous oil spill hit the central California coast. They knew the rates—well-documented and alarmingly rapid—at which the old-growth forests were being decimated.

By the time this meeting ended, the twenty-two scientists had learned enough to agree on this: The future of the marbled murrelet looked bleak, and it was their responsibility to do something about it. The first step was to show scientifically that significant numbers of marbled murrelets were in fact being affected by these threats *and* that the rate of mortality or effect on breeding productivity from these threats was contributing to a serious decline in the bird's population. To accomplish this, the biologists decided to spend the next year trying to collect historical and current data on the bird's population and then reconvene at the next

Pacific Seabird Group meeting to share their findings and to take action.

But what action? No matter how much data they collected, the scientists knew that they could not protect or save the marbled murrelet by themselves. They couldn't change logging practices, eliminate gill nets, or prevent oil tankers from polluting the ocean with spilled oil. These jobs belonged to the people who manage our forests and oceans and the wildlife in them.

When I say "our," I mean our government's. In the United States and Canada, every square inch of our land and water that is not privately or tribally owned is owned by the government—state, provincial, or federal. By virtue of our citizenship, tax dollars, and use fees, these lands are our lands. We can fish, hunt, hike, and camp in them; we can drive boats and off-road vehicles through them; we can eat seafood caught from our oceans; we can dig clams on our beaches; we can build homes with lumber harvested from our forests.

In the United States, most of the forests holding marbled murrelet nesting habitat are managed by federal agencies such as the Forest Service, National Park Service, Bureau of Land Management, and Fish and Wildlife Service. Within each state, there are also forests that are managed by state agencies such as the Alaska Department of Game, the Washington Department of Natural Resources, Oregon Department of Parks and Recreation, and the California Department of Forestry. The oceans where marbled murrelets forage are managed by organizations such as the National Institute of Marine Fisheries, the National Oceanic and Atmospheric Administration, the National Marine Sanctuaries, and the U.S. Navy. In British Columbia, the land and seas are owned and managed much the same way—by agencies such as the Canadian Wildlife Service, British Columbia Ministries of Forestry and the Environment, Parks Canada, and the Mineral Management Service.

Many of the managers of these agencies are also scientists with degrees in biology, wildlife ecology, forestry, environmental studies, or resource management. Their jobs, however, are less about fieldwork and data collection than about using the data collected by scientists in the field to set rules, establish policies, and write management plans that protect wildlife and habitat. Many of the scientists and the managers are in what they might refer to as a symbiotic relationship: They need each other. Without scientists and their data, managers cannot manage effectively. Without managers and their policies, scientists don't have funding and cannot expect their data to lead to action.

So the Pacific Seabird Group invited dozens of agency managers to a special 1987 meeting to talk about marbled murrelets. Thirty-nine managers and scientists gathered for two full days of meetings. The scientists had done their homework. They presented what they had learned about the marbled murrelet from published and unpublished scientific works; field guides; popular articles; avian atlases; local, regional, and state bird checklists; and publications such as *Bird-Lore, Audubon Field Notes,* and *American Birds*; scientific articles published in Russia and Japan; and phone conversations with people who had stories to tell about marbled murrelets. The managers were all ears.

By the end of the meeting, the group had formed the Marbled Murrelet Technical Committee, a number of subcommittees, and a very long list of research priorities. At the top of the list was finding marbled murrelet nesting habitat and estimating the current marbled murrelet population. Field research would begin the late spring of 1988 and would overlap the marbled murrelet breeding season. The committee would reconvene to share its findings the following September.

Most in the group could not resist the call to help. Energized by their shared concern, they felt an urgency to get into the forest and out to sea as soon as they could to learn about the ways of the marbled murrelet before it was too late. Many began their work during the summer of 1988 and have continued to this day.

I suspect that few of these researchers were aware of just how challenging the marbled murrelet could be both in the forests and on the sea. Perhaps this was a good thing. Had they known what lay ahead of them, they might not have answered the call of this bird, stepped out on a limb, taken that leap of faith that brought them from awareness to action. Just writing about the marbled murrelet would present me with similar challenges. When I began my work, I was unaware of how much of a commitment I would need to make. Moving my family west was part of that commitment, a big part, I thought. But it was only the beginning. Answering yes to the call of the marbled murrelet meant I had to keep answering yes, every day, every week, for nearly five years, as it turned out. I couldn't drop the ball, I couldn't bow out gracefully. No matter how many times I thought about doing so, I couldn't say no to this bird.

CHAPTER 15

*H*ello? Could you make this any more difficult for us?"
Lora Leschner was frustrated. It was the summer of
1987 and she had been trying to capture marbled murrelets
in Washington's Puget Sound for two days, but she was
having little luck. Leschner is a wildlife biologist with the
Washington Department of Fish and Wildlife. In 1986, she
was also the chairman of the Pacific Seabird Group. She had
embraced the plight of the marbled murrelet, organized all of
the early meetings, brought scientists and managers together,
and kept everyone motivated and moving forward in a spirit
of cooperation.

Now, Leschner was in a Boston whaler with three
colleagues, aiming a net gun at a marbled murrelet.

Leschner and her colleagues were experimenting with
techniques to capture and radio-tag marbled murrelets at sea.
By placing a radio tag on a bird, Leschner hoped that she
would be able to track it to its nest in a nearby forest—or
wherever the bird happened to nest. This technology for
tracking birds wasn't new in 1988, but it had been used
successfully on marbled murrelets only once and in southeastern Alaska. During the summers of 1983 and 1984, two
biologists captured and radio-tagged seventeen birds, but they
were able to track only one bird to its nest site in a moss-

covered old-growth mountain hemlock less than a mile from Kelp Bay. That nest—discovered a full ten years after the Big Basin "accident"—became the second tree nest ever to be found. Leschner hoped to repeat the successes of the Alaska team, but the marbled murrelets were making it difficult.

As soon as Leschner's boat came within range to shoot the net, the marbled murrelet dove out of sight. Following the path of the bubbles, Leschner tried to anticipate the spot where the bird would reappear—off the bow, off the stern, twenty yards that way, fifty yards this way—so she could fire the net onto the bird just as it resurfaced. But when she aimed and fired at the spot, the bird would pop up elsewhere. Or the gun would fail to fire. Or the net would get tangled before it reached the bird. The few times Leschner got the net on a bird, it slipped out and swam or flew away. Leschner and her stalwart cohorts even tried capturing the birds at night, using a bright spotlight to "freeze" the birds to make them easier to net.

The team spent weeks in pursuit of this cunning bird and, eventually, their persistence paid off. Using a process Leschner likens to cutting cattle out of a herd, they approached groups of foraging birds and were able to separate out two marbled murrelets, which they caught. But the birds were too weak, Leschner judged, to handle the stress of the radio-tagging procedure.

At the 1998 Pacific Seabird Group meeting, Leschner and her colleagues discussed their efforts in a presentation entitled "The Marine Road-Runner Show." The wily scientists had been left empty-handed, but with a drawing board full of new capture schemes.

The problem of catching marbled murrelets was, and still

is to a great extent, one of the biggest technical problems in the study of this bird. While net guns struck me as contraptions straight out of one of Wile E. Coyote's notebooks—something you could order by the crate from ACME Products—they weren't as far-fetched as the scheme of another group of scientists working on marbled murrelet capture techniques. This team had members of the U.S. Navy SEALs don scuba gear and attempt to catch the birds by sneaking up on them from below. Though no murrelets were caught this way, the researchers learned that marbled murrelets can outswim the fastest SEALs.

In 1990, Gary Kaiser, a wildlife biologist then with the Canadian Wildlife Service, tried capturing marbled murrelets in British Columbia using mist nets. Again, the technique was not new for avian studies, but it had never been tried on marbled murrelets. A mist net is a large, fine-meshed nylon net that is hung almost like a curtain by ropes or posts and placed strategically in a bird's flight path. Once an unsuspecting bird flies into the net, it is disentangled, then banded or tagged, and released unharmed. At least this is the way it usually works—but, as scientists found out the hard way, not with marbled murrelets.

Kaiser set up his mist nets in a narrow inlet on the British Columbia coast where he had earlier observed hundreds of marbled murrelets flying low over the water at dusk. Mist nets were attached to aluminum poles and then speared into foam floats so they could be placed on the water and then anchored to the shore. Early one evening, Kaiser spent four hours watching about two dozen marbled murrelets fly past—about twenty yards above the nets instead of low over the water. As the tide changed, the entire mist-net "system" tipped and was almost carried away when a small tree swept through the inlet.

Next, Kaiser and a crew of experienced mist-netters experimented with an underwater mist-net system—one that took hours to deploy. In the exceptionally clear waters of Desolation Sound, the scientists watched one murrelet approach the middle of the net, hesitate, and dive a little deeper to swim beneath it.

During the summer of 1991, Kaiser and his colleagues strung up four above-water nets and used a Rube Goldberg-esque system of bamboo poles, sport-fishing gear, foam floats, pulleys, and lead-ball anchors to keep the net taut in the breeze or changing tides. One fine June evening at 10 P.M., they caught one murrelet. "While we were busy congratulating ourselves," Kaiser told me, "a tugboat pulling a raft of logs approached, and we dismantled the nets in a panic. We couldn't work fast enough, and the boat carried off an anchor and float, and its wake damaged some of the rafts."

The following month, Kaiser rigged up the nets in another inlet where in three nights they caught fifteen marbled murrelets and were able to attach radio tags to each. They spent the rest of July searching for the signals by boat. They found about half of the radio tags—several days after they fell off the birds.

Despite the hard work and dedication of Gary Kaiser, Lora Leschner, and their many colleagues, no nests were located that summer. Though their work at times seemed like a comedy of errors, every mistake they made and each of the successes they enjoyed laid the groundwork for other field biologists who continued the radio-tagging effort. Not until

1994 would more mist-netted, radio-tagged marbled murrelets lead scientists to additional nests.

Not all researchers working at sea in the late 1980s and early 1990s were trying to catch marbled murrelets. Some were trying to estimate the bird's population and range—a job that could not be done in the forest, where the birds were all but invisible. In 1989, teams of scientists began working on estimating the size of the California population of marbled murrelets.

Most species of alcids and colonial nesting birds can be counted at their colonies where they nest. If the colonies are very large, such as those of the common murre, a pilot is hired to fly a helicopter or fixed-wing aircraft over the colony during the bird's breeding season to take a few aerial photographs. Scientists then count the number of small, bird-shaped specks on the enlarged photograph. Because marbled murrelets do not breed in conspicuous places or en masse, they have to be counted on the water. And they have to be counted according to a protocol.

Among scientists, the method for studying something is detailed in a written document called a *protocol*. For seabird biologists, such protocols include the time of year and time of day to conduct a study, what kind of boats to use, the duration of the study, what kinds of data to collect, what equipment to use for collecting the data, and even where to stand in the boat while recording the data. Without such standards, the studies are not considered scientific, and comparing data collected in different years, different locations, or by different scientists is like comparing apples to rocks.

In the summer of 1989, scientists began counting marbled murrelets. But they weren't just counting. They were trying to develop and standardize a protocol that could be used by other researchers to count them elsewhere and in the future. The protocol involves steering a boat at a certain distance from the shore—say six hundred meters—along a line (called a transect) that is roughly parallel to the shore. As the boat moves slowly forward at a set speed, surveyors scan the water on either side of the boat and count the birds they see within a set distance—one hundred meters, for example.

This sounded simple enough, until I imagined myself on the ocean in June in foul-weather gear, bobbing up and down on ten-foot swells in a small boat trying not to get seasick while looking at the choppy sea through binoculars for a small bird with a habit—well-documented since the days of Captain Cook—of diving when approached closely by a boat. Never mind actually describing the abundance of birds on the water in terms more useful than "not too abundant" or "seemingly invisible."

One of the more interesting problems that surfaced as the researchers refined at-sea protocols over the years was that not all surveyors could tell fifty meters from one hundred—or even fifty *yards* from one hundred. Nor could they accurately and consistently estimate the distance of a marbled murrelet from the boat. Judging distances is an art, a mastery of space, and an acquired talent. My lack of this talent is responsible for, among other disasters, my shearing off my car's outside mirror on a gatepost while backing out of my own driveway. To make certain that surveyors can judge distances accurately and consistently, the protocols require them to be trained in this art.

On the fine May morning I joined them, Rick Wood and
Lydia Miller were honing their distance-estimating skills on
Dabob Bay, a calm body of water in the southwest corner of
Puget Sound. Rick and Lydia are U.S. Forest Service biologists
who are part of a study of the marbled murrelet in
Washington State. They are two of the hundreds of men and
women who have signed up over the years for seasonal work
as marbled murrelet field technicians. They spend weeks in
training to learn the correct protocol and then spend one
summer—maybe more—collecting data that will enable
someone else (usually the project leader) to write a report,
make a presentation, or publish an article in a scientific
journal. Though Wood, Miller, and others may not be com-
mitted to the marbled murrelet over the long haul, their efforts
during just one season are intense and are critical to the
understanding of this species.

Rick Wood is an affable and easygoing biologist and
outdoorsman from Shelton, Washington, who has been
hunting, fishing, and birding in Washington State most of
his life. In the summer of 2004, Wood was training Lydia
Miller, a recently graduated biology major from Western
Washington University who was working as a summer field
technician. In just a few weeks, she had mastered the arts of
hitching and unhitching the boat trailer, driving and backing
up a 4 × 4 truck, launching and operating a Boston Whaler,
reading the boat's instrument panel, and identifying marbled
murrelets. The day I joined them, Miller and Wood were
judging distances.

"See that buoy?" Wood asked.

"Yep," Miller replied.

"Ninety meters," Wood said.

Miller paused. "Eight-five."

I said nothing.

Miller then aimed a handheld distance meter at the buoy. She pressed a button to fire a laser beam that struck the buoy and bounced back to the meter in two seconds. The meter flashed a number in red.

"One hundred twenty," she called out.

"Ouch!" Wood said, laughing.

"Okay, how about that dock piling?"

"Seventy-five," said Wood.

"Seventy," said Miller.

"Sixty it is."

My guess was so high as to be unspeakable. (Naturally I wanted to buy my own laser distance meter and judge distances on my own, but given its $400 price tag, I decided to practice backing out of my driveway instead.)

By the time Miller and Wood had taken measurements off of every buoy, piling, shrimp pot, snag, and other object in the bay large enough to bounce back an infrared beam, they had narrowed down their margin of error to about two meters. On a few occasions, their estimates matched the distance meter's exactly. Unfortunately, marbled murrelets are too small to bounce a beam off of, so Wood, Miller, and all other surveyors must rely on naked-eye judgments.

I had not joined Wood and Miller on Dabob Bay to look at buoys and dock pilings. I wanted to see marbled murrelets. Wood and Miller had seen eighty marbled murrelets the day before, so there was a good chance I'd get my wish as we

cruised around the bay—Miller driving and Wood scanning
the water with his binoculars.

"I think we got a pair," Wood said. "Let's move in."

Wood slowly moved the boat toward the pair.

"Two birds. See 'em?"

"Yep."

"We've got a pair. Wait. . . . Is it a . . . ? Wait. What *is* it?
Nope. It's not a murrelet. It's a harbor seal."

These two biologists know their birds, so it was hard for
me to see how they could mistake a seal for a bird, but at a
distance the mottled brownish nose and ear of a harbor seal—
sticking out of the water just so—is a dead ringer for a pair of
marbled murrelets. So were the pigeon guillemots. So were the
floating logs, plastic soda bottles, white-winged scoters, and
harlequin ducks. Mistaken identities are well-known to
anyone studying or watching birds.

Years after the pioneering work to develop an official at-
sea survey protocol, other scientists and statisticians have
now standardized it to work across California, Oregon, and
Washington. Modifications are still being made to apply the
protocol to surveys in British Columbia and Alaska. Creating
such a one-size-fits-all protocol has meant taking into
consideration the variations in climate, weather, topography,
coastal geology, currents, tides, fisheries, and human use of
the land. It has meant testing how different sizes and classes
of boats affect the survey results and how wind, glare, and
the presence of other bird species affect the surveyors' ability
to count marbled murrelets. It has required working out
equations to account for sampling errors—birds that are

missed during a dive or counted twice when they dive and resurface. It has meant more experimenting, testing, evaluating, tweaking, time, and money than anyone imagined. But the researchers have persisted, knowing that if they didn't, no one would.

CHAPTER 16

On a certain wide, mossy limb in the crown of a Douglas fir, the summer fog moves lightly over the slender beak, head, and back of a marbled murrelet. It is a male in marbled brown. Beneath its feathered body and pressed close to the warm skin on its breast is one pale green egg. Shortly before dawn, a similarly feathered bird lands abruptly on the mossy branch. This is the female arriving to relieve the male of his twenty-four-hour shift on the egg. The male instantly rises up off the egg, steps to the edge of the branch, and plunges into a steep, momentum-building dive. He makes his way out of the forest on whirring wings and calls a high-pitched *keer, keer, keer* as he circles over the forest canopy once, twice, three times before heading to the sea. The female settles herself carefully and completely onto the egg.

"Six-thirteen. Single bird, circling over the forest, multiple *keer* calls, last seen heading west."

Peter Paton is standing in the Lost Man Picnic Area. He is not lost, he is counting marbled murrelets. The picnic area—a few tables and benches—is in a clearing in an old-growth redwood forest near Lost Man Creek in Redwood National Park. Here, Paton has found an opening in the dense canopy—a small window onto the dawn sky.

It is May 15, 1988, and Paton is happy to be spending

his entire summer listening for the now-familiar calls of the marbled murrelet. Paton, then a biologist with the Redwood Sciences Laboratory in Humboldt County, remembers the first time he ever heard a marbled murrelet. It was in 1985 when he was surveying birds in an old-growth redwood forest nearby. One morning, Paton heard gull-like calls he couldn't identify. When he learned from a local birder that they belonged to marbled murrelets, he was excited that these unusual seabirds were residents in his neck of the woods. Paton urged his colleague at Redwood Sciences Laboratory, C. J. Ralph, to add the marbled murrelets to the list of birds they regularly surveyed. When the Pacific Seabird Group decided to spearhead marbled murrelet research efforts, Paton and Ralph were ready with a plan—a very ambitious plan.

During the summer of 1988, they would survey for marbled murrelet in the old-growth forests along the entire California coast, from Marin County, just north of San Francisco, all the way to Del Norte County at the Oregon border. First, though, they had to define their terms: What was *the coast*, and what exactly was *an old-growth forest?* Without working definitions, they wouldn't know where to place their feet when the survey season began.

For a nonscientist, the *coast* is probably synonymous with shoreline, beach, and seaside—that narrow band of rock or sand where the ocean meets the land. It's a place wide enough for a beach blanket or a stroll.

To forestry professionals like Paton and Ralph, however, the coast was much wider: a full forty kilometers, or twenty-five miles, inland from the water's edge. This was not an arbitrary distance or one established along topographic lines or vegetation zones. The marbled murrelet itself set the boundary—thirty-nine kilometers was the farthest distance inland birds had been detected in California, with one kilometer added for good measure. Within that strip, they needed to focus on old-growth forests; but what exactly did that mean?

Close your eyes, and you might imagine a cluster of massive, rough-barked redwood trunks soaring straight up from the forest floor. Few photographers with the widest of wide-angle lenses can capture even one of these enormous trees in its entirety. One of the few pictures I have ever seen was taken recently by photographer James Balog, who successfully captured a full-length image of a 242-foot-tall giant sequoia—a relative of the coast redwood. Working with a crew of tree riggers, Balog climbed an adjacent tree and, as he descended, took eight to fifteen pictures every fifteen feet. Then, with his collection of 451 pictures and a computer, he assembled a collage of the whole tree—complete with a rigger standing in its top for scale—to fit onto a single page of his latest coffee-table book of tree portraits. This picture is worth more than the thousand words writers have used to try to describe the grandeur of these trees. Big, immense, towering, ancient, virgin, majestic, grand—they all fall short.

Until the 1980s, scientists were hard-pressed to come up with a solid definition of an old-growth forest. But during the controversy over the spotted owl's habitat, push came to shove in the forests of the Pacific Northwest, and scientists produced and published a seven-page definition. The U.S. Forest Service distilled these pages into a convenient working definition: An old-growth forest is one that "has been largely unmodified by timber harvesting, and whose larger trees average over 200 years old or greater than 31 inches in diameter at breast height." The inconvenient part of the definition (and one that would take at least seven pages to do justice to here) describes the great complexity of such a forest—one that includes big, old living trees, as well as dead standing trees (snags), fallen trees (nurse logs), a multilevel canopy, an understory of younger trees and shrubs, and a variety of animals and plants that occur only in these forests.

The old-growth forest in my mind does not have snags, nurse logs, an understory, or any wildlife. There are only trees. After a few moments, I might conjure up a tidy green sea of delicate, low-growing oxalis for contrast. A wide, paved pathway might find its way into the picture—a trail that will lead me and my wide-angle lens right up to these trees. Some groves of old-growth trees appear like this in real life, especially along the most popular trails of our national and state parks, where most of us see our first old-growth redwoods. But these are not *real* old-growth forests. Old growth forests are messy.

Over the past twenty years, I have hiked and camped in old-growth forests in California, Oregon, Washington, and British Columbia, sometimes along paved trails, sometimes in the backcountry. It is always an uplifting experience. I feel humbled and exalted, weak and strong, insignificant and part of something profoundly magnificent. As soon as I tip my head back to see just how far up a tree I can see, I am transported, lifted up, exalted by the energy of the upward-soaring trees. I can imagine the water from the soggy earth rising up, cell by cell, through the xylem hidden beneath the thick bark. I can feel the yearning of young trees for the

canopy, the craving of leaves and flowers—flattened and
· parabolic—for sunlight.

I can also feel the rot. I can sense the downward pull of
the earth, the gravity of the trees spread wide at their bases.
Everything is weighty and waterlogged. Rain, wind, and time
have knocked down, drawn down, and shattered many of the
trees, their fallen columns turning the forest floor into an
acropolis of ruins. Stands of younger redwoods lay like pickup sticks, scattered by some fierce and hurling winds. What
was once vertical becomes horizontal; the canopy becomes the
forest floor.

The fallen trees teem with bacteria, yeast, spores, fungi,
beetles, termites, mites, and larvae that do not rest, mandibles
and hyphae working around the clock. Half-rotten trees, free
of their bark, disgorge their pithy insides onto the forest floor
and into the sunlight. Mosses, slime molds, and fungi pull the
trees' energy back into the soft, spongy forest floor, which
seems to be dissolving beneath your feet. High, then low, then
high as it flows over the buried trunks of fallen trees. The
understory is a tangle of vines and ferns and shrubs and
seedlings. An old-growth forest in good working order is all
life, all death, and all a big, beautiful mess.

Such forests don't suit everyone's taste. Some would
prefer to see these forests "cleaned up" so that the dead and
fallen trees don't become fuel for forest fires. But fire, too, is
a natural part of the old-growth forest, and many trees are
designed to endure it and even benefit from it. Fire is a force
that belongs in a forest, as much as wind, rain, snow, and
sunlight. After decades of Smokey Bear and the U.S. Forest
Service's fire suppression campaign, forest managers have

been selectively burning sections of forests to prevent catastrophic wildfires like those responsible for burning millions of acres in the West in recent years. These fires are used by some forest managers to justify cleaning up the forest of fallen and dead trees. The need to clean up our "messy" forests is presented as a safety issue and plays into our fear of what is dirty, dark, and unknown. Forests, especially the old ones, embody all these fears and harbor unknown or little-understood creatures that lurk, bite, sting, and make frightening noises. One has only to pick up a book of children's fairy tales to understand how early these fears are introduced into our lives. The forests of Little Red Riding Hood and Hansel and Gretel are not happy places.

I once helped tend a half-acre patch of oak-hickory forest on the property of my children's elementary school in Virginia. It was an old forest, with a few very mature oaks and a tangled understory surrounded by cornfields and homes with mowed lawns. Keeping the forest intact, the students at the school and their parents turned it into an outdoor classroom with a wood-chip trail, oak-stump benches, bird feeders, and interpretive signs. We created brush piles to attract birds, mice, snakes, and insects.

It was not a "scary" forest, but still, one of the women I worked with wasn't too thrilled about these brush piles. They were messy and offended her idea of an orderly, petunias-in-a-pot gardening style. Every time the woman suggested cleaning up the piles, I would explain how valuable they were for the small animals and hibernating butterflies and how decay was good for a forest—nature's way of recycling nutrients. This went on for several months until one day, as we

added a wheelbarrowful of clippings to the pile, she stood back
and pointed to the pile.

"Look at that," she said.

I braced for the criticism.

"Ain't that a beautiful pile of nothin'?"

Perhaps when the woman realized snakes and spiders
were not going to leap out of the brush piles onto her, she saw
the untidy piles as harmless, then as possibly beneficial, and
then as something to boast about. Or perhaps she did not
want to hear me extol the virtues of brush piles one more time.
Either way, it made me aware of what a struggle it is to allow
disorder, chaos, and what we fear into our idea of beauty, our
aesthetic of the natural world, and our understanding of how
a forest works.

Knowing how a forest works wasn't an issue for Peter
Paton and C. J. Ralph. Their problem was identifying old-
growth forests where marbled murrelets were most likely to be.
The solution came from a colleague with an aerial photograph
of the Pacific coastal forests taken by a U2 spy plane flying
65,000 feet above the earth. The photograph was taken with
infrared film and manipulated by researchers at the National
Aeronautics and Space Administration to show the different
vegetation types and stages of maturity. The photograph
showed four forest types quite distinctly: the old-growth redwood, the old-growth redwood and Douglas fir, the mature
redwood (trees eighty to two hundred years old), and those
with young trees less than eighty years old, plus the areas
where the redwoods had been clear-cut.

From this map, Paton and Ralph established their survey
sites in the old-growth and mature forests that measured fifty

acres or more. Even reduced this much, the survey territory was still vast—too vast for two men to cover alone. So they put out a call for help and in no time had assembled thirty qualified field assistants—thirty men and women willing, and even eager, to survey the forests for marbled murrelets for an entire summer. Most were biologists. Many were rangers from the national and state parks. One was Gary Strachan.

Strachan was a wildlife biologist who had been wind-surfing among the marbled murrelet since 1970, after he learned about the birds from Marge Keith, who, like Eleanor Pugh, was the wife of a California state park ranger and was also an enthusiastic and dedicated follower of the birds at Prairie Creek Redwoods State Park. For years afterward, Strachan had been conducting his own unofficial surveys of the small population of marbled murrelets along the northern California coast while surfing and windboarding. Though his surveys weren't exactly scientific, Strachan himself was a solid scientist and had collected enough data over the years to be of great value to the project. In 1988, Strachan was also the supervising ranger at Año Nuevo State Reserve, a nearly pris-tine wilderness on the coast side of the Santa Cruz Mountains, not far from Big Basin. Peter Paton and C. J. Ralph gave Strachan the job of coordinating the surveying effort in the Santa Cruz Mountains during the summer of 1988. Strachan wasn't recruited for his data sets, but for his energy. Ralph calls him "Mr. Enthusiasm."

When I visited Strachan at Año Nuevo one summer recently, he greeted me with an excited, "Come on up and look at my babies!" I followed the lean, blond, fifty-something ranger as he bounded up to the second floor of the farmhouse where he lives with his family at Año Nuevo. Strachan led me out to a glassed-in porch where his telescope was aimed toward a bed of kelp in the bay. I looked through the scope and saw several very small brownish birds sitting on the water—marbled murrelets.

Strachan is happy to talk about the marbled murrelet. In fact, it is difficult to stop him once he gets on a roll. In less than an hour, he told me about the grounded marbled murrelet chicks he raised, how they took off from the ground straight up like a helicopter, about the viability of the bird's population in California, about the talents of the local wildlife rehabilitator, about forestry practices along the coast, about the recent increase in the numbers of jays and ravens, which prey on marbled murrelets, and about the luau he hosted in the fall of 1974 to celebrate the discovery of the nest and chick in Big Basin. Only later, after several conversations with Strachan, did he reveal to me that his surfboard once sported a *Marbled Murrelet Club* decal. Back in the late 1970s, Strachan and a "dedicated pack of wildlife biology majors" at Humboldt State University formed the club and played it as a secret, somewhat cultish society of bird watchers. One of the club's activities was observing the marbled murrelets at Prairie Creek Redwoods State Park, where Strachan worked for several summers.

Strachan is clearly the right man to motivate and inspire a small army of soon-to-be-sleep-deprived surveyors. Forty-five minutes before sunrise on May 15, 1988, thirty surveyors went into the forests. Everyone had a tape recorder, a survey data sheet, a clipboard, a compass, and a headlamp. Everyone knew exactly where to place their feet. For two hours and fifteen minutes, they would walk or drive along the transect, stopping at each survey station to look and listen for marbled murrelets for ten minutes. When the surveyors detected a bird or birds by sight or sound, they recorded their observations. A typical detection would be described like this: "Six-thirteen. Single bird, circling over the forest, multiple *keer* calls, last seen heading west." After ten minutes, the surveyors moved to the next station. Mornings continued like this for two hours and fifteen minutes. Afterward, the surveyors transcribed the data from their tape recorders onto data forms, which become the official record of the survey—the scientific evidence of a marbled murrelet's existence.

The unit of measurement for a marbled murrelet during a survey is a "detection." A detection is the observation of a single bird or group of birds acting in a similar manner. Two birds flying together is one detection. Four birds circling together over the forest is one detection. Four keer calls—*keer, keer, keer, keer*—is one detection, unless each of those calls is more than five seconds apart. If they are, you've got four detections, not one.

It would seem that this protocol could result in both an underreporting and overreporting of marbled murrelets. And perhaps it does. But bird-surveying statisticians—the people C. J. Ralph refers to as "mathemagicians"—have figured out that the potential for underreporting is balanced by the potential for overreporting. The protocol was not designed to yield an exact number of birds, but to establish the presence of the marbled murrelet and its relative abundance in the forest.

In addition to the ten-minute-per-station surveys, surveyors also spent an entire two and a half hours around dawn at just one station. And, just to cover the bases, some surveys were also conducted around sunset.

During the summer-long surveys, researchers detected more than *keer* calls. They also heard very loud wing beats—an almost comical sound not unlike an amateurish impersonation of a helicopter—as the birds flew close overhead. During a few surveys, they heard a mechanical sound similar to a jet airplane. So loud and realistic was the sound that it sent more than one researcher running for cover. Not until later did they realize it was a marbled murrelet in a steep dive nearby. Scientists are still unsure how or why the birds make this bizarre sound.

By the middle of August, the team had recorded more than two thousand detections—some visual, most auditory—at about half the stations they surveyed. Marbled murrelets were present in Josephine County in southern Oregon, in Del Norte and Humboldt Counties in northern California, and in Santa Cruz and San Mateo counties south of San Francisco. They were absent in the three-hundred-mile-long gap between these two areas.

When Paton and Ralph compared the distribution of marbled murrelets to the distribution of the old-growth and mature forests on their high-tech map, some answers emerged. In the counties where the bird had been detected, there were remnant old-growth redwood and Douglas fir forests. These forests were almost entirely located in state and national parks and on lands owned by lumber companies. In the three-county gap where marbled murrelets had not been detected (but had been observed historically), virtually no old-growth remained. In their report, the two described the correlation between marbled murrelets and old-growth forests as "striking." They described the breeding habitat for marbled murrelets along the California coast—that one long, sinuous, and stunning piece of scenery—as "patchy."

What habitat remained was concentrated in the "big tree" parks and reserves, where the state's remnant old-growth forests were protected, and on private land where they weren't.

This did not sit well with Peter Paton, who petitioned the California Department of Fish and Game in 1988 to list the marbled murrelet as a threatened species in California. The state reviewed the evidence—much of it presented in Paton and Ralph's report—and decided that the marbled murrelet warranted greater protection. After evaluating the petition and other research presented subsequently, the state listed the bird as endangered in 1992. With this listing, the California Department of Fish and Game began funding research and taking steps to protect the bird's habitat at sea and inland. Listing petitions from researchers in Oregon and Washington soon followed. The Canadian government had already listed the murrelet as a threatened species in 1990.

CHAPTER 17

Though few of those who surveyed marbled murrelets that summer will admit it, what they really wanted to do was find a nest. Establishing absence and presence of the bird and estimating its abundance were critical, but almost like a lead-up to the thrill, the euphoria, the ornithological glory that would be theirs if only they could lay their eyes on a nest.

Steve Singer knew every old-growth forest in the Santa Cruz Mountains. He had a good idea of where the marbled murrelets were, though he hadn't been able to track one to its nest. Singer had been part of C. J. Ralph's survey team in 1988 and had seen hundreds of marbled murrelets during his surveys of Big Basin Redwoods State Park. Singer had seen dozens of low-flying stealth murrelets flying below and through the canopy, but the breeding season ended before he had a chance to find a nest or even see a bird landing in a tree. Singer was convinced that, given time the following summer, he could track those low, silent flights directly to a nest. The first tree nest discovery by Hoyt Foster had been an accident; Singer needed to find a way to find them intentionally and develop a protocol other researchers could follow to find more nests and learn the secrets of the marbled murrelet's breeding biology.

During the fall, winter, and spring of 1988 and 1989, Singer made plans and developed his strategy. He put together a small team that included his wife, Stephanie, an experienced birder; and Nancy Naslund, a graduate student at U.C. Santa Cruz hoping to do her thesis on marbled murrelets. Later, C. J. Ralph and Gary Strachan would add their support. With no funding and little in the way of equipment, this all-volunteer group set out for the woods in June to begin a summer of Dawn Stakeouts.

The stakeouts would begin well before dawn, when the forest and sky were still dark. Two, sometimes three, researchers would stand beneath a single three-hundred-year-old Douglas fir and turn their faces to look into the upper branches of the tree. For two hours they stood, watching, hoping to see a murrelet as it flew across the small space of pale sky above them and then into the tree. Based on the split-second timing of bird-tree interaction, the team hoped to determine whether the birds were actually landing in the tree, taking off from the tree, or merely passing by. When the timing confirmed the birds were using the tree, the observers repeated the Dawn Stakeout on subsequent mornings to try to locate the exact branch the birds were using. If the team was successful, they would spend the daylight hours monitoring the branch, the nesting marbled murrelet, the egg, the chick.

As fate would have it, the Dawn Stakeouts worked on the very first tree they selected. On June 3, 1989, the researchers spotted a bird flying out of the tree. On June 8, after five days of surveillance, they were able to pinpoint the branch it was landing on—one 160 feet up the tree. On June 10, after a two-day search for an unobstructed view of the nest, they saw an adult marbled murrelet sitting on the limb, incubating its egg. Singer and the other researchers were ecstatic. Their experimental protocol had worked.

For fifteen days, the Dawn Patrol stood watch. Steve and Stephanie Singer took time off work to observe the nest with Nancy Naslund, who also contributed monitoring equipment loaned from her school. Out came the telescopes, the high-powered eyepieces, the night-viewing attachments, and the telephoto lenses. Out came the thermoses of coffee as the Dawn Patrols became Dawn-to-Dusk-and-Beyond Patrols. No one knew precisely when the eggs had been laid, although they did know from other studies that the incubation period probably lasted about a month. The egg could hatch in a matter of moments, days, weeks . . . or in a month. Nest monitoring was continuous and, on a few occasions, around the clock. No one complained. No one called it quits. No one wanted to miss the big events—the never-before-seen hatching of a marbled murrelet chick or the never-before-seen fledging of a young bird.

In those fifteen days, researchers observed the nesting pair of murrelets working their incubation shifts in precise, clock-work fashion. Between six and twenty-three minutes before sunrise each morning, one adult would fly in low and silently toward the nesting tree, often making a low-pitched buzzing sound with its wings. Sometimes the bird would fly right past the tree and return a few minutes later to make a landing—a swoop-up and stall-out maneuver that ends with an audible thud of webbed feet making contact with the nest branch. The newly arrived bird then walked along the branch toward the nest—a distance of about four feet.

When I think of a marbled murrelet waddling purpose-fully (though perhaps a bit awkwardly) up to its mate on a branch 160 feet above the ground, I do not think "interesting avian breeding behavior," I think sitcom. Imagine the possible dialogue: "Honey, I'm home! Boy, I just flew in from the coast, and my arms are really tired!" Anthropomorphism—the bane of the scientist, the boon of the cartoonist, and the cheap thrill of the amateur naturalist.

In fact, a marbled murrelet rarely walks anywhere. At sea, their webbed feet are constantly paddling. In the air, feet are tucked back flush against the body. In the tree, they are spread out on either side of an egg. Outside Alaska, where some mar-bled murrelets have been found to nest on the ground, a tree limb is the only solid surface that a marbled murrelet ever puts its feet on. It's water, air, or tree limb. Unless it accidentally falls out of a tree, a marbled murrelet's tiny webbed feet never touch the earth.

That short stroll down the branch during the morning incubation exchanges was the most conspicuous activity sur-veyors observed. There was no greeting ceremony between the male and female, no bill rubbing, and no fussing about the nest while the birds prepare to settle down on the nest or fly off to the sea. Some of the fly-ins, however, were quite exciting. Observers saw one bird fly into the forest canopy, land on a branch about twenty feet below its nest, then shoot straight up, maneuvering deftly through the canopy before stopping on a dime on its nest branch. The acrobatics, Singer said, were stunning.

Singer and his colleagues hoped that the chick's first flight would be even more exciting. But, on the fifteenth day, a common raven landed on the nest branch. It moved toward the nest and displaced the marbled murrelet. Both the raven and the murrelet disappeared from the branch. Fifteen minutes later, an observer saw a raven—perhaps the same one—flying from the direction of the tree carrying what seemed to be a carcass in its bill. Judging from the size of the carcass, the observer guessed it was either the embryo from the egg or part of the adult. The Dawn Patrol, all murrelet lovers at heart, was devastated.

Only four days after the first nest failed, Nancy Naslund and Juliette Schear, a U.C. Santa Cruz undergrad, found a second nest by accident. They were walking along a park road after the dawn survey and happened to look up only to see a marbled murrelet sitting on a branch. The nest was in the incubation stage. The team monitored the nest continually during daylight hours on videotape. Some of the flights associated with the incubation exchanges were extraordinary. In one case, the video camera captured an incubating adult disappearing from the nest. Even after viewing the videotape a few times, the researchers couldn't catch the actual departure. Only when the tape was played in slow motion could they see what had happened: In a fraction of a second, the bird shot off the nest like a cannonball out of a cannon.

After thirty-two days, the researchers got their first glimpse of the chick. It had apparently hatched after dark the night before when researchers were off duty. Naslund, Schear, and a small crowd of other researchers gathered to watch the adults brooding and feeding the downy chick for two whole days.

On the morning of the third day, while the chick was left

unattended, a Steller's jay landed on the nest and removed the chick, apparently killing it. Forty-five minutes later, an adult murrelet returned with a fish but left soon after. Later that day, a Steller's jay was seen picking at eggshell fragments at the nest and, the next morning, an adult murrelet returned to the nest—presumably for brooding duty—but did not stay. The team monitored the nest periodically over the next few weeks, but no murrelets returned to attempt another nest. The nest branch remained empty of murrelets for the rest of the season.

At the end of the marbled murrelet breeding season, a bittersweet one for the Dawn Patrol, Steve Singer called in a tree climber. For the second time in the history of Big Basin Redwoods State Park, a man with spurs and ropes ascended a 200-foot-high Douglas fir to come face to face with a marbled murrelet nest. This time, however, there was no pugnacious chick to behold—only empty nests. One was in a depression on a moss-covered branch and was indistinguishable from the rest of the branch except for five intact bird droppings—the legacy of the chick. The other nest looked intentional, con-structed—more a thing than a place. It was an oval cup with sides and a bottom of small Douglas fir twigs and dead bits of lichen. Had the nest been built by a marbled murrelet or another species? Today, because no other similarly constructed nests have been found, scientists believe that the marbled mur-relet had simply occupied an abandoned band-tailed pigeon nest—another rare discovery in the ancient forest.

Two summers later, in 1991, Steve Singer made the first direct observations of a chick fledging from its tree nest—a nest Steve had been monitoring for two months at Big Basin. At nine o'clock in the morning on the big day, the chick was on its nest, still down-covered except for its head and throat. By seven o'clock that evening, the chick had preened or picked off much of its down, leaving only a few feathers on its wings. The chick spent most of its evening turning, standing, walking, preening, flapping its wings, and pecking at small flying insects. Just after eight-thirty, an adult murrelet flew to the nest without a fish in its bill and perched motionless near the nest for sixteen minutes and then departed to the south-southeast. Twelve seconds later, the chick moved to the opposite side of the branch and, with strong, audible wing beats, took off to the northwest without a peep. The adult did not lead the young from the nest or call to it from above the trees. Instead, the chick set its own flight path to the sea.

8 15pm July 1 97

What I was beginning to understand about the men and women who were pursuing the marbled murrelet was that they do not consider what they are doing unusual or beyond the call of duty. For them, giving up their hours of deepest sleep, working on weekends, taking time out from their paying jobs, or hiking into forests in the dark on behalf of a bird they might not see was just a matter of doing their job. There was nothing extraordinary about their effort. A little-known seabird needed some attention, and off they went, not giving a second thought to the comforts they were giving up or the extra work they were taking on.

During some point in my initial interview with each marbled murrelet researcher, there came a point where he or she would laugh and say something like, "I'm amazed you think my work is that interesting or important. I was just doing my job, doing what I was trained to do."

I think this is only partly true. Yes, they have been educated and trained to study or manage seabirds, but not the marbled murrelet. This bird requires more than a degree in wildlife biology and training in the field. It requires stamina, fortitude, and a belief that the job they set out to do is worth doing and that they can help preserve the magic of the living world. In my eyes, these qualities make these men and women as rare as the bird they are pursuing.

One of these women is Kim Nelson. In 1985, Nelson was an avid birder but had little to do with seabirds. She had been studying forest-bird communities and cavity-nesting birds for her graduate work at Oregon State University in Corvallis. One morning, in an old-growth grove of Douglas firs, hemlocks, and cedars in Oregon's Coast Ranges, Nelson began hearing strange gull-like calls she didn't recognize. She knew they didn't come from a gull.

"It was plain weird," she recalled. "I was thirty miles from the sea."

Nelson had read of the 1974 nest discovery in Big Basin and suspected that the calls might belong to the marbled murrelet, but all the observations of the birds she was aware of had been much closer to the coast. Nelson called Peter Paton, a childhood friend and birding pal, and described the strange calls to him. He told her about the calls he'd just started hearing in the redwoods in California and filled her in on what he knew.

The following spring, when Nelson heard the strange calls again, she got a glimpse of the birds that went with them. Indeed, they were no gulls. They were marbled murrelets. Nelson reported her sightings in the Oregon Field Ornithologists' newsletter, and she tracked down Spencer Sealy, Harry Carter, and Lora Leschner to find out who knew what about this species. They encouraged her to come to the next Pacific Seabird Group meeting to share her observations. Though Nelson was immersed in her thesis on woodpeckers and knew very little about seabirds, she felt compelled to make time for such an unusual bird.

Nelson claims to have known no one at the 1986 Pacific Seabird Group meeting, but the opposite seemed true when I first met her at the 2002 meeting. I had no idea what Nelson looked like, but it didn't take me long to pick her out of a crowd of two hundred seabird biologists gathered in an outside courtyard at the Santa Barbara Museum of Natural History in southern California. She was the one being greeted and hugged by everyone else. On that day, she wore a long, flowing skirt, T-shirt, and Birkenstocks (the preferred footwear among biologists), and her long, wavy red hair flowed over her shoulders.

A native of Colorado, Nelson spent most of her childhood outdoors in the mountains hiking, riding horses, and skiing. In sixth grade, she won the class award for writing the best paper on the ecology of the Rocky Mountain National Park. She ventured to the West Coast for college, wanting to be near the ocean. Little did she know that desire would lead her into the world of the marbled murrelet.

After the 1986 meeting, Nelson felt energized, excited, and ready to join the effort to learn about this little-known seabird. She planned a study to discover marbled murrelet habitat use and nesting behavior along the entire Oregon coast in selected stands of mature and old-growth trees and even in the clear-cuts of the Coast Range. In a land managed for timber since the early 1900s, such patches were isolated, but Nelson knew where to find them. She had spent years searching the trees for woodpecker nests; she knew what it was like to look for a needle in a haystack.

Nelson and her crew from Oregon State University spent a few field seasons doing Dawn Surveys and Dawn Stakeouts in the forest. They also recorded the birds' vocalizations and tried to call the birds near them—a technique no one had ever tried—but the murrelets were unresponsive. In the summer of 1990, Dawn Stakeouts led to the discovery of Oregon's first two active marbled murrelet nests. Nelson and her crew were able to observe several chicks on their first day of life. They set up twenty-four-hour watches, borrowed night-vision goggles from the National Guard, and began recording every move and noise from the nest.

Upon hatching, a marbled murrelet chick falls somewhere in between the downy, open-eyed, ready-to-swim-walk-and-fly chicks (a development stage of birds known as precocial) and the pink, featherless, wobbly, gaping, helpless ones (known as altricial). A marbled murrelet is considered semi-precocial. It hatches wide-eyed, fully feathered in down, briefly wobbly, and unable to feed itself. After a few days of brooding by its parents, the chick is able to keep itself warm—or thermoregulate. After this developmental milestone, the parents leave the chick and return only for feedings.

For all but a few minutes of its day, a marbled murrelet chick is left alone on its nest. The chick remains still, moving only occasionally to pick at moss or lichen, change its position, snap at flying insects, preen, stretch, and flap its wings. Just prior to the arrival of an adult murrelet at the nest, the nestling's behavior changes—from still and sleeping to awake and restless. Sometimes the chick begins making soft "begging" calls. Scientists weren't sure what triggers this behavior—a distant *keer* call, the quality of the light, the color of the sky, the melody of the robin, a rustling in the trees, or perhaps just a hungry stomach. How can anyone know what part of the universe wakes a sleeping bird? From studies on the birds' vocalizations, researchers suspect the chick is able to recognize the adult's call; there is evidence of individualistic calls as well. How comforting to imagine a sleeping bird—just a few days out of its shell—waking at the sound of its parent's familiar voice.

I had spent my time listening *for* the murrelets' calls, not *to* them. It never occurred to me that an individual bird might produce a call with a pitch, tone, and timbre that was instantly recognizable to its chick. Could a marbled murrelet chick somehow learn its parents' calls before it hatched? Could the vibrations of a murrelet's *keer* call penetrate the fragile wall of an eggshell?

Studies suggest that human babies learn the sound of their parents' voices in the womb, that women who play a guitar next to their pregnant bellies may produce more musical children, and that newborns respond differently to the voices of their mothers and fathers. Could a newly hatched marbled murrelet chick be so finely tuned?

Some of the most astonishing marbled murrelet behavior I have witnessed is a feeding visit videotaped by Kim Nelson. The scene opens in dim light with an adult murrelet standing motionless and holding in its beak a glistening fish before its begging, pitiable chick for a full ten minutes. (Others have stood as long as thirty!) I worried that the adult was going to either fly off without ever feeding its chick or accidentally (or maybe intentionally) drop the fish off the limb. Nelson suspects the adults behave this way because they are resting from their flight and making sure to remain undetected by any nearby predators.

Then, in one sudden gesture, the adult placed the fish—
a finger-sized sand lance that appeared longer than the
chick—crosswise in the chick's beak and departed. After two
minutes of holding the fish at its midpoint, the chick turned
its head, ear-to-shoulder style, and began a succession of quick
openings and closings of its beak. In the fraction of a second
the beak was open, the fish's head slid a few fractions of an
inch closer to the chick's mouth. When the beak was closed,
it clamped tightly on the fish. In less than a minute, the chick
had worked the fish so that the fish's gill was at the opening of
its beak. The chick then tossed its head back, straightened its
throat, and in a few gulps swallowed the fish headfirst.

I felt my jaw drop. I couldn't believe such a tiny bird
could accommodate such a large fish. I called my family in to
watch the video. Like me, they had seen their share of photographs of robins placing insects and worms into the gaping
beaks of their wobbly chicks. I felt it was important for them
to know how challenging, precarious, and close to impossible
the act of feeding was for a marbled murrelet chick. I wanted
them to understand how much depended on the precision
transfer, from one slender beak to another, of one small, hard-
earned bit of salty protein and fat. We take so much for
granted when we sit down to a meal.

I replayed the feeding scene several times and then,
because my sons didn't quite reach the level of awe I had
hoped for, I took things one step further. I gave my twelve-
year-old son a large carrot and had him bite down on it so that
both ends stuck out of his mouth like the fish's head and tail
in the murrelet chick's beak. Without using his hands, my
son's job was to work the carrot with his teeth and tongue so

that one end of it (the equivalent of the fish's head) was in his mouth. After five minutes and only two drops on the floor, my son succeeded. Then he took the carrot out of his mouth with his hand and ate it like a human being, bite by bite.

This bit of kitchen science made me wonder why marbled murrelet chicks aren't fed smaller fish, why the adults don't tear the fish into smaller pieces, and why they don't use the regurgitation method common among other seabirds. The answers have to do with energy. Because a marbled murrelet nests as far as twenty-five miles from the ocean, each trip means a huge expenditure of energy by the adult. Adults themselves feed on abundant small prey during the day: fish, squid, and creatures of the krill variety that are not much longer than the "baby" carrots sold in bags at the grocery story. When the adults are feeding a chick, however, they forage for fish up to twice that long. Such fish are less abundant and harder to catch, but they mean fewer trips to the nest. Depending on the age of the chick, the size of the fish, and the distance from foraging area to nest, adults fly inland to feed their chicks up to eight times a day.

By 1989, finding marbled murrelet nests was no longer a matter of chance; it was becoming a science. Thanks to the pioneering work of Kim Nelson, there was a nascent protocol other researchers could follow to locate nests. There was no real competition going on—certainly no hundred-dollar discovery rewards were being offered—but the excitement surrounding the marbled murrelet was wildly contagious.

In 1989, Tom Hamer caught the fever. Hamer, a wildlife ecologist with the Washington State Department of Wildlife, had been studying spotted owls and barred owls in

Washington for nine years and was tired of working all night, from 8 P.M. to 4:30 A.M., to survey them. He was sick of owls and ready for a new challenge. When Hamer first heard about the marbled murrelet from a colleague, he remembers thinking, "Boy, this is a strange creature. I need to see what these birds look and sound like."

So Hamer joined a few of his colleagues camping in the Mount Baker–Snoqualmie National Forest along the South Fork Nooksack River, the same place William Leon Dawson first reported hearing the birds eighty years earlier. When Hamer woke the first morning, sure enough, he heard and saw marbled murrelets flying up the river drainage. In 1990, he attended the Pacific Seabird Group meeting and found that "everyone at the meeting was so excited about taking on the challenge of learning about this secretive bird. It was a *huge* challenge. I *live* for challenge. I wanted to get involved."

So in 1990, Hamer's challenge was to find the first marbled murrelet nest in Washington. He talked with Kim Nelson and other researchers and then came up with his own strategy for finding nests while surveying the birds in the state's old-growth forest.

"I thought, 'Well . . . gee, the eggshells must fall out of the trees. . . . So at the end of every survey, why don't we just zigzag through the woods and look under the biggest and best trees to see if we can find some eggshells.' And we did! 'Whoa! Hey! There they are! Now we have to climb the tree to see if we can find this little guy.'"

And he did. And there, high above the eggshells, was his marbled murrelet nest—the first one ever discovered in Washington State. Using the same technique, Hamer found a second and third nest that same summer. This reminds me of some advice Annie Dillard wrote that she was given as a child for finding caterpillars: Find the caterpillar droppings and then look up.

During one of his summers in the field, Hamer was given a downy chick found on the forest floor by some colleagues. Hamer brought it home to care for it and release it; in exchange, the chick taught him about marbled murrelet fledging instincts. Hamer set up a four-foot-long section of a tree trunk with an artificial nest platform in the spare bedroom of his house, one with windows facing south. He fed the bird small fish from Puget Sound and kept a close eye on it. Soon, the chick's juvenal feathers started growing in, it lost and plucked out its down, and it grew increasingly restless. Two evenings in a row—at about the same time of day chicks in the wild fledged—the bird began pacing back and forth on the nest platform. It finally took off from the platform on its first flight, due west toward the ocean—but into the closet. Hamer picked up the bird and set it back on the platform. Again, the chick flew due west into the closet. After a third time, when Hamer realized the chick's instincts to head west might be fatal, he put the bird in a box and made plans to release it into Puget Sound the next morning. The bird immediately dove down into the water, resurfaced a few seconds later, and then repeatedly dove for fish as if it had been practicing for days. After watching the bird for a long while, Hamer and his two crew members lost track of time and the tide. Their small, motorless boat began drifting rapidly out into the sound. Waves were washing over the sides of the boat. They took turns rowing like mad to get to shore, but after thirty minutes weren't getting any closer. "We started getting worried," Hamer recalled, "and wishing we could swim like a murrelet." After another hour of rowing like there was no tomorrow, the crew reached the shore, feeling exhilarated by the successful release of the bird—and chagrined that an orphaned chick raised in a bedroom had better instincts about the water than they did.

As Steve Singer, Kim Nelson, and Tom Hamer were making their discoveries in the Lower Forty-Eight, marbled murrelet fever had worked its way north to British Columbia as well. Paul and Mavis Jones have owned a summer cabin on the Sunshine Coast of the B.C. mainland since the late 1960s. Their cabin is on a calm bight popular for salmon fishing and for marbled murrelets. Paul has been a serious birder and artist most of his life and worked as a professional forester for forty years before retiring in 1990. In that year, Paul and Mavis first learned of the aggressive logging that was going on behind their cabin in an old-growth hemlock and cedar forest of the Caren Range—a forest that had never been burned or blown down since the last ice age 10,000 years ago. Paul began making regular hiking and camping trips into the forest looking for spotted owls or marbled murrelets—threatened species that might stop or curtail the logging. Paul and Mavis helped form a conservation group, the Friends of Caren, to protect as much of this forest as they could.

One morning in June 1991, Paul heard the piercing *keer* calls from above the trees, but the Canadian Wildlife Service and the B.C. Forest Service were reluctant to believe him. That summer, Paul and Mavis began documenting their sightings of marbled murrelets in the forest and they talked with Gary Kaiser, Kim Nelson, and other marbled murrelet researchers to help develop a strategy for finding nests. Friends and other volunteers joined them on surveys and Dawn Stakeouts. They camped in the rain, hiked in the mud, and spent countless hours scanning the branches of Caren's oldest trees. In August 1993, in his third season of effort, Paul and three others watched an adult marbled murrelet land in a cedar tree and move down the branch toward the trunk of the tree to feed its chick. This marked the discovery of Canada's first active nest (an inactive one had been discovered in 1990). This active nest and Paul's efforts documenting thousand-year-old trees in the surrounding forest led to the creation of Spipyus Provincial Park.

From the flurry of marbled murrelet nests discovered in old-growth trees in the early 1990s, researchers were beginning to formulate a picture of what marbled murrelets were looking for in the forest. In 1995, Kim Nelson and Tom Hamer began collaborating on nest site studies and developed a protocol for finding marbled murrelet nests by climbing trees.

Nelson and Hamer climbed their share of trees, but they called in the professional cone harvesters to climb most of them over the years. These highly skilled tree climbers pick cones from the most healthy conifers by the bushel for refor-estation projects. They are usually hired by the U.S. Forest Service or private timber companies, but in the off-season, they are happy to climb for marbled murrelets.

To select which trees to climb, Nelson and Hamer laid a grid over an aerial photograph of the forest, then randomly selected a number of grids in stands known to be occupied. They hiked to the center of a grid and laid out a circular plot with a forty-meter radius. Within that plot, they identified all of the trees they thought had platforms wide enough and high enough to suit the nesting marbled murrelets. The climbers worked their way up the trees and examined the platforms for broken eggshells, fecal rings, cuplike depressions in the moss, worn spots, "landing pads" where the moss on the branch had been flattened by the murrelet's webbed feet through repeated landings, and even tiny scratch marks of marbled murrelets' toenails. I had never given much thought to a marbled murrelet's toenails, but how wonderful to think of them as emergency landing gear. Nelson and Hamer's climbers found fifteen marbled murrelet nests that year. Over the next several years, Nelson and Hamer sent climbers into more than three thousand trees in Washington and Oregon and tripled the number of known nests.

From what they knew of the sixty-one tree nests and nesting stands that had been discovered throughout the Pacific Northwest to date, Nelson and Hamer knew this: For human beings, real estate is all about location, location, location. For marbled murrelets, it's all about platforms, platforms, platforms. No matter the species, size, or age of the tree, the distance from the tree to the ocean, or the amount of moss on the limbs, if a marbled murrelet could find a platform at least four inches wide, at least thirty feet off the ground, and in the middle of the tree's live crown, it had found a home. Most platforms are much wider than this (the average is about eleven inches) and much higher (the average is one hundred and eighteen feet). When a tree attains old-growth stature, its upper branches may grow suitably wide for a murrelet naturally. In many cases, however, the platforms were created through unusual limb deformation (crooks, forks, furrows, buttresses), decadence (rotten areas on the limb), damage (broken limbs, snags), and dwarf mistletoe.

If you are imagining a small sprig of green leaves and white berries wired together for holiday kissing, you haven't seen mistletoe. Neither had I until I moved west and saw huge shrub-sized clumps of this yellowish green epiphyte growing on the top branches of pines in the mountains near my home. Not until an infestation of bark beetles started bringing these trees down did I get a chance to see close-up how dwarf mistletoe did its work. A semiparasitic plant, its roots penetrate the bark of its host branch, feed off the nutrients produced by the tree, and appear to fuse with the tree. As the mistletoe grows, it expands and deforms the branch from within so that, even on close inspection, it is difficult to tell where the tree bark ends and the mistletoe begins. Mistletoe has turned many unsuitable nesting platforms into suitable ones for the marbled murrelet.

But not just any platform will do for a marbled murrelet. Preferred platforms have overhead cover—another limb or foliage—which helps protect the marbled murrelet from weather and from detection by predators overhead. The platform is usually located near openings in the canopy and is at a sufficient height to allow jump-off departures and stall-out landings. Access to the platform is also critical and is a characteristic of forests where the trees are of uneven height and ages. This uneven quality creates a canopy that is multi-layered, variable, and broken—not "flat topped" as one would expect from a tree farm or barbershop buzz cut.

From their tireless work in the old-growth forests and at

sea, researchers learned more in several summers than naturalists, ornithologists, and other scientists had in the previous two centuries. But what this seabird needed was protection, not scrutiny. It needed a voice, not descriptions of its vocalizations. If the mountain of data the scientists had collected was to amount to anything, someone would have to step forward and speak out for the marbled murrelet.

D ave Marshall knew this. In 1985, Marshall was a wildlife biologist recently retired from a thirty-two-year career with the U.S. Fish and Wildlife Service. A native Oregonian, Marshall was a third-generation birder and naturalist whose parents, he says, practically raised him in the Audubon Society of Portland. Marshall first heard about the marbled murrelet in 1939, when he was thirteen years old. He had joined his parents on an Audubon field trip to Malheur National Wildlife Refuge in Oregon's southeastern corner. This was not marbled murrelet territory, but the weeklong trip was led by Stanley G. Jewett, Oregon's top professional ornithologist. There would be plenty of bird stories and plenty of time to tell them. Marshall remembers Jewett expounding on the "greatest mystery of Oregon ornithology"—the location of the marbled murrelet's nest. Jewett shared stories of his own searches.

Dave Marshall was fascinated by these stories but not captivated by the marbled murrelet until more than forty years later when Mike McAllister, the son of one of Marshall's boyhood birding pals, told Marshall of hearing and seeing the birds flying inland over the old-growth forests in Alaska and Washington. In 1986, he published an article on this bird in the *Warbler*, the newsletter of the Audubon Society of Portland. After a brief and objective summary of what was known about the bird at the time, Marshall decided it was time to speak out. He criticized the U.S. Forest Service—the principal holder of Oregon's coastal old-growth forests—for not even considering the species "while it continues with liquidation of trees the bird may depend on." He questioned the priorities of the U.S. Fish and Wildlife Service, which had virtually no research programs for any birds except those listed under the Endangered Species Act. "The lack of knowledge," Marshall would later write, "is, in itself, a threat to the species."

The Audubon Society of Portland had an active conservation committee with a track record of using science to inform and influence lawmakers—science-based advocacy, it is called. In 1986, Rick Brown was a member of that committee. He knew that the concerns and criticisms Dave Marshall had laid out in his article were legitimate. He also knew that conservation didn't work on a species-by-species basis. Brown was a forest service biologist who had spent many years working in Oregon's Mount Hood National Forest. He knew the old-growth forests weren't just spotted owl habitat. They were ecosystems and, Brown believed, needed to be considered and conserved as such. Only by working to understand and protect other old-growth species, including the marbled murrelet, could conservation work effectively. Rick Brown knew it was time for the Audubon Society of Portland to rally its troops.

Brown did not start a protest. He did not organize the society's 7,500 members for letter-writing campaigns, tree sittings, or nest-searching field trips. He called Dave Marshall to talk marbled murrelets. With only the slightest encouragement, Marshall signed a contract to write a full report on the biology and status of the marbled murrelet. Brown intended to submit that report along with a petition to the U.S. Fish and Wildlife Service to have the bird added to the list of federally threatened and endangered species.

The Endangered Species Act was approved by the U.S. Congress and first signed into law by President Nixon in 1973. It was a bold and long-overdue measure to protect and recover the nation's imperiled wildlife species, both plants and animals, that were sliding toward extinction. After centuries of environmental neglect—degradation of habitat, misuse of chemicals and pesticides, abuses of wildlife trade, excesses of hunting and fishing, and the unchecked invasion of exotic species—the Endangered Species Act was eleventh-hour stewardship.

The way the act works, a concerned organization, group, or individual files a petition and a bona fide report on a species' status to the U.S. Fish and Wildlife Service or the National Marine Fisheries Service. Those agencies review the petition, open the issue for public comment, and then decide if federally funded protection measures are warranted. A species listed as "endangered" is in danger of becoming extinct, and one listed as "threatened" is on the verge of becoming endangered. A "candidate" species is one whose listing is warranted but precluded because the federal agency lacks the necessary funding and personnel to take the needed measures to protect the species.

Though Dave Marshall had never done research on the marbled murrelet himself, he was supremely—and perhaps solely—qualified to write the status report. He had spent the last eight years of his career—1973 to 1981—with the endangered species program. He had worked in the program's Washington, D.C., office, and as head of the program in Washington State, Oregon, and California. Marshall had read hundreds of listing petitions and status reports. He knew exactly what to write and how to write it.

Marshall began by summarizing dozens of reports on *Brachyramphus marmoratus* dating back to George Cantwell's from 1898. Marshall talked with Steve Singer, Harry Carter, Kim Nelson, and other Pacific Seabird Group scientists who had worked on or knew about marbled murrelets. He gathered the latest information on the bird's biology, behavior, population, habitat associations, and nest sites. Marshall described the threats to its continued existence. By the end of 1987, he had produced a succinct and thorough account of the marbled murrelet.

The rough population estimates presented in the report stated that there were tens of millions of marbled murrelets in Alaska, several thousand in Oregon and Washington, and a few thousand in California—hardly, it would seem, numbers from the brink. Compared to the currently listed "endangered" birds—many whose populations had dwindled to a few breeding pairs—the marbled murrelets were thriving. But plot population numbers on the Y axis and decades along the X, and you'll see the suspected story line—a straight line that shoots down—drop, loss, plummet, crash, depression, extinction. There was little hope for an upswing. The destruction of the bird's old-growth habitat was ongoing, mortality from gill-net fisheries was increasing, and oil pollution and catastrophic spills were proven dangers.

Now it was up to the Audubon Society of Portland to flex its muscle. It sent Marshall's report and a petition to Audubon

Society chapters throughout the Pacific Northwest. The petition, endorsed by forty local chapters in Oregon, Washington, and California as well as the National Audubon Society, requested that the U.S. Fish and Wildlife Service list the marbled murrelet as a federally threatened species. Such a listing would provide the bird some protection under the laws of the Endangered Species Act. In January 1988, the U.S. Fish and Wildlife Service received the report and petition. Three months later, within the stipulated time frame, it responded: There was sufficient information to declare that federal listing *may be* warranted. During the first public comment period, scientists, lumber company executives, environmentalists, private landowners, fishing fleet operators, property rights advocates, eco-activists, wildlife managers, oil company representatives, and unemployed loggers all weighed in. Everyone, it seemed, had an opinion about the marbled murrelet and its habitat.

In 1989, the Fish and Wildlife Service declared the marbled murrelet a "candidate" for listing. Two years later, it announced its *intent* to list the marbled murrelet as a threatened species; a final decision would be forthcoming. In 1992, it announced that it was extending the time period in which to make its final decision for six months. That move spurred the Audubon Society of Portland to sue the U.S. Fish and Wildlife Service for not making its decision within the legal time frames set out in the Endangered Species Act. In September 1992, the marbled murrelet was officially listed as a federally threatened species. Now the hard work began.

It was up to the Fish and Wildlife Service to fulfill its promise to protect the marbled murrelet, stabilize its population, and remove or minimize the threats to its survival. This process is called the *recovery*.

Recover. Protect. Stabilize. Restore. I grew up thinking that this is what the Endangered Species Act is all about—just the way Earth Day is supposed to be about joining hands in the springtime, smiling and laughing with our neighbors, planting trees, and giving the planet a good scrub. When a species got listed under the Endangered Species Act, our government had done its job. Wolves would now run free, breed, and become bountiful. Bald eagles would soar over snow-capped peaks again for our children's and grandchildren's enjoyment, and there would be enough wild salmon and trout in the sparkling water for everyone. And, now, the marbled murrelet would be safe. Environmentalists and loggers had joined hands, compromised, and set aside their differences. Everyone could relax.

I never really got past these happy, sunlit images until it dawned on me that I didn't understand the first thing about what happened *after* a species got listed. I knew it didn't just magically recover, but I had no clue as to who was in charge of protecting and restoring the marbled murrelet and all the wildlife we take for granted.

That the recovery process is complex, politically fraught, and very expensive came as no surprise, though I guess I was hoping that if left alone and undisturbed, the species would simply recover on its own over a decade or two. In 1996, the Fish and Wildlife Service made the first designated 3,887,800 acres of old-growth forest in Washington, Oregon, and California "critical habitat" for the marbled murrelet. Most of this acreage was on federal lands, though some state, county, and private lands were also included. But these forests, which included both known and potential nesting sites, did not provide specific protections for the bird. The designation simply was a way of saying that these forests "may require special management considerations" in light of the needs of the marbled murrelet.

Not every listed species gets critical-habitat designation or a recovery plan. Time, budget constraints, and lack of public support sometimes put these benefits of the Endangered Species Act on the back burner. The marbled murrelet was one of the fortunate unfortunate species. It would have its own unique recovery plan created by a group of scientists appointed to serve on its recovery team. Before the U.S. Fish and Wildlife Service selected the team, though, they had to have one thing: fresh data.

When the marbled murrelet was listed in 1992, five years had passed since Dave Marshall had written his status report of the marbled murrelet. Since 1988, scientists had amassed mountains of data and had made quantum leaps in their understanding of the species. But where was all that data? It was swimming around in researchers' notebooks and computers. It was published in agency reports and scientific journals; it was on its way to the presses. The Fish and Wildlife Service needed to consolidate all the available information on the marbled murrelet—its biology, behavior, habitat requirements, population trends, distribution, and threats to its survival. It needed to figure out what *wasn't* known about the species and suggest ways to fill the critical gaps. It needed someone who would—very quickly—transform all of this information into a single document. Luckily for them, the U.S. Forest Service had just created a team, headed by C. J. Ralph, to do just that. That single document would be published as the *Ecology and Conservation of the Marbled Murrelet*—my dog-eared marbled murrelet bible.

Marbled murrelet research—once a sometime thing for C. J. Ralph—became a nearly full-time job in 1992. In an organizational tour de force, Ralph recruited a team of seventy marbled murrelet researchers and forestry experts from universities, federal and state agencies, conservation organizations, and timber companies in the Pacific Northwest. He created a hierarchy of working groups. Everyone had a role and a specific task—or several. Everyone was expected to work at breakneck speed.

This was nothing like the early days of marbled murrelet research, when inland sightings of adults and discoveries of grounded chicks were reported—here and there, now and then—over the long stretch of decades. With C. J. Ralph at the helm, the work was a multiagency, multi-multi-biologist, full-throttle, do-it-now, midnight-oil, manic endeavor. In less than a year, most of the report's forty-five authors had completed drafts of their reports.

During this frenzy of research, the U.S. Fish and Wildlife Service appointed six biologists, including Harry Carter and Tom Hamer, to the official marbled murrelet recovery team. With the assistance of Kim Nelson, several official consultants from the Fish and Wildlife Service, and a steady stream of new and unpublished data from the marbled murrelet biologists, the team began its work. The backbone of the recovery plan was the 1994 *Northwest Forest Plan*—the Clinton administration's management plan that covered 24 million acres of federal land in Oregon, Washington, and northern California.

The plan was established to end the impasse over the management of the forests in the range of the northern spotted owl. The plan, which used a new ecosystem approach to forest management, included some protections for both the owl and the marbled murrelet.

The *Recovery Plan for the Marbled Murrelet* is a beautiful, technical, scientific document. It is 203 pages long. It states its objective clearly: to maintain and/or increase the bird's population by maintaining and/or increasing its marine and terrestrial habitat and by removing and/or minimizing the threats from gill-net fisheries and oil spills. The plan features a five-point summary of how to recover the marbled murrelet. First, establish six conservation zones in the bird's range and develop management strategies for each one. Second, identify and protect terrestrial and marine habitat within each of these zones. Third, monitor the bird's populations and habitat and survey potential breeding habitat to find suitable nesting areas. Fourth, implement short-term actions to stabilize the marbled murrelet's population; and fifth, implement long-term actions to stop the decline and increase growth of the population. The Fish and Wildlife Service budget for these actions for the first ten years was set at $12,695,000.

Establish, identify, protect, monitor, survey, implement, stabilize, increase, stop. Any one of these verbs was a life's work. It all seemed so overwhelming, so impossible. Was there an army of scientists waiting in the wings? How were these admirable and lofty recovery goals going to translate into job descriptions? The text of the recovery plan does offer much conceptual guidance, but none that erased the image of Sisyphus from my mind.

I flipped through the recovery plan on several occasions, trying to get a sense of it as an instruction manual of some sort. I looked for one paragraph that described an action in terms of "attach A to B and then insert into C." This was not that document. All 203 pages of the recovery plan would be distributed to men and women working for land and wildlife management agencies, timber companies, conservation groups, university departments of wildlife ecology, colleges of forestry, and private environmental research groups. In minutes, they would find the pertinent paragraphs and their marching orders. Over the days, weeks, months, and years to come, they would generate memos, proposals, requests for funding, and new job descriptions. They would hire staffs, order equipment, establish boundaries and zones, and take to the woods and water.

Only after the fifth flipping through of the recovery plan did I notice that each of the five sections of the plan is separated by a beautiful full-page illustration of two marbled murrelets flying just beneath the canopy of a single Douglas-fir. The same image appears before each of the five sections, but the quotation beneath it changes.

"You take my life when you do take the means whereby I live."—*William Shakespeare,* The Merchant of Venice

"Every entity is only to be understood in terms of the way in which it is interwoven with the rest of the universe."—*Alfred North Whitehead*

"A species must be saved in many places *if it is to be saved at all."*—*Aldo Leopold,* A Sand County Almanac

"The rapidity of change and the speed with which new situations are created follow the impetuous and heedless pace of man rather than the deliberate pace of nature."—*Rachel Carson,* Silent Spring

"[A] thing is right when it tends to preserve the integrity, stability, and beauty of the biotic community. It is wrong when it tends otherwise."—*Aldo Leopold,* A Sand County Almanac

Never in any document I had read on the marbled murrelet had I encountered these authors or these sentiments. How strange to think that these powerful lines—drawn from different centuries, countries, and contexts—together form a kind of credo, one that transforms a list of action items into a moral imperative. No marbled murrelet researcher or manager has ever told me recovering the marbled murrelet was "right." They say their conservation efforts are just part of their jobs, though some confess they couldn't sleep at night if they didn't undertake them. I think that deep down, we may all believe Shakespeare, Whitehead, Leopold, and Carson; it is our choice to decide how deeply. I was tempted to track down the individual who chose to include the five quotations in the recovery plan. But I am going to let it go, let it remain a mystery, and let it speak volumes for good intentions and speedy recoveries.

PART FOUR
HOPE

his pointing forward
probably four inches to
Than adult at 6:45
down somewhere & to
e over need to have small down
6:07 am

Chick 6:57 begun
going W — adult has moved
of the chick & the
only inside. Chi
at 7:00 am pulled
& swallowed it u
adult waddled a
the branch giving

nest coming
my
it has nest.
pre we
saw it.

(marbled).
d underside ?
g N towards us

The ad
dick
7 26 a

Oicer
female

adult moved at
1. exhausted on the

There were twenty-eight of us standing in a meadow, silent and apart, like performers on a stage; men and women costumed in layers of shape-muffling fleece, wool, and Gore-Tex. In the dim light and hovering fog, we appeared as silhouettes, androgynous beings arrived from another planet. Against a backdrop of dark forest we waited. The fog moved over our heads. Our warm breath was visible in the wet, cool air. Small, bright lights shined from our heads like beacons as we stood, waiting. As the sky brightened, we turned out our lights and faced the sky and began counting.

It was April 2004, and I had come to this meadow to learn the official way to detect marbled murrelets. The meadow is in Prairie Creek Redwoods State Park, a fourteen-thousand-acre sanctuary of old-growth coastal redwoods in Humboldt County, California, set aside in the 1920s by the Save-the-Redwoods League. It is a World Heritage Site and an International Biosphere Reserve and a hot spot of marbled murrelet activity. During the spring, the park is the outdoor classroom for Mad River Biologists, an environmental consulting company that has been training people, usually professional biologists, to survey marbled murrelets and dozens of other birds since the 1980s.

Mad River Biologists' business began growing dramatically with the listing of the marbled murrelet as a state-endangered species in California in 1992, with its1993 federal listing, and with the 1997 *Recovery Plan*'s recommendations to monitor the bird's population. In forests where certain activities might impact marbled murrelets, surveys must be conducted in stands with at least one suitable nest platform. While many surveys are done to clear a timber sale or allow other activities that might disturb or harm the murrelets, others are conducted as research on the bird. Mad River Biologists has trained and certified hundreds of biologists over the years, none of them, I fear, quite as inept as I.

Our three instructors that day in April were experienced wildlife biologists and seasoned birders who had spent many a summer searching the dawn skies for marbled murrelets. The four-day course and evaluation is required of anyone who plans to survey marbled murrelets professionally. Most of my twenty-seven classmates had been hired by the Bureau of Land Management to survey a tract of Oregon forestlands in the Coast Ranges outside Roseburg for the summer. Most were recent college graduates with biology degrees who were hoping to parlay their seasonal work into full-time careers. Two were biologists in their late forties; one was exploring options for a second career, the other simply enjoyed the seminomadic lifestyle of a seasonal field technician.

The day before we had gathered at the Quality Inn in Arcata, California, to review the new, official, sixty-five-page survey protocol created by the Pacific Seabird Group. We learned the difference between a survey site, a survey station, a survey period, and a survey visit. We learned the optimal times to survey, what equipment to use, and what data to collect. We learned how to describe what we observed in the field into a tape recorder in such a way that we could easily transcribe it onto data sheets afterward.

On that 8½ × 11 sheet of paper, we would carefully write the numbers and codes that describe the details of a single detection—the time, initial detection direction, type (heard, seen, or both), type of call (*keer*, groan, or whistle), nonvocal sounds (wing sound or jet sound), number of birds seen, behavior (flight over, through, or below canopy; circling; landing in or departing from a tree; or calling from a fixed point), initial flight direction, height of the bird seen, closest distance from observer to bird, departing direction, and final detection direction. Oh yes, and there was a category for "notes" where we were to include the air temperature, changes in weather during the survey period (fog, rain, or wind), and extraneous noises such as those coming from common ravens (coded CORA), American robins (AMRO), varied thrushes (VATH), Steller's jays (STJA), automobile traffic, babbling streams, or aircraft flying overhead. A surveyor's data sheets must be detailed, accurate, and meticulous, as they become part of the permanent scientific record and a critical tool in the management of marbled murrelet habitat. At times, these notes become legal documents that are introduced into courts of law.

The protocol was overwhelming for someone like me who considered "Look! A hawk!" valuable data. All of my fellow trainees had experienced a few seasons of surveying spotted owls, salmon, tree voles, or other wildlife. I was the lone novice in the group. When I confessed this fact to one of the instructors, David Fix, he laughed. "By God, I could take a fry cook from Denny's on the I-5 and teach him how to survey for marbled murrelets."

Fix has been training marbled murrelet surveyors for ten years and leading Audubon Society birding trips for twenty-five. He is a serious professional birder, senior author of the book *Birds of Northern California*, and a birding guru in Humboldt County. The real key to detecting marbled murrelets, Fix tells his classes, is to be mindful. "You have to be wide awake and alert and actively scanning every piece of the sky all the time. You have to really want to see a bird. Imagine you are bristling with antennae trying to pick up the bird's signals out of the air. You're responsible for what's going on in a one-hundred-eighty-degree hemispherical bubble of reality overhead."

Not every surveyor is capable of this kind of focus and stamina at five in the morning. Many survey stations are set up in remote parts of the forest not accessible by trail, requiring surveyors to rise in the wee hours of the morning, drive an hour, and then hike another hour or so to reach the station at the protocol-mandated start time—forty-five minutes before sunrise. Snowpack, avalanche shutes, and blinding snowstorms add to the challenge of surveying marbled murrelets in the high-altitude forests in Washington State; early in the season, surveyors hiked half a day to their station and camped overnight so they could be in place before dawn.

But not everyone wants to see marbled murrelets. For property owners, seeing even one of these birds in their old-growth stands can kill a timber sale. David Fix recalls training one man, an "eighty-year-old lumberjack type," who told him in his rough, barroom voice exactly what he thought about marbled murrelets. "I don't like 'em. I want to know what they look like so when I see one I don't have to report it."

This is the joke that sums up Fix's mantra for surveyors: "Absence of evidence is not evidence of absence." Just because one surveyor did not hear or see marbled murrelets in a particular forest stand doesn't mean there are no murrelets in that stand. It means that the surveyor did not detect any during the two hours of the survey. The surveyor could have missed the birds, or they could have flown in or out sometime during the other twenty-two hours of the day. Or maybe the following week, or month, or year. There really is no such thing as absence in the surveyor's world, only *probable* absence.

Fix is an articulate, philosophical, and funny man in his late forties whose humor was mostly lost on the young and groggy group. After class, Fix told me that he didn't necessarily want his twenty-eight students to see marbled murrelets. He wanted them to *want to see* marbled murrelets. He wanted them to see the robins, jays, and varied thrushes, too. He wanted them to be mindful. Awake.

David Fix spent his early career with the U.S. Forest Service in Oregon as a timber cruiser—a person who works in the forest estimating the number of board feet of lumber that can be extracted from a tree, stand, or large section of forest. In the late 1980s, he began surveying spotted owls for the Forest Service and was caught in the middle of the battle for the Pacific Northwest forests. One day in 1992, he did what he calls a "karmic 180" after counting ninety-three fully loaded logging trucks passing by the road in front of his place of work before noon. Soon after he moved to Humboldt County and began looking for rare birds in the marshes, spits, and lagoons along the shore. Through the large and active birding community around Humboldt Bay, Fix found his way to Mad River Biologists as a wildlife surveyor and trainer. Though he is technically a wildlife biologist, he signs his unofficial e-mails "David Fix—poet, skeptic, and peeler of tangerines atop the mount. Also merlits surveyed." Clearly Fix falls in the passionate environmentalist camp, though he is careful to maintain his objectivity during the training.

The night before we started surveying, I studied the protocol, listened to my tape of marbled murrelet calls, and turned the lights out at 8:30. It took me a while to fall asleep with my not-yet-sleepy mind projecting images of flying murrelets across my closed eyelids.

I woke the following morning at 3:45 A.M., dressed in four layers of warm clothing, and left the hotel in the rain to make the forty-five-minute drive up Highway 101 toward Prairie Creek. The inside of my car became a steam room in no time. I was overheating in my birding uniform, and the car windows began fogging up. The car's defogger was slow, so I opened the windows. The fresh air cleared the windows and kept me from falling asleep to the rhythm of the wipers and the soothing roar of the defogger fan on high. I turned on the radio and picked up the official state park information recording on the AM station. I was told that it was foggy and raining, and that I should drive cautiously and yield to the park's resident Roosevelt elk. By the time I arrived in the parking lot at the visitor's center, I was tense and partially soaked from the rain. I was also quite early. It was 4:45—

twenty minutes ahead of the stipulated arrival time. I resisted the urge to tip my seat back for a quick nap and, instead, tried to find some music on the radio. It was all static but the park station. After listening to the recording about the elk six times, the warning became absurd and I started laughing. *What am I doing here?*

At 5:05, headlights appeared in the fog. A van and a few cars pulled in beside me and disgorged their androgynous passengers. We greeted each other in the parking lot and then shuffled off in our clunky boots behind David Fix and two other instructors toward the meadow. The meadow where we would conduct our surveys was a two-minute walk from the parking lot—a kind of drive-in survey station for beginners.

First we oriented ourselves to the compass points and located the tallest tree around the meadow. That tree—a three-hundred-foot redwood—established the height of the forest canopy. During a survey, the basic unit of measurement is one canopy. So, a bird flying 450 feet above the ground is flying at one and a half canopies. A bird flying at this height may be just passing through, but a bird flying at one canopy or below canopy is likely to be an adult on its way into the forest to attend an egg or chick. A stand of trees where a bird is detected at or below canopy is considered an occupied stand.

Establishing the height of the canopy was the easy part. We also had to estimate in meters, usually rounded to the nearest fifty, the distance between ourselves and any birds we might see. I was at a disadvantage on three counts. One, I had never needed to know precisely how far away something was from where I stood. Two, if I needed to estimate a distance—say, from the backyard volleyball net to the out-of-bounds line—I used my own pace. Three, I was metrically impaired. Clearly, the only way I was going to get through this survey training was to cheat.

Just before the survey began, I singled out a fellow surveyor and pointed to a nearby tree.

"How far away is that?" I whispered.

"About fifty meters," came the instant reply.

I pointed out another tree a bit farther off.

"And that?"

"About 150."

So, a bird that was very close was about 50 meters; close, about 100; far, 200; very far, 300.

At 5:19, ten minutes before the survey was to start, it began to rain. We pulled up our raincoat hoods and put our tape recorders into small plastic bags. I practiced hitting the On, Off, and Pause buttons through the plastic. Even this was a challenge because I had forgotten my gloves and my fingers were already wet and almost numb. Seeing the small black buttons wasn't an option; there wasn't enough light in the sky, and my raincoat hood didn't cover my glasses. Everything was an impressionistic rain-spattered smear, and the sound of rain on the hood of my raincoat was loud enough to block out other noises, possibly all the marbled murrelet calls. I pushed off my hood, took off my glasses, and decided to try surveying by ear until the rain let up. This was, after all, only a practice run. I had two days to get my act together before the exam.

At 5:29, everyone was in position, staring up into the pale fog, spinning slowly in place in the meadow. The dry, uncut grass crunched lightly under our boots as we shifted our weight from foot to foot, trying to stay warm and awake. The survey started, and within two minutes the meadow began to *click, click, click*. Everyone was turning on their tape recorders. I looked around to see my classmates looking into the same patch of sky and talking into their tape recorders. They were describing something—what? I didn't see anything. The tape recorders clicked off. A few minutes later this happened again. I was missing everything.

Ten minutes later, I did hear a bird. It was a single American robin. Its lilting song marked the beginning of the dawn chorus there at Prairie Creek. I described this in my tape recorder. In case I didn't detect a single marbled murrelet, I could still say that I had collected ornithological data in the redwoods.

Half an hour into the survey, the rain stopped. The tape recorders started clicking again. This time, one of them was mine. *Keer, keer*. I turned toward the sound in the west but couldn't see a bird. *Keer, keer*. I searched the sky. *Keer, keer, keer*. The sound was moving through the sky toward the east. I heard a distant and final *keer*, and then nothing.

In a barely audible voice, I spoke into my tape recorder: "Single bird, heard not seen, flying from the west over the meadow to the east at 6:09 A.M. Multiple *keer* calls, not over-lapping. Last heard in the east." I paused. "Two hundred meters distant." *Click*.

In the next ten minutes, I detected eleven different sets of *keer* calls, some single, some multiple, some overlapping. I had yet to see a single marbled murrelet. I opened my eyes extra wide. I scanned and turned and worked my little crop circle in the grass. I wanted to see a bird. I wanted to see its chunky body and its whirring wings. I wanted to be mindful.

When there was enough light in the sky to believe the sun would rise again, I spotted my first birds—a pair directly overhead, flying silently, at about two canopies, over the meadow and to the south. There was hope for me.

Things picked up dramatically at sunrise. I saw a silent single bird flying overhead. I turned on my tape recorder and started talking. Then two birds appeared from the south, their *keer* calls overlapping. Then three more birds materialized from the east, then another from the west. I tried to track each bird. The birds circled above the meadow at and above the canopy, splitting into singles and rejoining into pairs and trios. As this group disappeared over the trees to the south, a single silent marbled murrelet swooped in from nowhere and passed so close to my head that I ducked. Less than a minute later, four birds came in at canopy level and disappeared to the east. Then I heard calls from the southeast. Then the southwest. Then the north. Then I caught sight of two birds zipping right into the timber on the north of the meadow. I could hear their wings beating. It was dizzying. It was exhilarating. I was speechless—literally.

By 6:49, when the survey window closed, I guessed I had detected about sixty marbled murrelets in the space of an hour, though I suppose it could have been just ten birds putting on a really good show with several encores. As we walked back to our cars, students and instructors were engaged in conversations that went something like this:

"Did you see the one that flew right overhead at 6:12? I thought it was going to crash into me."

"Yeah, that was incredible. But how about that group at 6:19?"

"I couldn't even keep up with them, they were circling and swooping in so fast."

"The best one was the wing sounds at 6:15. That was so cool."

The enthusiastic commentary continued at Rolf's Café, a cozy German-style restaurant at the edge of the park that specializes in elk meat. The café had opened early that morning to serve us bleary-eyed bird people bottomless cups of coffee and lumberjack breakfasts. After our meal, we were handed separate checks by the waitress and blank data sheets by our instructors. We moved to empty tables elsewhere in the café and began the tedious process of transcribing what we recorded in the meadow into numbers and codes that fit into the blanks on the data sheets.

The high point of this activity was learning that I had gathered most of the required data for most of the detections. There were some instances, of course, where I forgot to record the departing flight direction or the closest distance from myself to the bird. But overall I would say I was on a par with a fry cook from Denny's. I felt pretty good about my efforts. Until I got to 6:14.

Apparently, as I had stood in the meadow trying to describe the surge of birds flying in all at once from different directions—the ones that were calling and circling and splitting and joining—I gave up trying to describe what was happening and simply said "Whoa!"

Those who pass the final evaluation (I did) spend their summer (I didn't) rising in the dark, hiking into the woods to their survey stations, staring at the sky for two hours, and (in some cases) avoiding encounters with bears, mountain lions, territorial marijuana growers, and armed public-land squat-ters. Neither the group from the Bureau of Land Management nor the timber company detected an abundance of marbled murrelets. It was not because they weren't qualified or because they didn't want to see the birds. It was because the forests they were surveying were at the far eastern edge of the Coast Range and are marginal murrelet habitat.

As for the timber company biologists, the property they surveyed in Humboldt County had been cleared of nearly all its old-growth stands. What were left were mostly second-growth forests with a few residual old-growth trees. In all like-lihood, they spent their summer not hearing and not seeing marbled murrelets in such forests.

Why bother to send paid surveyors into such marginal habitat in California or Oregon? Because you can never be too sure with marbled murrelets. After all, absence of evidence is not evidence of absence.

CHAPTER 21

The efforts of certified marbled murrelet surveyors—
whether to gain knowledge or clear a timber sale—are all
part of the official recovery plan for the species. Theoretically,
forest stands where the birds are detected are spared from logging, thus saving habitat and giving the birds an opportunity
to continue breeding. But it is unrealistic to believe that any
team of surveyors, any number of researchers and managers,
can bear the full responsibility for recovering the marbled
murrelet or even stabilizing its declining populations. It has
been said that it takes a village to raise a child, and, by the
same token, it takes a nation to save a species. The men and
women who study and manage and rally for the marbled
murrelet face the daunting challenges presented by the bird itself and by the political, economic, and cultural environment
of the counties and states in which they work. This environment is created by a population torn on issues of land use,
private property, ethics of conservation, and the "rightness" of
saving imperiled wildlife and habitats.

Throughout the marbled murrelet's range, these issues
define and divide communities. Flip through the Humboldt
County phone book, and you'll get a sense of what I mean.
In this county of 128,000 residents, there are thirty-three
timber companies; ten timber cruisers; twenty-nine forestry

consulting companies; thirteen environmental, conservation, and ecological organizations; and forty-two environmental and ecological services companies. In such an environment, marbled murrelets are both detested and revered with equal zeal.

And the fact remains that even under the best of circumstances, the process of recovery will be a heroic if not impossible undertaking.

Once the marbled murrelet became a state and federally endangered species, it became illegal for landowners to modify their property in ways that might lead—eventually or directly—to the death of an individual bird. For most landowners, "modifying their property" means harvesting old-growth trees or stands. The law applies to federal forests, state forests, county lands, tribal lands, timber company lands, and private backyards.

On public lands, such as national forests and parks, logging restrictions are strictly enforced. On private land, such as that owned by timber companies, enforcing the laws is not always possible. And, without enforcement, private landowners are essentially on an honor system to keep their chain saws out of groves where marbled murrelets did or could nest.

In 1985, with ancient redwood trees valued at around $100,000 each as lumber, the family-owned Pacific Lumber Company was purchased by the Maxxam Corporation, a Texas-based company. The next year, the company doubled its number of loggers and doubled the previous year's harvest. In 1990, when the marbled murrelet was being considered for listing as a federally threatened and state endangered species,

Pacific Lumber submitted its Timber Harvest Plan for 237 acres in an untouched redwood grove called Owl Creek, part of the sixty-thousand-acre Headwaters Forest.

The proposal was initially refused, but later the California Board of Forestry approved it, provided Pacific Lumber conducted surveys for marbled murrelets for two years. After initially refusing to conduct any surveys on the grounds that the bird wasn't officially listed, the company eventually agreed. Using a protocol of their own design, the biologists conducted their surveys in Owl Creek, mailed the data sheets in, and then, without waiting for approval, the company's president ordered a three-day weekend of logging in Owl Creek in June 1992. Some people don't call what Pacific Lumber did to twenty acres of the Owl Creek grove logging; they call it a massacre. Over five days, the company cut down about a million dollars' worth of ancient redwoods before the California Department of Fish and Game intervened.

Pacific Lumber's logging permit was revoked. Representatives of Pacific Lumber, the Fish and Wildlife Service, the California Department of Fish and Game, the California Board of Forestry, and the California Department of Forestry were locked in heated negotiations for the entire summer of 1992, and things got even hotter in September, when the marbled murrelet was officially declared a federally threatened species. In November, federal and state agencies were still at a total impasse with Pacific Lumber. Neither side was willing to budge, though they decided to take a break from negotiations over the Thanksgiving weekend. During that holiday, Pacific Lumber sent loggers into the old-growth groves of Owl Creek for a second round. This time, they were not alone.

When Pacific Lumber began moving its equipment into the grove, activists from EarthFirst! rushed in to physically stop the logging. When they couldn't, they notified the Environmental Protection Information Center (EPIC), a watchdog organization in nearby Garberville. Mark Harris, one of EPIC's lawyers, put in calls to the sheriff's office, the Fish and Wildlife Service, the Department of Fish and Game, the California Department of Forestry, and even the Federal Bureau of Investigation, but no one would stop the logging. The time was ripe for a battle.

In 1993, lawyers with EPIC sued Pacific Lumber in federal court for violating the Endangered Species Act in Owl Creek, but the lawyers of the Pacific Lumber Company overwhelmed the small staff at EPIC with mountains of documentation and motions. In 1994, Colorado environmental attorney Macon Cowles—fresh from a recent victory in the *Exxon Valdez* oil spill case—stepped in.

The case of the *Marbled Murrelet v. Pacific Lumber Company* went to trial in U.S. District Court in San Francisco in 1994. Pacific Lumber initially testified that its surveyors had not detected enough marbled murrelets to indicate that the Owl Creek stand was occupied by the birds. Pacific Lumber revealed that the surveyors working in Owl Creek had been ordered to keep two different sets of survey data sheets—the originals and a replicated set altered by Pacific Lumber to minimize the detections of murrelets. The original survey sheets were stored in a closet in the home of the owner of the surveying firm hired by Pacific Lumber; the replicated survey sheets were sent to the Department of Fish and Game a few days after the start of the illegal logging in June 1992 and also to EPIC's lawyers before the trial. It was also revealed that at the end of the 1992 survey season, a member of Pacific Lumber's staff hosted a party at his home for the company's forestry staff, which included the murrelet surveyors. At the party there was a target of a marbled murrelet on a dartboard, at which the attendees where throwing darts.

In February 1995, Judge Louis Bechtle ruled that the Pacific Lumber Company was prohibited from logging its ancient redwood groves in Owl Creek. In his sixty-page decision, Bechtle stated that Pacific Lumber had violated the laws of the Endangered Species Act by removing habitat known to be occupied by a threatened and endangered species. Though the Act limits only *killing* birds, Judge Bechtle's interpretation of the law made habitat removal and killing synonymous in light of the precarious state of the marbled murrelet and the high probability that it would become extinct in California. Judge Bechtle did not look kindly on Pacific Lumber's disregard for the official survey protocol, stating that in addition to falsifying data, the company had not used "an independent and impartial third party using the scientific method to determine whether the Owl Creek stand is occupied by the marbled murrelet."

Judge Bechtle's ruling was a victory for EPIC and for the marbled murrelet. It was the first time in history that the laws of the Endangered Species Act were enforced on private lands.

Pacific Lumber appealed the Owl Creek ruling all the way to the Supreme Court, but its appeal was denied. But the battles were far from over. Under the Endangered Species Act, a landowner *can* log its old-growth groves if it prepares and gets approval of a Habitat Conservation Plan. Such a plan outlines ways of maintaining, enhancing, and protecting one area of habitat while logging in another area. If a company's Habitat Conservation Plan is approved, it is issued an "incidental take" permit that allows it to take (kill) marbled murrelets legally as long as the activity that results in the take is legal.

In 1996, the Pacific Lumber Company applied for a Habitat Conservation Plan for its entire 210,000-acre property. After the California Board of Forestry refused to approve the plan, Pacific Lumber sued both the state and federal government, demanding to be paid the presumed value of the forest it couldn't log.

Rather than engage Pacific Lumber in another costly court battle, the U.S. government and the state of California approved a Habitat Conservation Plan that allowed the company to log some stands occupied by marbled murrelets in exchange for saving others. This Headwaters Deal included the federal and state governments' purchase of twelve thousand acres of Pacific Lumber's timberlands, including three thousand acres of old-growth redwoods in the Headwaters Forest. The price? A mere $480 million.

Since these are your tax dollars at work, you can visit the Headwaters Forest Reserve, the largest protected virgin redwood forest in the country. I did—or at least I tried to. The reserve is managed by the Bureau of Land Management, which allows public access from a county road south of the town of Eureka. When I arrived at the reserve entrance one afternoon, I was the only one in the parking lot. I thought twice about wandering around in a three-thousand-acre forest alone, then got out of my car and strode over to the information kiosk, where I picked up a brochure stating that access to the old-growth groves, including Owl Creek, was through ranger-led hikes conducted four days a week. The day I showed up was not one of them. I could, however, walk along an abandoned logging road that leads to a vantage point overlooking one of the Headwaters groves. The eleven-mile round-trip was described as starting out on moderate terrain and ending with an "arduous hike over extremely steep terrain." The entire trip would take nine hours. It was 2 P.M. I could never make it to the grove overlook and back by dark. I felt disappointed, excluded, denied, disfranchised—and just fine about it. Keeping people out of marbled murrelet habitat—whether they are carrying chain saws or cameras—might be the best way to give this bird a fighting chance.

CHAPTER 22

As a private company trying to make a profit from the land they own, Pacific Lumber is clearly not happy about having to compete with the marbled murrelet. Many people demonize the company, but I wanted to form my own opinion about the murrelet's rights versus private property owners'. I wondered if amid all the illegal logging, the massacres, the fist pounding, and the courtroom dramas, there was another story. So I planned to conduct a series of interviews with Pacific Lumber management—from past presidents on down. I showed up on Pacific Lumber Company's doorstep in Scotia, California, in June 2004. Little did I know that my first interview at the company would be my last.

Jeff Barrett is an environmental biologist who had worked as a consultant to timber companies and the U.S. Forest Service before joining Pacific Lumber in 1996. His first job there was to negotiate the aquatics issues—mostly spawning salmon and stream sedimentation—of the Habitat Conservation Plan during the sale of the Headwaters Forest. Since 1998, he has been the director of fish and wildlife programs on Pacific Lumber property and is involved with all Habitat Conservation Plan negotiations.

I had a list of questions for Barrett but decided to hold back in order to see where a first conversation about marbled murrelets would naturally go. Barrett began talking about Habitat Conservation Plans and Sustainable Yield Plans, describing the latter as a plan to achieve "maximum yield for the long term; you can't rape and pillage now." He told me that 83 percent of Pacific Lumber's old growth is under a Habitat Conservation Plan for the next fifty years. He told me they have six biologists who survey for marbled murrelets every year. He told me he doesn't believe that the loss of old-growth forests is the main problem for the marbled murrelet. He was convinced it is something else—perhaps a decline in ocean productivity or some larger problem scientists have yet to discover.

Barrett is not soft-spoken. He was quick to tell me that he is "known for being fairly outrageous and direct." This said, he began with a riff on the lack of data on marbled murrelets.

"What are the marbled murrelets doing in the forest? Don't know. When do they come into the forest? Don't know. What's their productivity? Don't know. What exactly do they need in an old-growth forest? Don't know."

I knew this wasn't entirely correct, but I just kept listening.

"I have no antipathy toward the marbled murrelet," Barrett continued. "They're kind of cool. I respect alcids in general, marbled murrelets specifically. Everyone wants these birds to do well."

I wasn't sure this was true either and wondered where he was going with this.

Barrett went on to say that he thinks that biodiversity, ecosystem health, and private property rights are important, and that "you can have it all." He thinks that the conservation of the marbled murrelet is not Pacific Lumber's problem—it's the government's.

"There is over two million acres of marbled murrelet habitat in California, Oregon, and Washington. Pacific Lumber owns thirty-four-hundred-some acres of that. Most of the habitat is on federal lands, national forests, national parks, and state parks. This is government land."

Barrett continued. "We want to camp under old-growth redwoods, but we want to save the trees and the birds. We want cheap oil, but we don't want to drill in Alaska. We want electricity with the flip of a switch, but we don't want a power plant. We want lumber to build a house, but we don't want to log the forests. We want to save the forests, but we won't ask for green-certified wood. We are a society of hypocrites."

I found myself nodding in agreement. Though the conversation seemed veering away from Pacific Lumber Company and marbled murrelets, I think he was on to something—something deep in the heart of every conservation issue.

"How much," Barrett asked, "were state and federal land managers—the owners of the overwhelming majority of the old-growth forests—prepared to restrict their activities, including camping, hiking, picnicking, to protect this species? Pacific Lumber isn't even allowed to drive through some of our murrelet stands! In other stands we have to follow onerous rules such as entering the stand—at 15 m.p.h.—no sooner than two hours after sunrise or later than two hours before sunset. Is our society willing to support such restrictions on the old-growth stands in the state parks and national forests?"

I had to think about that one. I had been camping with my family at Big Basin Redwoods State Park recently, and we pitched our tents in the middle of a stand of old-growth Douglas firs. Would I vote for a law that blocked off that campground? Would I be grateful to the park managers for barricading trails that lead into the ancient groves? Would I attend meetings to protest a housing development that encroached on a mature Douglas fir forest? Never mind what *society* was willing to support; what was I willing to do for a rare, threatened, or endangered species?

I left the Pacific Lumber Company knowing that I wouldn't be back, knowing that I wouldn't need to interview anyone else. I had gotten all that I needed from them—one really good, hard question.

I strolled across the street from Barrett's office to the Scotia Museum, a one-room, casually curated repository of the town's logging history. There were old photographs of nine-teenth-century loggers, of oxen pulling felled trees out of the forest, of coal-fired locomotives transporting timber, of the town the company built.

Before Scotia was Scotia, it was a town called Forestville. The name Scotia was chosen in 1888, when the town got its first post office, because so many of the Pacific Lumber Company millworkers were from Nova Scotia. Over the years, Pacific Lumber has built employee housing, stores, a school, hospital, skating rink, church, and theater in Scotia. In 1998, Pacific Lumber had jobs for sixteen hundred people and was Humboldt County's largest private employer. That Scotia is a company town and proud of it is evident everywhere in the museum. Prominently displayed in the front of the museum is an enlarged collage of photographs depicting a dad playing basketball with his kids, some baby ducks, and a family feeding some birds. The caption reads, "Scotia remains home to Pacific Lumber and to more than 250 families, many of whom are the second and third generation in the area. Scotia is a great place to spend a day or lifetime."

I strolled around the museum, gazing at the axes, drag saws, band saws, and metal wedges. They were the tools from a bygone era of logging—tools without motors, electrical cords, OSHA safety warnings, or two-cycle engines—tools in shapes that no longer exist. I found myself admiring a hand-forged broadax hung at eye level on the wall. I had never seen such a tool, though I wielded it through metaphor—as writer Annie Dillard suggested—to cut out of my life what kept me from writing. It was a powerful tool. Its blade was lustrous steel; its long, wooden handle was worn smooth with use. I longed to take it down off its hooks, feel its weight in my hands, and feel whatever would course through my veins when I held it. Adrenaline? Fear? Power? What would the muscles in my arms and back feel like if I raised it over my head? What would its blade have sounded like cutting into the thick, rough bark of a redwood? I walked on.

There were several glass cases of logging camp relics—tin cups, plates, and the like—interspersed with old sepia-toned photographs of loggers in the forest. In the photographs, the loggers are not working. They are posing with their axes in front of fallen trees and enormous stumps. They are wearing their work clothes—long-sleeved, button-down shirts, denim overalls, wool pants, leather boots, and brimmed hats. They are lean and clean-shaven or sport large mustaches. They are serious, proud, and washed in sepia. They cannot tell me what I have learned elsewhere: that to bring down the ancient tree they stand before required them to toil for weeks with their axes before taking up the cross-cut saws—"misery whips," they called them. They cannot tell me the story of their conquest. They cannot show me what I can imagine—their calloused hands, their aching backs, their empty pockets where they will put a few dollars at the end of the day.

. What they are showing me is how big the trees were. In every photograph, the loggers pose in such a way that I can know the size of the tree. In one photograph, seven men stand shoulder to shoulder on the stump of one tree. In another, twelve men and a dog stand on a single stump. And in another, one man stands before a felled tree—the diameter of the trunk is more than twice the man's height, I'd guess about twelve feet. Hold your arms out to your sides. The distance from fingertip to fingertip is between five and six feet. Double that.

These were thousand-year-old trees that might have held marbled murrelets—the birds these men named "fog larks." These loggers must have heard plenty of marbled murrelets circling and calling above their heads. They must have learned to recognize the birds' silhouettes as their view of the sky opened with each tree they felled. After just one summer, they likely knew more about marbled murrelets than any naturalist at the time. But what were they to do with their knowledge? Who were they to tell of the mossy limbs, broken eggshells, flightless chicks, and stunned adults—and why? If they had known how rare a tree-nesting seabird was, what stories we might have heard from their sepia lips.

Standing in front of these images, I realize I have seen
these pictures before—if not these exact pictures, ones just like
them. It must have been in elementary school that I first saw
them, stock photos in the inevitable "Westward, Ho!" chapter
of my social studies books. I am certain I saw them in my
American history book in high school. The photographs are
not about trees. They are not about the forest or the environment. They are about America—its strength, its can-do,
larger-than-life spirit. These photographs are icons, the loggers
are folk heroes—men who tamed the wilderness and won the
West. Their labor produced the lumber that built homes for a
growing nation in the nineteenth and twentieth centuries.
These same men panned for gold, mined silver, and built rail-
roads. They were proud of their work, their efforts, and their
sacrifices to supply their countrymen with what they needed.
What need could they have had of an elusive bird?

Leaving the museum, I drove through the Van Duzen
River Valley to Carlotta, a rural town south of Scotia. Back in
the 1920s and 1930s, Joseph Grinnell and William Leon
Dawson made regular trips to Carlotta to visit H. E. Wilder,
a friend and fellow birder whose property backed Pacific
Lumber Company land. All three men had seen and heard
marbled murrelets flying over Wilder's property. Though it
was too late in the day for murrelets, I was curious to see if
Wilder's home still existed and how much the landscape had
changed.

The hills I could see from the highway looked like a dog
with mange. They had been cut over and the forest that
remained had grown back in patches. The hills were not
cloaked or blanketed in trees, they were draped in second-

growth rags. Individually, the trees were lovely and larger than most growing elsewhere in the world. But seeing clumps of them surrounded by clear-cuts was disturbing.

I stopped in at the Carlotta post office to ask the postmistress if she knew of anyone in the town with the last name of Wilder. She said no, but that there was a Wilder Road just a quarter mile farther down the highway. I found it and followed it a few hundred yards to where it turned into a dirt road and then forked left and right into two driveways. I drove up the driveway to the right, where I could see a small house built in what looked to be the Craftsman style popular in the early 1900s. It was the only house that old along the road. When I got to the top of the driveway, I was sure this was H. E. Wilder's place; it had a commanding view of the valley and of the Trinity Mountains. The house backed up on a redwood forest and hills that looked as if they had been "lumbered off" in the 1920s, as Joseph Grinnell had described in his field notes. I parked and knocked at the door, hoping to meet H. E. Wilder's great-granddaughter and learn some stories from her. No one answered.

As I walked back to my car, I took a moment to look at the house and imagine how cozy it would look before dawn with a few lights on to guide the earlier birders to their clothes, coffee, and binoculars. I think I spotted the second-story window William Dawson mentioned using in 1916 in his *Birds of California*: "On the morning of July 1st," he writes "having spent the night with Mr. and Mrs. H. E. Wilder of Carlotta, we rose for an early start, and were immediately greeted by Murrelets. Thrusting head out of window, I distinctly heard two birds as they made their way down the valley. This time we were twenty miles from tide-water. Somewhere on the slopes of the Trinity Mountains there is a breeding colony of Marbled Murrelets!"

I gazed across the valley toward the mountains. While Dawson, Grinnell, and Wilder saw and heard marbled murrelets, what I saw as I got into my car to leave was a double-propeller helicopter working the backside of the hills. These helicopters are used for steep-slope logging—to remove cut logs in places too steep for roads and heavy equipment. I watched several logs being transported out of the forest, probably to a truck waiting on a nearby road. As the enormous, branchless trunks dangled in the air, I wondered why anyone was going to such extremes for redwood lumber, for old-growth wood. What was it about the wood that made it so valuable? What fueled the demand that Pacific Lumber and other lumber companies were satisfying?

On the Frequently Asked Questions page of the California Redwood Association's Web site, I found some answers.

Q: Why should I use redwood for my project?

A: Use redwood for its long-lasting beauty. No other softwood has the rich beauty or long-lasting performance of redwood. Use redwood for its natural durability. Redwood heartwood is naturally resistant to decay. Use redwood simply because it is a pleasure to use.

Long-lasting, rich, beautiful, naturally durable, resistant to decay, pleasurable. These were words that appear in advertisements for most any product that is advertised, from skin cream, shampoo, and nail polish to automobile tires, all-leather interiors, furniture polish, and house paint. Clearly someone in the redwood marketing department was tapping into something other than trees. Was the desire for redwood, I wondered, tied to a basic human desire to possess these qualities in ourselves, some universal aesthetic? Does it really matter what the product is? How many of my consumer choices were made because of some subliminal message that the product would make me be or feel rich, beautiful, long-lasting, pleasurable—even resistant to decay? What was I willing to pay—and at what cost—for such products? I shudder to think.

I left Humboldt County and took a flight home via the Seattle-Tacoma airport, where I passed a huge, ceiling-to-floor, Plexiglas panel that was decorated with some brown-colored abstract pattern. I stopped in my tracks. It was the life-size cross section of an enormous tree—the abstract pattern was actually the concentric growth rings. It was a novel design for a wall—the panels were subtle, functional, and quite beautiful. I started walking toward the panel to run my fingers over the rings, but something made me stop. Something was wrong. My synapses were misfiring, my pleasant memories of counting growth rings were tainted, and my idea of beauty was being unwired. What was I willing to sacrifice?

CHAPTER 23

L oss of nesting habitat from logging is a significant threat to marbled murrelets, but it is not the only threat they face in the forest. Nest predation is considered a major cause of marbled murrelet mortality. Of all the marbled murrelet's many predators, the most successful are thought to be the common raven and Steller's jay. These birds are members of the corvid family and are what marbled murrelets aren't: bold, aggressive, wary, clever, *adaptable*. Over the last decade, as marbled murrelet populations have been declining, corvid populations have been exploding and their range expanding in the western United States due to rapid urbanization and the fragmentation of forestlands. Such drastic landscape changes threaten the marbled murrelet and plenty of other species—but make the living easier for the ravens and jays.

In the last twenty-five years, common raven populations have increased ten to fifteen times across much of the western United States. To understand the effects of this boom on marbled murrelets, scientists at the University of Washington in Seattle began a multiyear study of the problem in 1995.

John Marzluff, a wildlife biologist and an associate professor of ecosystem sciences at the university's College of Forest Resources, is the king of corvid research in the Pacific Northwest. Marzluff's personal interest in and enthusiasm for the highly intelligent corvids—especially jays, crows, and ravens—is evident from the moment you step onto the university campus, where hundreds of crows are banded as part of one of Marzluff's studies. The interior of his office is a shrine to corvids. The walls and bulletin boards are covered with postcards, photographs, Native American–style artwork, carved wooden models, tchotchkes, and knickknacks depicting the members of his much-adored family of birds. And there, in the middle of it, is John Marzluff with his thick, raven-black hair.

When I asked Marzluff why the marbled murrelets were so, so . . . when I paused to find the right adjective for their apparent inability to adapt to less-than-ideal nesting habitat, Marzluff quickly filled in.

"So stupid?"

Marzluff believes that if marbled murrelets can't learn to nest in younger trees or on the ground, the changing landscape might spell their doom. Marzluff knows that marbled murrelets can't just up and change, as the corvids do so brilliantly, so he developed a study of marbled murrelet nest predators.

The first step was to identify the potential predators at the nest sites. I saw one major problem with this—John Marzluff needed nests. When he started his study in 1995, there were only three known nests in the entire state of Washington, so Marzluff designed a study using artificial nests. All he needed was 337 eggs, 334 stuffed chickens, $215,000, six years, and a constant supply of highly motivated graduate students.

The study—the first of its kind for a marbled murrelet—

would be conducted primarily in forests on the west side of the Olympic Peninsula, near major concentrations of marbled murrelets. Several weeks before marbled murrelet breeding season commenced, John Marzluff sent his graduate students out into the rain-drenched forests of the Hoh, Soleduc, and Quinault river valleys looking for the perfect study sites. In the first year of the study, they selected eighteen forest stands ranging from fifty to two hundred acres. The dominant trees were either western hemlock, Sitka spruce, or silver fir. Marzluff hired one of his graduate students, John Luginbuhl, to be the project coordinator. It was largely up to John to develop a protocol for the study, as none existed. John started work well before the first field season and spent months experimenting with equipment and developing procedures as he went along.

John Luginbuhl's first job was to create an artificial nest, even though the marbled murrelet does not make a nest. An artificial nest was more about artificial eggs. The egg making started with a bulk order of plastic Easter eggs. Within each egg, John placed a custom-designed, motion-sensitive radio transmitter. Each transmitter was encased in resin that had been molded to fit perfectly inside the plastic egg. Imagine, if you will, the transmitter as a hard-boiled egg: The transmitter itself is the egg yolk, the resin the egg white around it. Once this tidy package of technology was placed in the tree, the transmitter would send out a signal when the egg was jiggled, jostled, or carried off in a beak.

Of course, no predator is going to fall for a hot pink murrelet egg. John got fellow graduate students to paint each egg with hobby-store model paint to resemble the pale green, dark-speckled marbled murrelet egg. Once the paint dried, the eggs were coated in several layers of paraffin. The paraffin was nothing special, just the paraffin you can buy at the grocery store for topping off your homemade fruit preserves. I have always found the sight of such household items—paraffin, plastic ice-cube trays, pipe cleaners, tongue depressors, and baby-food jars—in a science lab amusing. Can't they afford *real* equipment? But scientific equipment doesn't always have to be state-of-the-art, it just has to work. The paraffin was known to work for capturing the imprints of the predators' beaks, teeth, or claws.

Once the paraffin cooled, the eggs were stored in cedar chips (another hardware store purchase) to reduce the scent of human hands that might be lingering on the paraffin. Since marbled murrelet chicks were also potential prey, Luginbuhl made models of nestlings from specimens of domestic chicken chicks preserved with borax and salt. The preserved skins were stuffed not with cotton batting but with finely crushed cedar chips and a radio transmitter. Luginbuhl coated the surface of the transmitter with paraffin—again to preserve the predators' telltale imprints.

Luginbuhl and his colleagues headed into the temperate rain forests of the Olympic Peninsula with backpacks loaded with the fake eggs, crossbows, cameras, lumber, and climbing rope. The polypro and Gore-Tex clothing they wore had been stored in cedar chips for the past twenty-four hours to reduce any trace of a human scent they might have brought into the trees—a scent known to deter small-mammal predators. They took a box of thin, latex gloves to use for the same reason. To minimize the impact of climbing on potential murrelet nesting trees, Luginbuhl did not use spurs or a flipline but climbed without making contact with the tree. Using a crossbow he retrofitted with a spool of fishing line and his climbing ropes, he shot his climbing line into the tree and over a sturdy branch. Using ascenders and a climbing harness, he worked his way up to the nest branch—a wide one about forty-five feet above the ground and protected by overhead branches. Still dangling from the tree in his harness, Luginbuhl set the artificial egg in a patch of moss close to the trunk, then strapped a 35-millimeter camera equipped with auto advance and a date and time imprint onto the branch nearby. The camera had a built-in auto flash and was attached to an active infrared motion detection system. If a potential predator passed in front of the infrared beam, it would be *lights! camera! action!*

On good days, Luginbuhl and his colleagues could set up a nest in about ninety minutes. Rigging each study site— typically with six artificial nests placed in six different trees— required a full day of effort. A bad day might start with heavy rain and continue when the fishing line shot from the crossbow snapped or got tangled in the tree. Things might get worse when, once the climbing line was set and tested, the branch would break and send the climber into a ten- or twenty-foot free fall. Just when such a bad day was starting to look good, tree-nesting hornets and yellow jackets might attack the climbers—an event that turned a bad day into an unredeemable one.

Despite these logistical challenges, Luginbuhl and his colleagues had enough good days to set up and monitor hundreds of nests in the study area. During the monitoring phase of the study, they camped in their trucks or at a campground near the study site. Once they received the signal—a fast pulsing from the transmitter—they would head into the woods with telemetry antennae tuned to the unique radio frequency of the transmitter. Once they located the artificial nest tree, they climbed it and retrieved the artificial egg or chick and the film from the camera. On one occasion they located a disturbed egg five hundred yards from its original location, jammed into the broken top of a fifty-foot-high rotten snag. The plastic shell was shattered and the paraffin clearly showed many raven-bite marks. Luginbuhl and his crew also found the skin and bone of one artificial chick devoured, despite the borax and salt. They found the transmitter fifty feet above in the tree—buried in a flying squirrel nest. The paraffin was covered in little incisor marks. "These events, small as they are," Luginbuhl told me, "make all the slogging worthwhile."

From the hundreds of photographs and hundreds of waxy imprints that John Luginbuhl and his colleagues collected, they learned that 82 percent of the nests were preyed on during a period of a month. This rate of predation was high but similar to the rates found by other researchers at real marbled murrelet nests. They identified eleven animals at the nest sites capable of preying on murrelet eggs or chicks.

Among the birds, the scientists rounded up some of the usual suspects: Steller's jays, gray jays, common ravens, American crows, and Cooper's hawks. But they also found a surprising number of small mammals—northern flying squirrels, *Peromyscus* mice, bushy-tailed wood rats, Douglas's squirrels, Townsend's chipmunks, and mustellids (ermine or mink). The study showed that corvids preyed more heavily on eggs and that mammals, because of their keen sense of smell, were more adept at locating and preying on the stuffed artificial nestlings. Because this was an artificial nest study, with no adult marbled murrelets or chicks fending off these predators, it is difficult for scientists to know how many of these *potential* predators would be *actual* predators at a real nest. What John Luginbuhl suspects is that marbled murrelets are threatened by not just a few corvid species in the forest, but by an entire community of birds and mammals whose complex interactions and relationships in the food web are little understood. While a flying squirrel might never prey on a live marbled murrelet chick, its very presence at a nest site could theoretically attract another bird or mammal that would prey on the chick. Of the nest failures scientists have documented, 78 percent have resulted from predation.

Even if we could stop all logging of old-growth forests and keep the ocean free of oil pollution and full of fish, the marbled murrelets might not endure in the face of predation. This predation isn't altogether natural. Studies by scientists such as John Marzluff are showing that what a crow or raven does may be influenced by human behavior. They link the corvid population boom to our increasingly urbanized landscape and its increase in garbage—a food source exploited heavily by the omnivorous and opportunistic corvids. As these birds move into and exploit new territories, they find that our once-dense forests—now fragmented, patchy, and edged by roads, parking lots, clear-cuts, and campgrounds—are easily accessible and feature trees where marbled murrelet eggs, chicks, and adults are easy pickings.

   Scientists have yet to address the issue of controlling corvids in marbled murrelet territory, but one researcher joked that the West Nile virus epidemic, which has wiped out corvid populations in some areas of the United States, may be the "best thing that ever happened to the marbled murrelet." Strange to think of a mosquito carrying a virus as an ally of the marbled murrelet, but then again, this bird needs all the help it can get.

CHAPTER 24

During the summer of 1978, biologist Kathy Kuletz spent her entire summer, from May through August, on Naked Island—a small, forested island in the middle of Alaska's Prince William Sound. She and one other field technician had been hired by the U.S. Fish and Wildlife Service in Anchorage to study the island's bird and marine mammal populations. Getting there required being ferried from the Whittier harbor on a chartered fishing vessel loaded with enough gear to set up camp for four months. The trip was three hours one way, in good weather. As the boat made its way across the long stretch of open water to the island, Kuletz's senior colleagues at the Fish and Wildlife Service pointed out the various inlets, islets, sea lions, harbor seals, eagles, puffins, and pigeon guillemots. Kuletz noticed the marbled murrelets; it was her first glimpse of these small seabirds.

"They were everywhere on the water—hundreds and hundreds of them," she remembers, "but nobody knew anything about them. I found that very strange."

During her four years of working on Naked Island, Kuletz slept in a tent or plastic "weatherport" and woke every morning to the sound of rain and marbled murrelets calling as they flew over the island. On many mornings, Kuletz scrambled out of her tent at the first call to watch the show against the pale sky. She watched the acrobatic flights of single birds, pairs, and groups of birds as they swooped and circled and dove over the tops of the trees. She listened to their *keer* calls, strange groaning calls, and fluttering wing beats. She was awestruck—and curious. What attracted these birds to Naked Island? Kuletz was especially intrigued by the numbers of marbled murrelets flying into the groves of trees with fish in their bills.

Kuletz began reading about the biology and behavior of the marbled murrelets. She soon learned that others long before her had been as fascinated and as puzzled as she was by this species. What she didn't understand was how the marbled murrelet, clearly *the* most abundant bird in Prince William Sound in the summer, could be so poorly understood—almost ignored—after so many years of surveys and research in the sound. Kuletz vowed that one day she would return to search those groves on Naked Island for nests. Little did she know that her research on marbled murrelets would come under the worst possible circumstances.

On March 24, 1989, the supertanker *Exxon Valdez* left the port of Valdez bound for California, its hull brimming with 53 million gallons of crude oil from the Alaska pipeline. Just after midnight, the tanker ran aground on Bligh's Reef, ruptured, and sent 11 million gallons of thick, black oil into Prince William Sound. That much oil would fill 125 Olympic-sized swimming pools. Waves and currents eventually spread the oil along 1,300 miles of the rocky Alaskan coast. The spill killed as many as 2,800 sea otters, 300 harbor seals, 22 killer whales, billions of salmon and herring eggs, 150 bald eagles, and 250,000 seabirds, including 8,400 marbled murrelets. That number was based on estimates of marbled murrelet populations at sea—710,000 in the spill zone alone—and on the numbers of oiled carcasses recovered by biologists on Prince William Sound's rocky shores. The number of murrelets would have been higher, but the spill occurred in March, when most of the populations were farther offshore.

Kathy Kuletz remembers watching the news of the spill on television. "It was devastating," she recalls. "I kept thinking they were going to control it, but after three days it was clearly out of control. It was just a matter of tracking the oil as it moved along the coast. It was a slow-motion nightmare."

Among the thousands of oiled marbled murrelets, thirty-three were found alive and brought to rehabilitation centers. A team of professionals and dozens of volunteers, including veterinarians, set up a cleaning facility and recovery facility. Dawn dishwashing detergent was the cleaning agent. Only three marbled murrelets were released back to the sea.

The oil reached Naked Island in three days. At the time of the spill, Kathy Kuletz was not working as a biologist. She and her husband were building a house on the Kenai Peninsula and raising their three-year-old son. But when the calls started coming in from the U.S. Fish and Wildlife Service office in Anchorage, Kuletz decided to attend its planning sessions and meetings to decide what action to take. "In the course of all the meetings," Kuletz recalls, "no one mentioned marbled murrelets. No one had even considered them."

The estimated three thousand marbled murrelets that come to Naked Island in the summer were still far from shore at their winter foraging grounds and were beyond the direct impact of the spill. In June, however, they would be moving toward shore and would likely encounter the oil that clung to the rocky shore and eat fish that had ingested oil. Kuletz wanted to do something for the marbled murrelets, so she proposed a damage assessment study specific to species in Prince William Sound. Her work began in June of 1989 and would be followed by years of studies oriented toward the restoration of the damaged population.

In 1991, the Exxon Corporation was charged by the State of Alaska and the U.S. government for their criminal and civil crimes. The settlement included $900 million for restoring the resources that suffered from the spill. In 1994, a restoration plan was adopted with money dedicated to habitat protection and acquisition; research, monitoring, and restoration of fish and wildlife in the spill region. The goal of the plan was to return the marbled murrelet population and many other injured species to the conditions that would have existed had the spill not occurred. To a certain degree, this plan roughly parallels the recovery plan of the U.S. Fish and Wildlife Service in Washington, Oregon, and California.

Largely through oil-spill funds, Kathy Kuletz has been researching marbled murrelets for fifteen years. She has published a dozen papers on this seabird, and in early 2005 she finished her PhD dissertation on it. The marbled murrelet can be a life's work, and restoring a damaged ecosystem will require generations of effort from people like Kathy Kuletz.

Oil pollution demons don't always take the form of huge tankers like the *Exxon Valdez*. The demons assume a myriad shapes and sizes, and they lurk everywhere—in all our waters, all the time.

I learned about these demons at an all-day Oil and California's Seabirds symposium at the Pacific Seabird Group meeting in Santa Barbara in 2002. The lecture hall at the Museum of Natural History was packed. Ten scientists had papers to present. Harry Carter opened the symposium with a five-minute overview of the forty-five oil spills that had occurred in California between 1969 and 1999. He spoke of catastrophic spills from oil tankers, marine vessels, sunken ships, oil-drilling platforms, and pipelines. Of course I had heard of the *Exxon Valdez*, but not the *Apex Houston, Puerto Rican, Cape Mohican, American Trader, Command, Stuyvesant, Kure, Platform Irene,* or *Jacob Luckenbach* spills. Carter's presentation was grim, matter of fact, and listed in the program as Welcoming Remarks.

One of the most mysterious oil spills involved the *Jacob Luckenbach,* a steamship freighter en route from San Francisco to Japan in 1953. Just seventeen miles from the Golden Gate Bridge, it collided with another ship in heavy fog, sank in thirty minutes, and disappeared. For nearly fifty years, the sunken vessel lay unnoticed in 176 feet of water—though it sent regular oily messages to shore. In 1992, scientists began picking up thousands of oiled seabirds, mostly common murres, on the beaches of Sonoma and Monterey counties; oil and congealed petroleum, called tarballs, were discovered in the water and along the shoreline. No one could figure out the source of the San Mateo mystery spill. Currents and winds from winter storms helped push the oil and dead birds to shore again in 1997. And again in 1999. And again in 2001.

Finally, in February 2002, just a few weeks before the Pacific Seabird Group symposium I was attending, environmental sleuths found archived records of the ship, then the wreck, and then the oil floating on the water above it. Those sleuths included recreational divers, beachcombers, and staffs of the Naval Historian's office, the U.S. Coast Guard, the California Department of Fish and Game, the California Office of Oil Spill Prevention and Response, Vortex Diving Company, the State Lands Commission, and the state's Petroleum Chemistry Laboratory, which matched the "fingerprint" of the oil on the birds and shore to the oil leaking from the *Jacob Luckenbach*. Based on the number of oiled birds found, scientists estimate that some forty thousand birds could have been lost since 1992, when they first became aware of the problem. That staggering number does not include possible damage done in the forty years prior to that. During the summer of 2002, dive teams living in pressurized chambers worked to locate and pump out the remaining oil. They managed to remove 2,380 barrels of oil—about 20 percent of the original total on board. They sealed and buried leaking vents and pipes, containing an estimated 690 barrels. Because no legally responsible party exists, the $19 million for cleanup and restoration activities is being sought through the Oil Spill Liability Trust Fund, which collects from oil companies a five-cents-per-barrel fee on domestic and imported oil. The S.S. *Jacob Luckenbach* is one of hundreds of sunken ships off the Pacific Coast.

One speaker offered some good news: Recovery and rehabilitation efforts have become more effective for many species of seabirds. And some bad: The marbled murrelet isn't one of them.

Among seabirds, marbled murrelets have one of the highest susceptibilities to oil spills. Because of their nearshore foraging habits, they are inevitably in the path of the oil as it washes ashore. Because of their small size, their feathers are quickly covered in oil and lose their ability to trap air and repel water. The birds cannot maintain their body heat, and they consequently suffer hypothermia and die. Oiled feathers also make it difficult—and sometimes impossible—for the mar- bled murrelets to fly, dive, and forage. Birds also die when they ingest oil, either directly from their feathers as they preen them or indirectly when they feed on oil-contaminated fish and other marine life. Once oiled, most marbled murrelets drown, sink, and are never recovered on the beach. Of the small num- bers that are recovered, few are successfully rehabilitated.

The next speaker was from the U.S. government's Minerals Management Service, which runs the federal offshore oil and gas operations—thirty-three drilling platforms' worth—in nearly 2 billion acres along the southern coast of California. Some good news: Large, offshore oil platform spills have de- clined dramatically in California thanks to oil-spill prevention measures mandated by federal and state agencies in 1969.

Following this, good news from scientists at California's Office of Oil Spill Prevention and Response: Though 650 bil- lion barrels of petroleum products are transferred through California waters every year, seabird mortality cannot be at- tributed to accidental tanker spills. And the bad news? Thousands of recent seabird deaths can be attributed to other causes—oil pipeline breaks, nontanker vessel spills, chronic oiling, and bilge dumping.

Before I met the marbled murrelet, I would never have sat through such a lecture on how barges and oil tankers are cleaned, but there I sat, rapt. Each tanker has tanks for holding its crude oil payload. It also has tanks for holding the diesel fuel to run its engine and tanks to hold the oil dripping from the engine. It also has a bilge to hold any oils and fuels that leak or overflow. Twice a month, the tanks are emptied down to the "last drop" of fuel and oily wastes before they are cleaned with high-pressure hoses spraying hot water or vegetable oil. This "last drop," regulations stipulate, can be no more than twelve thousand gallons. Gulp. That's four Olympic-sized swimming pools' worth of oily gunk. These twelve thousand gallons of waste can be legally discharged at sea 100 miles from shore at the rate of 50 gallons a mile over 240 miles. At this rate, a tank washing takes about four days. In reality, this time-consuming process is often done illegally—closer to shore and in just one or two days. The discharged waste—a mixture of crude oil, gasoline, bunker oil, diesel oil, and water—can do as much damage to seabirds as a full-fledged, catastrophic oil spill. Another biologist discussed the difficulty of monitoring tank washings and small accidental oil spills at sea. Still another discussed the importance of beached-bird surveys—a line of work not too different from beachcombing.

Jan Roletto coordinates the surveys along the central California coast within a strip of shoreline protected by the Gulf of the Farallones National Marine Sanctuary and the northern portion of the Montery Bay National Marine Sanctuary. These sanctuaries encompass 2,300 square miles of ocean that are off limits to oil and gas exploration, discharge of effluent (from vessels during tank cleaning or other sources from the water and mainland), disturbance to wildlife by aircraft, alteration or construction on the seabed (such as the building of bridges and pilings), and the passage of oil tankers, barges, or merchant vessels (in certain areas). These activities are considered threats to marine ecosystems, which include the marbled murrelet and its prey species. The Gulf of the Farallones and Monterey Bay are two of the five National Marine Sanctuaries on the Pacific Coast that protect more than ten thousand square miles of the ocean—much of marbled murrelet territory. The sanctuaries are not off limits to the public, but they do regulate boating and vessel access in some areas. They offer the marbled murrelet at sea what the national and state parks offer the bird on land—a place where some of the threats to their survival are lessened.

Sanctuary scientists like Jan Roletto and a corps of a hundred volunteer citizen-scientists are part of "Beach Watch," a citizen-scientist program that helps to detect oil spills soon after they occur. Trained volunteers regularly stroll along their assigned beach, identify and count live and beached (dead) marine animals, count and collect carcasses, photograph marine life and human activity on the beaches, conduct water sampling tests, and document oil and tarball deposition. They are the "eyes" of the sanctuary.

Though most oiled marbled murrelets rarely make it to shore, the Beach Watch program makes sure they will be identified and reported when they do. When oiled seabirds are recovered, feather samples are sent to chemistry laboratories where scientists study the "fingerprint" of the oil—the unique chemical signature that can be used to match the crime to its source.

Hundreds of live oiled birds found by Beach Watch volunteers over three recent winters helped in tracking the source of the 2001 San Mateo mystery spill and the 1997–1998 Point Reyes tarball event back to the *Jacob Luckenbach*. Beached carcasses collected by volunteers in the wake of other spills helped scientists estimate the total number of killed seabirds. Such estimates are critical for calculating how much the responsible party owes the state and federal agencies who will oversee the restoration activities of the damaged natural resources.

The threat of catastrophic oil spills and chronic oil pollution looms large on the horizon. Other menaces lurk just below the water's surface—fishing nets. In 1979–1980, Harry Carter and Spencer Sealy first documented the link between commercial gill nets and hundreds of marbled murrelet deaths along the coast of British Columbia. Other scientists soon discovered that gill nets were a problem for marbled murrelets elsewhere along the Pacific Coast.

Gill nets are not the quaint rope fishing nets that are draped on the walls of seafood restaurants or that are tossed off fairy-tale boats by such "fishermen" as Wynken, Blynken, and Nod. To get these ridiculously quaint images out of my mind, I had to do some research. Gill nets are mesh nets made of monofilament (single-strand) fishing line, the kind that is virtually invisible in the water. Gill nets come in two basic sizes: four football fields long and three football fields long. They are almost too immense to imagine. Like ladies' "fishnet" stockings, gill nets are mesh. The size of the mesh (the opening) depends on the type of fish being sought. Four-inch mesh is generally used for sockeye salmon, which are caught in the relatively shallow (30-feet-deep) nearshore waters where the marbled murrelets forage. When deployed, salmon gill nets are left out for several hours at night. As the salmon swims forward through the mesh, it gets as far as its gills—and then becomes stuck. When it startles, it backs up to escape and the thin nylon line cuts into its gills.

While the salmon are getting entangled in the mesh, so are the marbled murrelets that are chasing smaller prey that pass easily through the net. Because marbled murrelets frequently feed in low light, they have an especially difficult time seeing the nets. As they "fly" underwater in pursuit of their prey or dive to avoid the fishing boats, the murrelets become entangled in the gill nets, usually around their wings. Trapped and unable to come up for air, the birds quickly drown.

Gill-net fisheries have operated in waters off the Pacific Coast since the early twentieth century, so it is likely that marbled murrelets have been drowning in these nets since then. Until recently, no one has kept track of numbers of gill-netted marbled murrelets, or most other seabirds and mammals for that matter. Scientists today estimate that the salmon gill-net fisheries in Alaska may kill some 3,300 marbled murrelets each year; a bycatch study done in Prince William Sound in 1990 reported 1,231 gill-netted marbled murrelets. Because the marbled murrelet is not a listed species in Alaska, there are no laws banning gill netting there. Protection might be in its future, however, as the U.S. Fish and Wildlife Service is considering listing the less abundant and equally threatened Kittlitz's murrelet, which forages alongside the marbled murrelet in Alaska.

Elsewhere in the marine habitats of the marbled murrelet, gill-netting restrictions vary. In British Columbia, gill netting is not restricted. In Oregon, gill netting has been prohibited since 1942; in northern California, since 1993; in central California, since 2002. In Washington State, the situation is complex, as Puget Sound is one of the largest salmon fisheries in the country and drives many local economies, especially those of the Makah, Lummi, and other tribal nations that are not subject to state or federal fishing regulations. Reducing bycatch, it was feared, would reduce catch and the economic well-being of these communities.

In 1995, the Washington Department of Fish and Game closed some nontribal fisheries to protect marbled murrelets. In 1997, the hours of gill-net fishing for nontribal fishermen were restricted to daylight only; fishing around dawn and at night when marbled murrelets forage was prohibited. In addition, fishermen had to replace the upper seven feet of their gill nets with highly visible white mesh. Some tribal fisheries are making these changes and equipment amendments voluntarily. After several years, these simple measures seem to be reducing the rates of bycatch for marbled murrelets and for other seabirds as well.

When I first learned about gill-net fishing and marbled murrelet bycatch, I felt remote from the issue. I was still living on the East Coast and felt that the problem—a Pacific Coast one—was being well-handled by the commercial fishermen, federal and state agencies, gill-net manufacturers, scientists, and Audubon Society advocacy groups. But then I looked at what I ate.

Mind you, I am not a holier-than-thou eco-femme, nor a shop-till-you-drop consumer. I fall somewhere in the middle. I do try to make conscious choices about what I buy, who I vote for, and which causes I support, but I am guilty of making some bad, or at least ill-informed, decisions on behalf of our wildlife.

Here's my confession: I have been eating sushi for the past twenty years, never worrying about how the fish were caught or that the oceans might one day run out of the fish that I loved and that other creatures, such as marbled murrelets, needed. A few years ago, a group of conservation organizations published a wallet-sized seafood guide to inform consumers about selecting a fish based on its abundance and on the fishing methods used to harvest it. I obtained a small stack of these guides and passed them out to my friends and family. I told my parents that I wasn't eating salmon because they were on the list and were murrelet food. They said I had gone around the bend. When I ate at a seafood restaurant, I would tuck one of the guides into the menu after I placed my order, hoping I could influence the seafood selection of the next diner. But despite my best intentions, even I couldn't always refrain from eating the fish on the "avoid" list when the "best choice" fish were unavailable.

Feeling like a real hypocrite, I decided to challenge myself to order cucumber rolls and mixed vegetable rolls instead of sushi. A small gesture to be sure, but one that requires me to unwire twenty years of pleasurable habit. So far, it's working. With enough wasabi, soy sauce, and ginger, anything tastes like sushi.

Ten thousand years ago, the meadow where I spent my first morning with marbled murrelets was a pristine forest dominated by coastal redwoods and Douglas firs. There were no roads, only the narrow paths left by deer, elk, mountain lions, rabbits, and the Costanoan people who hunted them. No one can say how many marbled murrelets nested in those trees back then. The Costanoans most certainly saw and heard the birds but left no records of them.

The forests of Gazos Creek survived the arrival of the Europeans in the early seventeenth century and the settlement of coastal lands by Spanish missionaries in the eighteenth century. They did not fare well when rancheros, pioneers, gold diggers, and loggers arrived in waves in the nineteenth century. In 1871, the Pacific Lumber Company opened the first sawmill on the property and began large-scale logging the surrounding forests. Most of the lumber went into building (and then rebuilding) the city of San Francisco. Over the next seventy years, the mill at Gazos Creek was kept in operation by a succession of lumber companies who logged what they could of the old-growth and the second-growth forests as well. In 1962, the mill shut down. The forests along Gazos Creek were reduced to a scattering of old-growth redwoods and Douglas firs, some stands of second-growth trees, smaller deciduous trees, clear-cuts, enormous stumps, dirt roads, and a stagnant millpond. A 120-acre parcel of forest was acquired to be part of a tree farm.

In 1965, Chuck and Margaret Taylor leased the property for a summer youth camp. They built a lodge room, kitchen, dining hall, amphitheatre, and twenty rustic bunkhouses to accommodate one hundred and twenty campers. The millpond was stocked with trout; rowboats and canoes were set on its banks; part of it was lined with concrete to create a swimming area. The old log landings and building pads were paved for an archery range, basketball courts, and tennis courts. For nearly thirty summers, Mountain Camp offered some ten thousand boys and girls classic summer camp fun. In 1989, Chuck Taylor passed away and the camp was sold to a Korean evangelical Christian group from Richmond who re-opened it as a summer church camp. They sold it in 1992 to a Taiwanese foundation in the business of promoting Pacific culture.

By accounts from neighbors living within earshot of the property, what was being promoted on the property was only marginally cultural and not at all pacific. A large hall with two cashier's windows was added to the dining room; when the rifle range was cleaned up later, shell casings of heavy gunnery were found in abundance. The barely electrified camp was now as bright as a city thanks to new heavy-duty, gasoline-powered generators. Year-round, busloads of Taiwanese men from Oakland and San Francisco came to the redwood forest to enjoy their wild weekends. Needless to say, no one was paying any attention to the marbled murrelets or the ancient trees. Nor were they paying attention to the gasoline cans in the generator room.

Neighbors said they could hear the explosion for miles. No one was killed, but the fire burned several structures to the ground and caused a mass exodus of revelers. The group's insurance was cancelled and the property was abandoned in 1997. You can still see the burn marks—blackened bark—on the trunk of one old redwood tree that silently witnessed it all—and probably saw it coming.

The property went on the market for $1.45 million—a hefty price, but this was the California coast and there were redwoods on the property. But who would want a partially burnt and mostly ramshackle camp? Who would buy a parcel of forest knowing they weren't likely to be issued permits to log the old-growth trees? Who would pay such a price and not dream about developing it into pricey Gazos Glen Estates, Redwood Mountain Resort, or Lucky Pacific Culture Ranch? Who? The Sempervirens Fund.

Since 1900, this nonprofit organization has had one singular and successful goal: to acquire redwood forests in the Santa Cruz Mountains for permanent conservation. Its name is taken from *Sequoia sempervirens*, the scientific name of the coastal redwoods (*Sempervirens* means "ever-living"). Through real-estate savvy, creative funding strategies, and a remarkable amount of patience, the group has purchased a total of 21,000 acres of forests, mostly in hundred- or thousand-acre patches. As each patch is acquired, it is transferred to the California Department of Parks and Recreation to become a state park— or part of one. Big Basin Redwoods State Park, Butano State Park, Portola Redwoods State Park, and Castle Rock State Park are part of the Sempervirens Fund legacy. It is the vision of the Sempervirens Fund to patch the parks together into one glorious, contiguous, unfragmented redwood forest. Such a long-range vision takes persistence and perseverance.

Brian Steen, the fund's executive director, has been trying to purchase one privately owned 580-acre property since 1999, when he joined the staff. Files on the property go back to 1990. The owners, an older couple that has lived on the property most of their lives want to log it.

"I told her there was a problem with that," Steen says. "Marbled murrelets."

"You mean fog larks?" came the response to Steen. "Those are just stupid little birds you environmentalists put on the property so we can't log it."

In 1996, the Sempervirens Fund couldn't afford the Gazos Creek property *unless* it had marbled murrelets on it. Ten years earlier, eleven marbled murrelets had been killed when the *Apex Houston* transportation barge spilled 26,100 gallons of crude oil along the coast between San Francisco and Monterey. State and federal laws required the Apex Oil Company of Clayton, Missouri, to fund efforts to restore heavily impacted species. Most of the 1994 settlement money has gone into restoring a population of common murres—a species which suffered 6,000 deaths in the spill. Though 11 marbled murrelets may seem trivial in comparison, they were a state-endangered and federally threatened species and there-fore deserved special consideration. The birds got nine years of consideration and $500,000 for the acquisition of marbled murrelet breeding habitat in the area of the spill. That's about $45,000 of compensation for each of the eleven marbled murrelet.

When the Gazos Creek site came on the market in 1997,

the Sempervirens Fund was ready to pounce, but not without the murrelets.

The Fund hired Steve Singer to tour the property and determine if the old-growth redwoods on the property were potential marbled murrelet nesting habitat. Singer reported that there was one twenty-acre stand that could be considered, at best, "marginal breeding habitat." One day in the future, it might serve the needs of one or two nesting pairs of murrelets. Maybe. There was also a ten-acre stand where Singer had seen marbled murrelets flying in low and below the canopy. The stand was not far from a meadow, Singer noted, that seemed to be a very important area for the marbled murrelets. They regularly flew over it and circled and called above it during the breeding season.

This was *the* meadow. Once a tennis court, it was now something more than a meadow. It was a piece of earth where a man—or woman—could stand, look up, and see a hundred marbled murrelets doing what they have always done, oblivious to what had gone on on the ground below. It is a place where a man could stand, breathe deeply, and feel real hope that what he wrote in a letter twenty years earlier might come to pass: that the marbled murrelets might always be with us. If only those birds could have known how glad Steve Singer was to see them.

With the good news from Singer, the Sempervirens Fund acquired the Gazos Creek property in 1998. The $1.45 million was split three ways: the Fund paid $550,000, the Apex Oil Company paid $500,000, and the Save-the-Redwoods League paid $400,000. The property was transferred to the California Department of State Parks in 1999, which has leased it to the Pescadero Conservation Alliance, for restoration as the Field Research Station, a small center for environmental restoration and education. Crews of volunteers have been working steadily over the years to erase the years of neglect and misuse of the property and hope to have the research station open in the summer of 2006.

Meanwhile, Steve Singer returns to Gazos Creek every summer to survey the marbled murrelets as part of a long-term study funded by the *Apex Houston* oil spill settlement. Singer spends some of his time doing dawn surveys of the birds from the meadow and some of his time working with Tom Hamer on a radar study of the marbled murrelets on the property. The study takes place in a small camper mounted with a marine radar and parked on a hillside just downstream from the meadow. Inside the truck is twenty-five-year-old Melanie Spies, a radar technician hired to track marbled murrelets every morning. The radar sends ultrahigh-frequency radio waves into the airspace above Melanie's truck and the radio waves that bounce off flying objects (marbled murrelets, band-tailed pigeons, bats) reflect back to a receiver that generates tiny blips. From inside the truck, Spies watches the small radar screen for the marbled murrelet's signature blip. Between well-earned yawns, she counts the blips and notes the direction and the time of the bird's flight on a data sheet.

On the morning I visited, Spies had detected 109 marbled murrelets—about twice as many as Singer had detected with his naked-eye survey. No one can best radar in terms of marbled murrelet detections in certain situations; it produces highly accurate counts of birds, but nothing about how high or low the bird was flying or what kinds of calls it made as it flew. No technology can best the human eye or ear in terms of marbled murrelet behavior in any situation. Only a human observer can see the below-canopy flights or hear the silence of a single bird flying into the forest to its nest.

I returned to the meadow at Gazos Creek recently to take Steve Singer's place in the meadow. There were a few July mornings that Singer was too busy to do the required dawn surveys and, since I was still a certified surveyor, I gladly agreed. So did my husband and two sons, then ages eight and ten. I was eager to introduce them to the meadow, a rare bird, and the rigors of dawn surveying.

Thanks to the hospitality of Randy Bennett of the Pescadero Conservation Alliance, we stayed in one of the renovated bunkhouses at the Mountain Camp. This meant we had only a brisk five-minute walk to the survey site.

At 4:30 on the morning of July 1, we woke in the dark, dressed in a total of sixteen layers of warm clothing, put on our headlamps, and marched to the meadow. It was 39 degrees Fahrenheit. We set up a few chairs, established the canopy height, checked the tape recorder, and began scanning the skies. Twelve minutes later I heard two distant *keer* calls.

"Did you hear that?" I asked.

"Hear what?" they replied.

A minute later, I heard several calls, then watched as a single bird flew over the meadow just above the canopy.

"Did you see that?

"See what?" they replied.

I couldn't take the time to explain what they had missed. Another single bird flew over, then another. At 5:35, the birds started calling from somewhere beyond the trees encircling the meadow. My family thought I was imagining things.

"Can we go home now?" asked my eight-year-old. "I'm freezing."

"I'll take him back to the cabin," my groggy husband offered quickly. "I'll have some hot tea ready when you get back."

But my ten-year-old wanted to stay. Though four is a small sample size, I imagine it is large enough to draw out this conclusion: Half the people who sign up to survey marbled murrelets at dawn would happily buy their way out after twenty minutes.

So mother and son continued, happy to be awake, outdoors, and shivering. When my son heard his first bird, it was as if he had discovered gold. When he saw his first bird swooping in below the canopy, he said, "Whoa!"

My son caught on quickly. He learned to point to part of the sky (rather than call out "murrelet!") when he heard the *keer* calls. It was a pleasure—a gift—to see him trying so hard to get a glimpse of these rare birds, to hear their distant calls. I know that two is a statistically insignificant sample size, but it is large enough for me to make this conclusion: For me and my son, the shared pleasure of his first marbled murrelets will always be with us.

CHAPTER 26

It was springtime in British Columbia. Three young graduate students from Simon Fraser University were laughing, singing sea chanties, and fumbling around in pitch-black dark. It was one o'clock in the morning, and they were having the time of their lives. They were cruising the waters of Desolation Sound in an inflatable raft. They were not on spring break, they were seabird biologists at work, trying to net marbled murrelets for banding, blood sampling, and radio tagging. They were on the water most of this night—cold, exhausted, and excited—their small boat carrying a light load of equipment but a lot of stamina and savvy. They were scientists on the cutting edge—cowboys on the frontier of science.

Russell Bradley was steering the boat, more or less straight, about three miles offshore. The boat was a sixteen-foot Zodiac with an outboard motor. Laura McFarlane Tranquilla was leaning out over the front of the boat trying to hold a salmon net on an eight-foot-long pole just above the water. Peggy Yen was leaning off the front, carefully balancing her weight against Tranquilla's as she moved a million-candle-power marine spotlight just above the surface of the water. They were three miles offshore and well out of sight of their base camp at Theodosia Inlet. They were all wearing insulated survival suits, several layers of clothing, fingerless gloves, wool hats, and skid-proof boots. It was April, and the water and nighttime air temperatures hovered around 42 degrees—well above freezing but far from balmy.

As soon as Yen spotted a pair of birds on the water, she shined the light directly on them. Bradley slowed the outboard motor to murrelet-swimming speed. The birds paddled away, but Bradley steered the boat to follow. Tranquilla tightened her grip on the handle of the salmon net and slowly dipped the net several inches below the surface of the water. Everyone in the boat was very awake, very tense, and speaking in whispers. As the boat glided toward the birds, one began to fly off, but Tranquilla deftly lifted the net up in time to catch the other, and, with a quick twist of the handle, closed the opening of the net. Tranquilla described it as a bit like an alien abduction.

Tranquilla brought the netted murrelet into the center of the boat and to a makeshift processing table—the top of a plastic storage container. Yen carefully took the bird out of the net and placed it in a dark-colored cloth bag. Though the murrelet didn't peck at the bag, flap its wings, or try to escape, it called a muted *keer* from within the bag. Its mate, still on the water, called back—a touching moment that motivated the students to work even more efficiently.

With the Zodiac bobbing up and down on the water, Yen slid the bag off the bird enough to expose its body but keep its head covered. She held the bird still while Tranquilla used a pair of vise grips to place a metal identification band around its ankle. They took measurements of its wing and bill. They looked for a brood patch, measured it and used Spencer Sealy's rating system to assign it a score. They examined the pattern and color of the bird's feathers, which might help them determine the bird's age and stage in the molting cycle. Then, with a sterilized pin, Tranquilla pricked the tarsal vein of the bird and collected one drop of blood. The DNA in that one drop would later be analyzed at a lab at Simon Fraser University to determine the gender of the bird. The banding took one minute. Taking blood took another two.

Then came the tricky part—the radio tagging. Tranquilla turned the murrelet carefully onto its stomach and parted a few feathers between its shoulder blades. She swabbed the exposed skin with rubbing alcohol and then inserted an 18-gauge needle in about an eighth of an inch. With the skill of a surgeon, she removed the needle and then inserted a metal wire tipped with a tiny hook. She twisted it ever so slightly counterclockwise to anchor it under the bird's skin. Yen put a drop of glue—a type called Vetbond Surgical Adhesive—at the point where the anchor met the bird's skin to help it stay in place. The wire was attached to a tiny lithium battery, a transmitter, and an antenna that measured about four inches in length. This whole contraption looks like a funky, dangly earring, but it is a subcutaneous avian transmitter—a radio tag. The tagging was completed in twenty minutes. Yen gently put the bird over the edge of the boat and back onto the water. It gave the side of the boat a sharp peck and then swam off toward the calls of its mate.

Each tag is tuned to a different radio frequency and will send out a signal that can be picked up by a telemetry antenna. If and when the tagged bird flies inland, researchers can track the signal into the forest and, with any luck, to its nest. This technology is effective for locating marbled murrelet nests, but it is controversial since the impact of the radio tagging on the birds themselves has not been thoroughly studied. Some scientists believe that tagging places undue stress on the bird and may interrupt its breeding cycle. In fact, some marbled murrelets with well-developed brood patches were tagged but failed to initiate nesting after capture. Experimenting with ways to reduce this stress, some scientists in California have tried sedating the marbled murrelets with an inhalation anesthetic prior to the radio attachment. Though all the birds were alert and exhibited normal behavior—flying, diving, preening—they exhibited significant behavior differences. In one year, the anesthetized birds began nesting much later than untreated birds; in the next year, only 18 percent of the treated birds initiated nests after capture as compared to 58 percent of birds that were not anesthetized. Scientists have not yet isolated the cause for the low nesting rates; it is likely related to the use of anesthesia, but many factors may be involved.

Tranquilla, Yen, and Bradley are well aware of the potential stress and trauma their work can place on the marbled murrelets they capture. They have sympathy for their subjects and work as quickly and steadily as they can. Even with Tranquilla's rock-steady hands, not all procedures can be performed on the Zodiac. To take more than a drop of blood from a captured bird requires the use of a needle and syringe and thus a trip to shore to work on land. More than a drop in this case is two grams (.07 ounces) of blood. Lab technicians will measure the levels of corticosterone—a stress hormone released by all vertebrates during events such as food shortages, storms, disturbance, predation, or capture and handling by researchers. The lab will also test the blood for vitellogenin, a protein found in egg-producing female birds. Gone are the days when scientists had to collect and dissect the birds to study their fertility.

Just forty-five minutes after the capture, banding, blood sampling, and radio tagging, the scientists return the bird to the spot where they captured it. If all goes well, the students will catch four or five more birds every night they go out. On a bad night, when the marbled murrelets successfully evade capture, the trio amuse themselves by watching the stars and the bioluminescence. Good nights and bad, by the end of the summer they hope to catch three to four hundred birds, band and collect blood from all of them, and place radio tags on seventy to one hundred of them.

When marbled murrelets are not being chased and tagged, they are being watched. Researchers return daily to Desolation Sound, to the area where they tagged the birds, to pick up their radio signals by antennae. Early in the season, the researchers find most of the tagged birds on the water. As breeding season progresses, the researchers will pick up some signals on the water every second day—a pattern they describe as "on-off." What they hope this means is that the tagged bird is part of a breeding pair and that it is "on" the water one day, and "off" the next when it is in the forest incubating an egg.

To find that egg, a hired professional helicopter pilot flies over the forest with two researchers and a telemetry antenna. Once the team picks up a bird's signal, the helicopter pilot hovers over the site until the researchers get the strongest signal and the most precise location of the nest. Even with the best pilots, "precise" is the size of a football field. Working with Global Positioning System (GPS) technology and a handheld antenna, a ground crew tracks the signal to the stand and to the nest tree. After the breeding season, researchers climb the trees to look for the nest. Though radio tracking is as high-tech as marbled murrelet research gets these days, it is not just a matter of pointing an antenna into a tree and saying "there's the nest." Tracking a bird is intense and physically exhausting work; it can take as long as two weeks to zoom in on the nest tree once its signal has been detected.

Between 1998 and 2001, the scientists from Simon Fraser University radio-tagged 290 marbled murrelets—169 of these tagged birds were radio-tracked to inland nesting locations. They discovered 71 nests, 66 in old-growth conifers (one tree held two nests). Four nests were discovered in very unusual locations.

One was in a deciduous tree—a 130-year-old red alder in an unlogged deciduous-coniferous forest close by Theodosia Inlet. The nest was about sixty feet up the hundred-foot-tall alder on a wide limb heavily covered by moss. Three were found on the ground—on cliffs as far as thirteen miles inland—in areas without large trees with potential nesting platforms nearby.

Nests in a deciduous tree and on the cliffs are very rare, Russell Bradley tells me, and should not be seen as evidence that marbled murrelets aren't dependent on old-growth coniferous forests. "The nests in the alder and on the cliffs had the same critical attributes as conventional sites," he says. "A wide platform with thick moss as substrate, adequate cover, and easy access in and out. Such features are generated in mature and old-growth forests and not in second-growth forests. These birds are *very* specific in their habitat requirements."

The thought of spending all night on the water in a Zodiac chasing seabirds sounded fascinating. Just being on the water under a canopy of stars sounded strange, exciting, humbling, a bit eerie, potentially dangerous, and very attractive. I say "sounded" because what I knew of radio tagging I had only heard secondhand—from the Simon Fraser students and other researchers. Deep down, I was hoping I wouldn't have to actually get in a Zodiac myself and experience this potentially dangerous fieldwork firsthand.

Several years ago, when I began writing a book on fire fighting, I attended a few training classes and asked a 911 dispatcher and the local fire chief a thousand questions so I could put together a step-by-step narrative on how firefighters put out a house fire. After my ninety-ninth "and then what did you do?" question, the fire chief said, "You know what? You need to feel some heat."

I knew what he meant, and he was right. Before I had time to panic, I was putting on eighty pounds of fire-fighting gear, breathing with a regulator and air tank, and following five firefighters up a dark staircase in a burning building. It was a practice burn in a controlled setting, but the fire was real and very hot. Nothing a firefighter will ever tell me could replace that firsthand experience. Now, years later, it was time to stop asking questions and "feel the heat." I needed to get myself into a Zodiac and understand what is involved in meeting the marbled murrelet on its own terms: on the water. By the time I had convinced myself of this fact, the Simon Fraser crew had finished their radio-tagging project. Luckily, there were other scientist-cowboys rounding up and tagging murrelets elsewhere along on the coast.

In April 2004, I called Marty Raphael at the U.S. Forest Service's Pacific Northwest Research Station in Olympia, Washington. Raphael has been involved with marbled murrelets since 1992, when he began a long-term monitoring study of the birds as part of the Northwest Forest Plan. Raphael and his colleagues and crews had done years of dawn surveys, years of radar studies, and in 2004 they started their first radio-tagging project in Puget Sound and in the Straits of Juan de Fuca. I asked Raphael if I could tag along.

Raphael made it clear that there might not be room for me in one of the two three-person Zodiacs they were using. Raphael and his lead biologists were still assembling and training their tagging crews, and the boats might be full by the time I arrived in mid-May.

If there *was* room in a boat, Raphael warned the weather and the water might not cooperate; crews don't go out in rain or in water with swells over two feet.

If the skies and seas were calm, Raphael continued, he couldn't guarantee that I would actually see any marbled murrelets. It was still early in the marbled murrelet breeding season, and the birds were still offshore.

If I *did* see marbled murrelets, he said, there was no guarantee anyone would be able to catch them. The birds were boat shy and very, very difficult to catch.

If they managed to capture a bird, Raphael said I probably wouldn't get to see it being tagged. I would be in the back-up boat, not the tagging boat.

I decided to take my chances, and, as luck would have it, Raphael called on my first night in Port Angeles to say the crews were going out and that there was room for me in the back-up boat. As I have come to expect from following the call of the marbled murrelet, the experience was not what I had expected.

At 10 P.M., I drove to a boat launch at Ediz Hook to meet Raphael and four other Forest Service biologists. I was given a full-length padded survival suit, one with an emergency whistle in the upper left pocket. If I went overboard and expected anyone to find me in the dark, this tiny whistle would save me. I pulled the suit on over my clothes while the crew unloaded two Zodiacs, the *Keer* and the *Fog Lark*, from the trailers and onto the boat ramp.

I stepped into the *Fog Lark* with Raphael and Lydia Miller, the biologist I had met earlier on Dabob Bay. After an equipment check and a boat-safety lesson, we headed out from shore around 11 P.M.

The sky may have been full of stars, comets, and fireworks, but I wasn't going to see them that night. As soon as I tipped my head back to look for the Pleiades, Raphael handed me a million-candlepower marine spotlight. I wasn't taking up space on this boat to stargaze or watch Miller do all the work—I was going to search the seas for marbled murrelets. Though only one boat does the actual radio-tagging, both boats look for birds and capture them if they can. We kept in contact with the *Keer* by two-way radio.

You do not try to sit like a normal person in such a boat. Your legs are denied their full range of motion because you are wearing something not unlike the overstuffed snowsuit your mother made you wear when you were six. You flop over the front of the boat so that all your weight is on your stomach and every wavelet feels like a Heimlich maneuver. To prevent yourself from lurching forward suddenly, falling out of the boat, and being run over by it, you rest some of your weight on your knees. If you are in charge of the marine spotlight (I was), you must shine this light toward the horizon so that the bottom edge of the beam just barely grazes the top of the water. Then, you begin scanning to the left and right so that you cover an area just shy of 90 degrees on either side of the boat. If you scan past 90 degrees, the beam (powered by a car battery) will shine in the eyes of the boat driver. Raphael had to remind me of this fact more than once.

So, while Raphael was driving the boat out a few miles from shore, I was swiveling left and right on my elbows, scanning the water, looking for small, light-colored objects on the water—the marbled murrelets. I was scanning, shifting, scanning, searching, twisting, lifting, steadying, looking, seeking, and swiveling. I saw nothing that looked like a bird. After just fifteen minutes, staying focused on what's at the end of the beam becomes difficult. My eyes followed the long beam of light but got lost in the part of the beam that is about five feet from my face. There was no water, no boat, just part of a light beam, a fuzzy whiteness that does not contain marbled murrelets. The wind was drying my eyes out. I blinked and scanned and scanned and blinked. My head was sinking, and my shoulders were rising up to meet my ears. My left leg fell asleep. It was Miller's turn.

When I sat up, I looked up to the sky and to the brightest Milky Way I'd seen in years. There were too many stars to be able to pick out any familiar constellations. As my eyes adjusted, I caught a few shooting stars. For a moment I thought they were marbled murrelets in flight.

Miller scanned the water for twenty minutes. When I saw her head sinking and shoulders slouching, we switched places. I took a deep breath and started scanning.

"What's that?" I asked.

Raphael cut the engine.

"Did you see something?"

"It was something white off to the left. Maybe two birds," I replied, pointing and hoping.

"Keep the spotlight on it."

Raphael steered the boat toward the two white objects and then put the engine in neutral.

"Those are rhinoceros auklets," he said.

We lingered for a minute, watching these chunky birds with largish beaks with a small rhino-style horn. Raphael turned the boat back around, and we moved on.

"What's that?" I asked again a few minutes later.

"A Pacific loon," Raphael replied. We moved on.

"What's that?" Raphael asked.

We moved close and discovered it was a very large gull.

I was weary and ready to apologize to Raphael, curl up in the bottom of the boat, and fall asleep. Only three more hours.

"What's tha—?" I began.

It was a whitecap. Two of them.

"Easy mistake," Raphael said.

So were the murrelet-shaped bits of kelp I kept spotting. And the other whitecaps, the wisps of fog on the water, the piece of bark, the stick, and the bottle. The hours passed like this. Miller and I took regular turns with the spotlight.

Finally, I caught two very small white objects in the spotlight. There they were 50 feet away—two marbled murrelets bobbing on the water, the first ones I had ever seen at sea. Raphael instructed me to keep the spotlight on them, to freeze them like deer in the headlights as he maneuvered the boat toward them. Miller held the net low in the water. Raphael radioed to the other boat. We were moving in for the capture.

I cannot say exactly what happened next, other than the birds disappeared. I may have blinked, moved the spotlight off the birds during the jolt of a wave, or lost sight of the two birds behind a wave or among the whitecaps. Whatever happened, those two birds were gone. There was no chance of them ending up in Miller's net or anywhere near a radio tag.

We continued our search for another few hours, but then we turned back around 3 A.M. when the wind picked up and turned the water into an enormous flock of whitecaps. On shore, we unloaded the gear and loaded the boats back onto the trailers. I was disappointed, but not too badly.

By August, the crews had captured twenty-eight birds and had tracked three to their nests. Though Raphael seemed disappointed that this number fell so shy of the forty birds he had hoped to capture and tag, I saw it as a stunning victory. No matter how many multidegreed biologists you can fit in a boat, a marbled murrelet is never going to yield its secrets willingly—except, perhaps, to another marbled murrelet. Until someone invents a gizmo to call, lure, entice, or inveigle a marbled murrelet, researchers have few options but to chase after them with all the energy they can muster.

After my adventures in the Straits of Juan de Fuca, I made a brief stop in Tacoma, at the Slater Museum of Natural History on the campus of the University of Puget Sound. I wanted to see the egg that, seventy-three years earlier, Stanley

Warburton, his wife, and Earl Osburn had discovered on the ground in Alaska. Though Warburton and Osburn were convinced it belonged to a ground-nesting marbled murrelet, no one had ever proven this scientifically. No marbled murrelet researcher or oologists had revisited the egg and compared it to a bona fide marbled murrelet egg. Without questioning my credentials—did I have any?—or motivation, Dennis Paulson, the director emeritus of the museum, brought me a tray of auk eggs that included the Warburton-Osburn egg.

It was in nine pieces. It was mostly whole with the thin, white albumen sagging like a deflated balloon inside the shell. It was about the size of a chicken egg. I found it hard to imagine a bird the size of a marbled murrelet doing much more than waddling a few steps with such a burden. Flying seemed out of the question. To my eye, the egg color was pale green with spots of lavender-gray and brown that formed a kind of Milky Way band around its lower third. The closer I looked at the spots, however, the less willing I was to call them gray or brown. The gray had the cast of silver, the brown seemed both bronze and gold. It was a very beautiful egg.

HANDLE WITH EXTREME CARE read a small note next to it. I dared not pick it up, so I took out my camera to take a photograph. Naturally, I had forgotten to buy film. So I decided to sketch the egg in my notebook. And then I sat there, staring at the egg. Though many marbled murrelet researchers knew about the egg, none I had talked to had ever seen it. There were only two people I could think of who would be interested in this egg—Harry Carter and Spencer Sealy, who were collaborating on an article about the early breeding records of the species. I thought that a photograph might be useful to them and might possibly prevent the egg from remaining in oological limbo.

As fate would have it, the Slater Museum had just acquired a high-resolution digital camera, and Paulson kindly agreed to photograph the egg and send images to me, Carter, and Sealy by e-mail.

In the spring of 2005, Harry Carter and Spencer Sealy published an article in the *Northwestern Naturalist* (the old *Murrelet*) entitled "Who Solved the Mystery of the Marbled Murrelet?" Though I had expected the answer to be Hoyt Foster, the authors credited Stanley Warburton and Earl Osburn. After examining the photograph of the egg and consulting a noted egg expert, they agreed that this egg is evidence of the first confirmed nest (of any kind) as well as the first confirmed ground nest of the marbled murrelet. They don't feel, however, that Warburton's and Osburn's names should replace Hoyt Foster's. They believe that these men should share the limelight (dim as it is so late in the show) with E. J. Booth, W. Feyer, R. D. Harris, and A. B. Johnson—men whose discoveries of eggs, dead chicks, orphaned chicks, and stunned adult murrelets can now be considered "first" breeding records of the marbled murrelet despite the fact that no one could prove it at the time. I was thrilled to know that Warburton's beautiful, cracked egg still had a story to tell.

CHAPTER 27

I cannot tell you exactly why I needed to see that cracked egg. Nor why I felt an urgency to ride a Zodiac at midnight, sit in a lawn chair in a meadow at dawn, see the window where naturalist William Dawson thrust his head, or lay my eyes on a metal plate that marks the missing branch where a strange seabird made its nest thirty years ago. That I sought out these experiences is a mystery to me. That I continue to treasure them is even more mysterious. With all the bigger, grander, and more popular attractions in the world, why would I choose to spend my time pursuing the story of a rare bird that requires me to be inconvenienced, uncomfortable, relentless, and often exhausted?

Perhaps it is because I felt a small thrill of discovery when I first learned about this bird—a bird few people had heard of and even fewer knew much about. I had made a connection to another species—a rare one—that would allow me to step out of myself for a little while and follow an unbeaten path. Little did I know my path would lead me to people who had also chosen to step out of their lives among human beings and become engaged, obsessed, and entangled with a bird. All recognized that quality that makes a thing worth protecting, saving, losing sleep over. They belong in my pantheon of heroes, of rare birds.

Included in that pantheon is a man named Carl Schurz, the first U.S. Secretary of the Interior, under Rutherford B. Hayes. In 1879, Schurz proposed to establish a national park to protect the redwood forests of northern California. Even back then, concern was growing for the future of the redwood forests and the continued abuse of the forestlands from logging. Schurz's proposal was not approved, nor were any of the numerous proposals and legislation introduced in the following decades to preserve the ancient forests. In 1918, a group of conservation-minded citizens formed the Save-the-Redwoods League and began purchasing redwood forests through private donations.

Though neither Secretary Schurz nor any member of the Save-the-Redwoods League might have ever seen or heard a marbled murrelet or known the names of any of the creatures of the redwood forests, they knew the redwoods were unusual, rare, and worth saving. Beyond the trees themselves, they must have been convinced that such forests held mysteries that, too, were unusual, rare, and worth saving. Though such mysteries might take several lifetimes to understand, these early conservationists had the foresight—and generosity—to allow future generations the chance to understand the forests' long-held secrets. Nearly a century of conservation pressure paid off. In 1968, President Lyndon Johnson authorized the establishment of Redwood National Park.

Today, the original park is part of Redwood National and State Parks (which includes Prairie Creek, Del Norte, and Jedediah Smith Redwoods State Parks) and has an estimated forty thousand acres of suitable (potential) marbled murrelet habitat. In 2001, researchers at Humboldt State University in

Arcata began a four-year radio-tagging study of marbled murrelets in the park. Percy Hébert and Rick Golightly were the
lead scientists on the study, which required the time and talents of seventy individuals, mostly biologists from the university and state and federal agencies. Their goal was to determine
whether marbled murrelets (chicks and adults) respond to
human disturbance—people hiking along a trail, the noise of
traffic and car doors slamming, and the sound of chain saws
used for the maintenance of public trails in the park.
Researchers radio-tagged one hundred birds and were able to
observe twenty-four of them at their nest sites during several
disturbance trials. The videotaped birds—both chicks and
adults—did spend more time in "alert postures," but did not
flush when disturbed. Some birds initiated nests, others didn't.
Some eggs were predated, others weren't. Some chicks fledged,
others didn't. Researchers may not be able to determine what
influence the actual disturbances had on the bird's productivity,
but they can confirm that the bird's current rate of reproduction is not adequate to sustain its population in California.
Predation at the nest by corvids is still the major issue. Even
in Redwood National and State Parks, where the quantity of
potential nesting habitat is great, the presence of ravens and
jays decreases the quality of that habitat for marbled murrelets.
Percy Hébert and Rick Golightly believe that the abundance
of these nest predators in the parks is directly linked to the
presence of human beings, specifically, to their food.

"People get such a reward, such personal pleasure, from
feeding wildlife," says Golightly, "that it is very hard to break
that habit. But it's a real problem. People bring food into the
forest and the corvids have learned to follow the people into

the forest where they don't usually go—even if it's for just one potato chip. It doesn't take much to feed a jay or for a jay to connect the slamming of a car door to that potato chip. In the parks here, the rangers have started saying 'feed a jay, kill a murrelet.' That's not out of line. That's not extreme."

The researchers from Humboldt State University also learned from their radio-tagging study that the murrelets will reuse the same nest year after year, that they do fly into the forest and land on branches even if they are not nesting, and that they use stands of pristine old-growth forest. All the nests they discovered were in coastal redwoods and Douglas firs on wide platforms—the conventional marbled murrelet nest site. One of the Douglas firs grew near Little Lost Man Creek. This fir was one hundred and fifty feet tall, four feet wide, and hundreds of years old. It took Percy Hébert and a crew of surveyors three weeks to find this tree. It took me two hours to find it on a hike through the drainage of what I now call Nearly Lost Woman Creek.

I wanted to make this hike so that I could learn firsthand what kind of work scientists do *after* they tag a marbled murrelet. Rick Golightly told me to "dress warm" and meet his two biologists at 3:15 A.M. in the parking lot outside the university's wildlife department. My day began at 2:45, with the usual layering on of clothing followed by a drive along the foggy coastal highway. I was to meet my guides, Steve Mullin and James Hall, in the parking lot at 3:15. Mullin is an undergraduate and Hall is a graduate student in wildlife biology. Both are at Humboldt State University and both have been hired to assist Golightly and Hébert in monitoring several of the nest sites in the park. That morning, we were hiking to one tree to listen and watch for a murrelet that Hébert and another crew member had tracked there the previous year but had not detected in the tree since.

"How did you get interested in marbled murrelets, James?" I asked during our half-hour drive to Little Lost Man Creek.

Hall responded in that enthusiastic, rapid-fire style that marks many people affiliated with marbled murrelets.

"Well, let's see. I went to UC–Davis to study wildlife ecology as an undergrad, and then after graduating, I decided to study shorebirds for my master's at Humboldt State. I started surveying snowy plovers, which, as you probably know, are a threatened species and nest in protected beaches along the coast here in Humboldt County. I really enjoyed that job, so when I heard about this marbled murrelet project I went to Rick Golightly—you've met Rick, right?—and he said they could use someone like me, someone with some surveying experience. The job's great for me since my wife works at the university, and I am not really sure what I am going to do next. I like being in the woods."

"How about you, Steve?" I asked, "How did you get involved with this very odd seabird?"

"Bad luck."

I waited for him to laugh and then elaborate. He chose not to.

When we arrived at the Little Lost Man Creek parking lot, we put on our headlamps and backpacks with snacks and water and walked toward the trailhead.

"Here, you might need this." Steve handed me a sturdy, five-foot-long stick.

"Oh, no thanks," I replied, "I don't usually use a walking stick. I'll be okay."

"It's for the mountain lions."

"Oh," I said, waiting for him to laugh. He chose not to, but he did elaborate.

"We've seen mountain lions around here the last few times we've been out on surveys. Last month we had to abort one of our surveys because there was one right along the trail. We stopped, but it wouldn't back off. We waited as long as we could, but after ten minutes we turned back."

"Oh," I said, taking the stick.

We started down a trail at a brisk pace, Steve in the lead. As it was still too dark to get a view of the forest, I kept my gaze on the few feet of ground covered by my headlamp. We turned off the trail, walked along the creek for a ways, and then stepped across it on a path of rocks—most of which I missed. Once over the creek, we began bushwhacking our way through the forest—an obstacle course of fallen trees, rotting trunks, switch-size saplings, ferns, and vines. I kept close to Steve as he seemed to be following a path of sorts, though I didn't see any signs of a trail.

"How do you know where you're going?" I asked.

Steve bent down a twig of a nearby tree to show me an inch-wide piece of yellow-green reflective tape. The previous summer, the Humboldt State University crew had attached the tape to various branches to mark out a path leading to the nest tree once they found it. They weren't exactly generous with the tape, but Steve found piece after piece without a single wrong turn.

We continued hiking, and I was chatting, a bit loudly for
the sake of the mountain lion. The forest was muggy and quite
a bit warmer than I had expected. I was probably a wee bit
overdressed, but when I am told to "dress warm" by a scientist,
I do so. The terrain began to get steeper. We were climbing up
the drainage. I stopped talking so I could get enough air into
my lungs. Steve was hiking full steam. We had to get to the
tree by 4:45 to start the survey, and Steve didn't want to be
late. I was starting to breathe harder. We were crawling under
gigantic fallen logs on our bellies, our backpacks scraping on
the undersides of the trees. Soon I was sweating. I do not
mean perspiring. I was dripping.

With a quick apology, I stopped, took off one of my
jackets, and took a quick swig of water from the bottle in my
knapsack. Refreshed, I continued. Up. The slope may not have
been *exactly* 89.5 degrees—just shy of impossible—but it sure
felt like it. Even Steve's and James's pace slowed. Every step was
like climbing an attic staircase with treads two feet apart. I
grabbed onto saplings and branches to pull myself up. The
ground was soft and my footing unsure. I was really sweating.
My long underwear shirt was clinging to my skin. My neck
was wet. Not only that, I was getting light-headed. I tried to
breathe deeply, steadily, and put one foot in front of the next
until it passed. I stopped and offered to let James go ahead of
me. He declined.

I walked on a few more labored paces, still light-headed,
verging on dizzy. I had never experienced this before, but
neither had I spent any time climbing straight up in the dark
before breakfast.

Suddenly, and probably just in time, I realized that neither James nor Steve was going to ask "Are you okay?" or make sure I survived to tell the tale. How were they supposed to know how many layers of clothes I had put on? How could they know I was seeing stars? I was faced with two choices: I could collapse and be left in the woods as mountain lion bait while James and Steve went bird-watching, or I could apologize (again) and take off all my clothes. "I am sorry," I announced as casually as I could. "I have to stop a minute. I think I'm overheating."

Silence.

"Okay. Whatever. Fine. We can stop a minute."

In that minute, I took off my fleece shirt, my boots, my water-resistant overpants, my fleece sweatpants, my T-shirt, my long underwear pants. I stood there in my underwear, my long undershirt, and my wool socks. I took a long swig of water and felt a welcome chill. I breathed as deeply and slowly as I could, then put back on the lightest shirt and loosest pants I had. I stuffed the rest of the wretched layers into my knapsack.

I do not know what James and Steve were doing while I was having my near-death experience. I was so focused on breathing and staying alive, I didn't even look around. I imagine they were trying to divert their eyes from the whole scene, hoping I would rally for the final ascent, or wishing Rick or Percy had sent along a real stripper. After a few minutes, we continued hiking—up, of course—another fifteen minutes before we reached the nest tree. It was a beauty. So was the small rotting log I sat down on. We all rummaged through our backpacks for snacks and water bottles and then settled into silence to start the dawn watch.

While we sat there—waiting for a single bird to land in one tree—I had to ask myself: Why am I doing this? If an experience of this bird takes this much work, would anyone miss it should it become extinct? Who in their right mind would hike this far into the forest for the possibility of seeing or hearing a rare bird? Would I have hiked this far to see a common raven? Why does the fate of this bird matter to me?

I thought about the work James, Steve, and the hundreds of other biologists have been doing since the mid-1980s. Twenty years' and at least a billion dollars' worth of effort to learn enough about a bird to realize that it probably cannot be recovered. Is it hubris to think that in just a few decades we can recover a species that began evolving some twelve million years ago during the Miocene? Deep down, do we believe that we can recover it—or even stabilize the bird's population—without recovering its lost habitat? Little of the already logged areas will ever return to old-growth forest; most will be harvested again before they are a century old. It seems absurd to expect the marbled murrelet to survive in the patches and fragments we have left it, in a forest full of predators we have encouraged to thrive, in an ocean we cannot keep clean or free from entangling nets. Perhaps no one really expects to recover this bird, but they cannot bring themselves to stop trying, to say out loud that this bird costs too much to save.

We heard a few distant *keer* calls in Little Lost Man Creek that morning, but none of us saw or heard any bird in the tree. Perhaps we had missed it. Perhaps the bird never showed up. It was a long way to come to detect a probable absence.

Because it was now light out and I had regained my equi-
librium, I could enjoy the forest. What I enjoyed most was the
sound of the ground under my feet—soft, hollow, pithy. It
had a strange thump to it when I tapped it with my stick. All
of a sudden, I felt the soles of my feet. They had never walked
so far off the beaten path in such a forest. I wasn't walking on
dirt, possibly not even on earth. I was standing, firmly rooted,
on thousands and thousands of years of fallen redwood needles and trees. I wondered where the original forest floor was
before the trees fell here and raised up the floor six, ten, twelve
feet—the diameter of their trunks. I was standing on a huge
raft of wood, floating. I was almost giddy with joy.

It was a feeling I had again while standing in the middle
of a meadow in Prairie Creek Redwood State Park one
morning, not long after my climb with James and Steve. I was
with Heather Brown, one of the Mad River Biologists who
conducts survey training courses. I had a plane to catch home
later that morning, and I wanted to squeeze in one more dawn
survey before I left marbled murrelet country for the year.

Heather had been surveying marbled murrelets in
northern California for ten years. She is as good as surveyors
get, but she had just finished a week of surveys at a nearby site
where she didn't see many birds. Worried that she might have
lost her touch (or her acute sense of hearing or sight), Heather
was back at Prairie Creek for one dawn survey that would tell
her where the problem lay. Within five seconds of our arrival
in the meadow, I knew that the problem was not Heather's.
She detected a dozen or so marbled murrelets a full ten minutes before I saw anything but floaters in my eyes. To help me
out, she pointed to the piece of sky where the birds were. I

looked and followed her finger as she traced their arcing flight over the meadow. But I saw nothing.

When the sky began to brighten, I started seeing birds. Singly, in pairs, and in groups as large as six they flew in from the sea, circled and called over the meadow, and spun off in different directions over the canopy. In no time Heather reached the minimum of thirty detections needed to prove that her eyes and ears were working just fine. I thought Heather would now pack her binoculars and head home to bed. Why do more work than you have to? I thought that after ten years of marbled murrelet surveys—ten summers of sleep deprivation, hundreds of mornings of *keer* calls, circling flights, and below-canopy behaviors—the thrill would be gone. But Heather Brown didn't take off. She put her tape recorder away and just stood there to watch the rest of the show.

"Wow!" she yelled. "Did you see that?" Luckily, I had. Eight birds had come wheeling in over the meadow, intent on impressing us with their acrobatics. They were swooping and diving and circling with energy like I had never seen.

A single bird came flying in low and silently not five feet above our heads. We could hear its buzzing wings.

"Whoa!" Heather yelled, as we ducked our heads.

We watched for a full half-hour as if we were watching fireworks on the Fourth of July. "Wow!" "That was awesome!" "Whoa!" "That was amazing." Heather pulled out her binoculars and followed two birds flying close together just above the canopy. And then Heather said something I've never heard a marbled murrelet surveyor say: "They're so pudgy and cute!"

I laughed, but it's true. Marbled murrelets are pudgy and cute. And they are chunky and neckless. They are fast, camouflaged, and crepuscular. They are *still* secretive, elusive, and yes, mysterious. They are divers, auks, and murrelets. They are fog larks, marbleds, buzz bombs, and merlits. They are magnificent and spectacular.

And I was standing in a meadow, on top of the world, grateful to be in their universe.

EPILOGUE
2005

Under the Endangered Species Act, the U.S. Fish and Wildlife Service must review the status of its listed species every five years. Such a review is based on the "best available scientific and commercial information" to determine whether a change in listing status is warranted. The marbled murrelet was due for such a review in 1997, but not until 2002, when it was sued by a timber industry group, did the service take steps to conduct the review.

In January 2003, the service began its requests for the "best available" information since its 1992 listing. A second request was made in July 2003. The U.S. Fish and Wildlife Service's regional office in Portland, Oregon, received more than 450 documents, reports, data sets, and comment letters. After creating a database of all the information, the service hired EDAW, an environmental consulting company based in Seattle, to synthesize the information for the report. EDAW organized a panel of scientists with expertise in seabird biology, genetics, and marine and forest ecology. Tom Hamer, Harry Carter, and Kim Nelson were among the seven panelists. The panelists spent five months reviewing the database and preparing their report. In March 2004, the report was completed.

From the available information, the report concluded that "the long-term survival of the marbled murrelet in Washington, Oregon, and California is not certain." The world population of marbled murrelets the scientists reported was estimated at 947,500 birds, with 91 percent in

Alaska, 7 percent in British Columbia, and 2 percent total in three states where it is federally listed. The scientists predicted a continued population decline over the next forty years, with the largest relative declines in California—especially in the Santa Cruz Mountains, where local extinction may be a concern. The population declines, they stated, were due primarily to the effects of old-growth logging combined with poor reproductive success from corvid predation in there maining forest patches, especially those near human settlements. Though mortality from gill-net fishing has been reduced dramatically, mortality from oil pollution has continued. "At present and for the foreseeable future, [the] remnant populations are struggling to be self-sustaining . . . and face potential extinction during the next century."

The report was sent to the regional Fish and Wildlife Service Pacific Regional Office in Portland for review. In April, the two reviewers confirmed that the marbled murrelet deserved continued protection and recommended no change in its status as a federally threatened species. The reviewers in Portland sent the study and their recommendation to the Department of the Interior in Washington, D.C. Three days later, the Department of the Interior requested that the Portland office delay the official announcement of its position for four months. That amount of time, the Department of the Interior explained, was needed for thoroughly reviewing the documents.

The official announcement came on September 1, 2004 from Assistant Secretary of the Interior Craig Manson. Going against its own scientists at the Portland regional office, the administration of President George W. Bush decided that, though the marbled murrelet populations continue to decline, the Washington-Oregon-California populations should not be considered a distinct population segment worthy of protection. Translated, since the estimated Alaska population of the birds is over 800,000 (without special protection) and the British Columbia population of birds is between 55,000 and 78,000 (with some protection), the federal government questioned the need to continue the costly protection of a bird over three states that it believed constituted the southern edge of its range in North America.

To its credit, the U.S. Fish and Wildlife Service did not immediately delist the bird. It asked for more information. In early 2005, it funded a genetic study of the bird across its entire range to determine scientifically if indeed the "southern" population in the tri-state area forms a distinct genetic population segment. Once this study is completed, the U.S. Fish and Wildlife Service will have a year to decide whether to continue federal protection of the marbled murrelet or to remove the protections—a decision that could ultimately increase logging in old-growth coastal forests and reduce the amount of habitat the government acquires for the bird. The delisting process would involve a year of meetings, a public comment period, and any number of lawsuits from environmental groups. The big question facing decision makers—from the Department of the Interior to individual members of the public (birders or not)—is whether or not we have the political or moral obligation to save this rare bird and its vanishing habitat.

... going ...

... as the ... from our nest ... confirmed by ... who saw it leave nest minutes or less before we saw it.

It's mottled underside (marbled). then left flying towards us branch.

Second adult returned at 7:05 am and lay exhausted on branch with a larger ...

A NEW EPILOGUE FOR A
STILL RARE BIRD
2013

With this Mountaineers Books edition of *Rare Bird*, I have the opportunity to reflect on the changes that have occurred in the life of the marbled murrelet since 2005. There is a little good news, much bad news, and the looming question we cannot yet answer: Can this imperiled seabird be saved?

The good news is that, despite constant pressure from the timber industry and because of constant pressure from conservation groups, the marbled murrelet is still on the list of federally threatened species in the United States (outside Alaska) and Canada. This may sound like bad news, but I consider it good news because the murrelet cannot survive as a species without such protection. When I finished writing *Rare Bird* in 2005, I didn't realize how close the murrelet was to losing this protection in the United States—protection that has been provided to it by the Endangered Species Act since 1992.

By 2005, the U.S. Fish and Wildlife Service had requested a rangewide genetic study of the murrelet to help determine whether or not the birds in Washington, Oregon, and California—birds representing just 2 percent of the entire population—qualified as a "distinct population segment." Under the Endangered Species Act, the federal government must protect not only entire populations of listed species but also subspecies and subgroups considered to be distinct population segments. The study was commissioned under pressure from the timber industry, which was pushing for delisting murrelets in the Lower

48 so their protected forest habitat could be logged. The industry's argument, essentially, was that there are enough murrelets
in Alaska and British Columbia, and that the 2 percent in the
Lower 48 is not distinct and not worth saving.

In 2004, the Fish and Wildlife Service's major scientific review
of the murrelet's status had showed that the birds in the tri-state
area qualified as a distinct population segment, but the agency's
headquarters announced plans to delist the bird anyway, claiming
that the studies were flawed. An official delisting proposal, however, never appeared—only the call for a rangewide study.

At the time, I thought the agency was simply being extra
cautious, seeking to ensure that it had the best available scientific data before making a decision of such import. It wasn't until
February 2008 that the real story emerged: High-level officials in
the Department of the Interior had tampered with and ultimately
reversed the findings of the Fish and Wildlife Service's 2004 report
so that the timber industry would "get what they want"—access
to the millions of acres of federally owned old-growth forests protected for murrelets. This revelation (brought to light by the law
firm Earthjustice) led to the vindication of the wronged scientists
and the decision by the Fish and Wildlife Service that delisting
should not be proposed.

I was feeling pretty good about science triumphing over poli-
tics on behalf of the murrelet, but alas, that glimmer of good news
was extinguished by yet more timber-industry lawsuits coinciding
with the crash of the U.S. financial markets in late 2008. Since
then, recovering the murrelet has taken a backseat to recovering
the economy. For many timber-dependent counties in the Pacific
Northwest, this means logging. For the Fish and Wildlife Service,
this means intense pressure from the timber industry to delist the

murrelet and scrap protections on its forest habitat. And pressure from the timber industry means equal and opposite pressure from conservation groups, so the Fish and Wildlife Service finds itself frequently in court to resolve its murrelet management problems.

In the midst of these battles, the population of marbled murrelets is crashing. The most recent report shows a decline of nearly 30 percent in Washington, Oregon, and California between 2001 and 2010. In Alaska, where the murrelet receives no special protection, populations have declined about 70 percent in the past twenty-five years. In British Columbia, where the species has been listed as threatened by the Canadian government since 1990, scientists suspect similar declines. Since *Rare Bird* was first published, the total murrelet population has dropped from 947,500 to between 358,000 and 418,000. Clearly, recovery efforts have failed to halt or slow the bird's dive toward extinction. Why is this? Because recovering a species is complex and expensive—more so than anyone ever imagined.

In the late 1980s, scientists identified three major threats to the marbled murrelet's survival—loss of nesting habitat, gillnetting, and oil spills. The most recent status reports, completed in 2009 by the Fish and Wildlife Service and also by the Committee on the Status of Endangered Wildlife in Canada, are full of newly documented and potential threats. But "threats" really isn't the right word anymore. The damage is not impending—much of it has been and continues to be inflicted. Twenty-plus years of scientific data show the degradation of the ocean where the murrelet swims and forages, reveal the ruination of the ancient forests where it breeds, and point to the seemingly unavoidable loss of this extraordinary species. The reports read like a script of the apocalypse.

The main cause of the murrelet's population crash continues
to be the ongoing and historic loss of its forest nesting habitat—
which is caused almost exclusively by logging. Scientists believe
that the recent population declines are from the lag effect of logging begun in the mid-nineteenth century. The once-abundant
murrelet population is not responding well to the removal of
nearly 90 percent of old-growth forests. Little high-quality
nesting habitat remains, and when faced with less than suitable
nesting sites, these birds may choose not to breed at all.

Despite protections on federal, state, and provincial forest,
tens of thousands of acres of mature and old-growth forest are
still being logged or degraded. Between 2004 and 2008, the Fish
and Wildlife Service authorized the removal of 16,423 acres of
potential or known murrelet nesting habitat, the degradation
of 23,449 additional acres, and the removal of 2,450 individual
potential nest trees. Other causes of habitat loss—wildfires, insect
outbreaks, tree disease, and windstorms—have increased dramatically in recent years. Though considered natural, these events
are exacerbated by logging and the newly documented effects of
climate change. Scientists predict that warming temperatures and
drier conditions will increase the frequency, severity, and magni-
tude of wildfires.

Add to this the booming population of murrelet nest predators—ravens, jays, and crows—that continues to benefit from
fragmented forests and forest edges adjacent to newly cleared
areas. Predation rates on murrelet eggs and chicks on the nest
remain high as these clever corvids are provided with easier and
deeper access into the forest.

But we should not revert to the outworn black-and-white,
environmentalist-versus-logger arguments about preserving old-

growth forests. Some of our favorite recreational sites were carved out of the finest old-growth forests and are fragmented and full of edges created by roads, parking lots, amphitheaters, campgrounds, and hiking trails. A recent study conducted in Redwood National and State Parks in California—prime murrelet nesting habitat— showed that nest predators cause more than half of nest failures each year. Logging and development may have allowed these predators to penetrate the forest in the first place, but our trash and snack foods keep them coming back.

Nest predation is just one factor contributing to a larger and increasingly complex problem for murrelets: low breeding success. The quantity and quality of the small fish the murrelets eat—especially the rockfish, herring, and smelt—continue to decline from overfishing and the degradation of these prey species' spawning grounds. Depleted fishing stocks in California have forced murrelets to begin feeding on krill—tiny larval forms of fish and other marine creatures. Adult murrelets that cannot adequately feed themselves may not initiate nests or, if they do, may decrease the time spent incubating eggs or reduce the number of feeding visits, especially if fish are difficult to obtain. These changes can lead to the direct mortality of eggs or chicks, or to an increased vulnerability to nest predators. Reproductive rates in Washington, Oregon, and California are less than a tenth of what scientists believe is necessary to sustain murrelet populations.

Marbled murrelets also face a sea of troubles in the coastal waters where they spend 95 percent of their lives. While progress has been made to reduce oil pollution and catastrophic oil spills, these pernicious threats are likely to increase in both the United States and Canada with the recent push for domestic oil production. Increases in offshore oil drilling, gas-platform development, and shipping traffic (including oil tankers) in coastal waters put the species at high risk. Proposed overland oil and natural-gas pipelines and terminals throughout the inland range of the murrelet will likely cause major habitat losses. Gillnet fishing, though banned in California and Oregon, is still practiced in Washington, Alaska, and British Columbia. In British Columbia alone, about 550 murrelets drown by entanglement each year as bycatch.

As if this weren't enough, newly documented threats at sea include entrapment in "derelict fishing gear"—abandoned gillnets, purse seines, crab pots, and other fishing lines. Climate change is associated with warming ocean temperatures, changes in upwelling patterns, and ocean acidification—all of which affect marine food webs and murrelet prey species. Biotoxins (such as PCBs and PDBEs) contaminate the fish the murrelets eat. Increased aquaculture displaces murrelets from foraging habitat and degrades the spawning grounds of their prey fish. Sea-level rise inundates the spawning grounds of many of these fish. Harmful algal blooms produce compounds that reduce feather waterproofing and cause seabird deaths through hypothermia. Increased levels of domoic acid cause neurological damage to seabirds. Elevated underwater sound disturbances, such as pile driving and detonations, have been shown to disrupt foraging behavior and cause injuries and death to seabirds. Even so-called green energy has a cost: Murrelets risk collision with massive underwater wave and tidal turbines in their foraging grounds and with onshore and offshore wind turbines in their sea-to-forest flight paths.

It is hard to avoid the grim conclusion that the time has come to change the murrelet's status from threatened to endangered. A threatened species is one likely to become endangered; an endangered one is likely to become extinct. It pains me to write "marbled murrelet" and "extinct" in the same paragraph, when I so wanted to be able to type "saved," "stabilized," or "recovered" instead.

When faced with such hopelessness, I often turn to the last few pages of *Hope Is the Thing with Feathers: A Personal Chronicle of Vanished Birds*, by Christopher Cokinos: "... I have learned much from this history and have realized, finally, that sadness at loss is our best *first* response. It should not be our only response. We know that the world gives us life, beauty, and solace. We would be ungrateful if we failed to give that back."

The good news for the marbled murrelet is, I believe, that we are trying to give that back. We are not giving completely or perfectly, but we are trying.

And by "we" I mean the scientists, the environmentalists, the advocates for wildlife and the wilderness, the letter writers, the email petition signers, the public hearing attendees, the hikers and campers, the park rangers, the careful timber managers, and the beleaguered U.S. Fish and Wildlife Service—the agency charged just forty years ago with the job of understanding and managing ecosystems eons in the making. And by "we" I also mean the lawyers and judges—federal and state—who grapple with the intent and language of the Endangered Species Act in order to clarify the meaning of terms such as "critical habitat," "adversely affect," "distinct," "jeopardize," "take," and "recover."

Bird by bird, some corvid populations are being controlled. Line by line, much derelict fishing gear is being hauled out of the water. And, thanks to ongoing scientific research, we are learning more and more about the murrelets and the problems they face.

Although our efforts are not yet paying off, we continue trying. But clearly, we need to try harder. Trying harder is easier if we remember that there is a living, breathing bird—one we may never hear or see—in the middle of all this. And that this bird, this wisp of life, is helping to hold our beautiful and fragile ecosystems together.

Over the past several years, I have had the privilege of talking about the marbled murrelet with audiences at bookstores, book clubs, conservation organizations, birding groups, and schools all over the West Coast. Typically, I read a few passages from *Rare Bird*, play a recording of the murrelet's calls, and show a set of slides that chronicle the stages of its life—from egg to adult. Most images of this hard-to-photograph bird elicit comments, questions, or various versions of "oh my!" When I show the image of the downy murrelet chick on its nest, I invariably get a great big "awwww" from the audience. When I tell the story of how this chick first leaves its forest nest for the sea, I can hear a pin drop. It is always then—in the silence of the darkened room—that the enormous space between the mossy nest and the crashing waves becomes real, that those listening join me in urging the fledging chick toward its destination, that the distance between our two species seems to disappear. It is then that I feel most hopeful and most inspired to return the life, beauty, and solace that this rare bird has given me.

While it is safe to say that any action you take to reduce your footprint on the planet will ultimately help the marbled murrelet, some specific actions you can take now will help more directly.

Help control murrelet predators. Keep your food to yourself when visiting old-growth coastal forests in or adjacent to national parks, state parks, or other public lands. Refrain from feeding wildlife—especially the corvids. Pick up any bits of food you may have accidentally dropped. When camping, use metal food-storage lockers or animal-resistant food containers (bear canisters).

Help restore the murrelet's food supply. Purchase fish caught or farmed using environmentally friendly practices. Regional seafood buying guides for the continental United States are available at www.seafood watch.org.

Help keep murrelet waters clean. Reduce use of pesticides, fertilizers, and other chemicals on your lawn and garden. Through city and farmland runoff, these and other chemical pollutants flow into estuaries and coastal waters, thereby degrading the habitat of the fish the murrelets feed on and the water where they spend 95 percent of their lives.

Advocate. Dozens of conservation groups are working to protect the marbled murrelet, and you can help in many ways: writing emails, lobbying your legislators, joining annual bird counts, attending public meetings, making a financial contribution, and more. To begin, visit www.mariaruthbooks .com for a list of worthy organizations.

Encounter a marbled murrelet. You can see these birds in many places along the Pacific coast, especially in the spring-summer breeding season. When the murrelets are at sea, you can spot them from a boat on the water (with binoculars) or from land at the coast's edge (using a spotting scope). To fully appreciate them, however, you must go into the forest and watch for them flying over the treetops or circling above a meadow in the predawn light. The timing of their inland flights varies according to latitude, and the local sunrise determines the best time for observing them. Visit www.mariaruthbooks.com for detailed information.

ACKNOWLEDGMENTS

I am deeply grateful to the staff of Mountaineers Books for bringing my tale of the marbled murrelet to new readers at such a critical time for this species. Thank you for the care you've taken with my book. Thank you for the care you've taken encouraging your readers to enjoy, understand, and conserve the wild places we love.

A special thanks to Maxine Dunkelman of the Olympia Mountaineers for connecting people, places, and books with such enthusiasm.

This book would be but a pamphlet were it not for the men and women of the Pacific Seabird Group, who have worked tirelessly over the years to understand and protect the marbled murrelet. Their dedication has kept me inspired, energized, and in awe throughout this project. A special thanks to Steve Singer, Spencer Sealy, Kim Nelson, and Harry Carter for their insights and careful reading of the manuscript during various stages.

For guiding me into this bird's habitat, thanks to David Fix, Rick Golightly, Marty Raphael, and Steve Singer.

For resources well beyond my reach, thanks to Ernst Bauernfeind of the Natural History Museum in Vienna, Austria; Karen Carter of the San Bernardino County Museum; Dennis Paulson of the Slater Museum of Natural History; Ray Gonyea of the Eiteljorg Museum of American Indians and Western Art; Kristen Marshall of the Zoology Library of the Natural History Museum in London; Russell Johnson of the UCLA History and Special Collections Division of the Louise M. Darling Biomedical Library; and Pamela Ford of Mount San Jacinto College.

Five decades worth of gratitude go to my father for his encouragement, generosity, and humor, and for giving me the spirit of inquiry. And, finally, to my mother, who left the earth with grace and beauty, *grazie—grazie mille.*

INDEX

ABOUT THE AUTHOR

Maria Mudd Ruth has written more than a dozen books on natural history topics for children, young adults, and adults. She first encountered the marbled murrelet in 1999 while living in Virginia. She moved her family to Southern California in 2001 to be closer to murrelet habitat while researching and writing *Rare Bird*. In 2006 she moved her family again, this time to Olympia, Washington, where she is happily pursuing the mystery of clouds for her next book. For more information on the marbled murrelet and Maria's other projects, visit www.mariaruth books.com.

ABOUT THE ILLUSTRATOR

Paul Jones grew up in India, where he illustrated a book on the birds of Burma under the guidance of his father, A. E. Jones, one of India's best-known ornithologists. Paul became a forester and later a conservationist. In the 1990s he found two active nests of marbled murrelets, and in so doing saved what has turned out to be Canada's oldest closed-canopy forest; the area is now a provincial park. Paul's sketches have documented previously unknown nesting behaviors of the murrelet, and his writings and drawings have appeared in numerous articles. His book, *The Marbled Murrelets of the Caren Range and Middlepoint Bight,* was published by the Western Canada Wilderness Committee in 2001.